# The Tenth Amendment and State Sovereignty

# The Tenth Amendment and State Sovereignty

## Constitutional History and Contemporary Issues

EDITED BY MARK R. KILLENBECK

ROWMAN & LITTLEFIELD PUBLISHERS, INC.
*Lanham • Boulder • New York • Oxford*

BERKELEY PUBLIC POLICY PRESS
*Berkeley, California*

ROWMAN & LITTLEFIELD PUBLISHERS, INC.

Published in the United States of America
by Rowman & Littlefield Publishers, Inc.
4720 Boston Way, Lanham, Maryland 20706
www.rowmanlittlefield.com

12 Hid's Copse Road, Cumnor Hill, Oxford OX2 9JJ, England

British Library Cataloguing in Publication Information Available

**Library of Congress Cataloging-in-Publication Data Available**

ISBN 0-7425-1879-5  (cl. : alk. paper)
ISBN 0-7425-1880-9  (pbk. : alk. paper)

Printed in the United States of America

♾™ The paper used in this publication meets the minimum requirements of American National Standard for Information Sciences—Permanence of Paper for Printed Library Materials, ANSI/NISO Z39.48-1992.

# Acknowledgments

This collection owes its origins to the University of California, Berkeley. A gathering there, *The Concept of Reserved Powers in American Constitutional Law and History,* was cosponsored by the Jefferson Memorial Lecture Program, the Center for Law and Society, and the Boalt Hall School of Law. It was organized by Daniel B. Rodriguez, then a professor of law at Boalt Hall and now dean and professor at the University of San Diego School of Law. We owe a debt of gratitude to Dan for bringing a group of talented individuals together and providing the impetus that led to the decision to collect these essays.

We are also deeply grateful to Harry N. Scheiber, the Stefan N. Riesenfeld Professor of Law and History and director of the Center for the Study of Law and Society at Boalt Hall. It was Harry who arranged for Bill Leuchtenburg to deliver the Jefferson Memorial Lecture in conjunction with the original gathering, and it has been Harry over the years who has nurtured and sustained the Seminars on Federalism and resulting publications that provided the pattern and foundation for this volume. Harry is both a preeminent authority on federalism and someone who cares deeply about facilitating the work of those who share his interests in and enthusiasm for this important topic.

Finally, the editor and authors want to express their thanks to Maria Wolf from the Institute of Governmental Studies for her patient and expert editing of the text and to Jean Wu, a student at Boalt Hall, who provided invaluable assistance compiling the Case and Subject Indexes for this volume.

# Contents

CHAPTER ONE

# No Harm in Such a Declaration?

## Mark R. Killenbeck

> The powers not delegated to the United States by the Constitution, nor prohib-
> ited by it to the States, are reserved to the States respectively, or to the people.
> United States Constitution, Amendment X.

Is the Tenth Amendment misunderstood? Or is it merely the unfortunate victim
of the company it keeps? Is it simply a truism, standing for nothing more than
the proposition that those powers not given to the federal government have been
withheld? Or is it a vital first principle with its own substantive force, articulating a precept that limits and binds?

These are not idle inquiries. For while the fortunes of the Tenth Amendment
itself have waxed and waned, the issue it encapsulates in twenty-eight simple
words is quite properly regarded as "perhaps our oldest question of constitutional law,"[1] one that, Chief Justice John Marshall observed, "is perpetually arising, and will continue to arise as long as our system shall exist."[2] This is especially the case as we enter the twenty-first century, not simply in the Supreme
Court of the United States, which has of late given the Tenth Amendment a stature never before enjoyed, but also in the body politic, within which these issues

---

[1] New York v. United States, 505 U.S. 144, 149 (1992).
[2] M'Culloch v. Maryland, 4 Wheat. 316, 405 (1819).

have assumed increasing importance as we contemplate lessons both express and implied in an ongoing dialogue between Court, Congress, and the states.

The threshold issue is deceptively simple. In this Compound Republic, what is the "proper division of authority between the Federal Government and the States"?[3] We know, because the Constitution itself tells us, that it, "and the Laws of the United States which shall be made in Pursuance thereof; and all Treaties made, or which shall be made, under the Authority of the United States, shall be the supreme Law of the Land; and the judges in every State shall be bound thereby, any Thing in the Constitution or Laws of any State to the Contrary notwithstanding."[4] But what are we to make of the fact that the states are arguably the senior partners in this union, entities that prior to ratification "were sovereign, were completely independent, and were connected with each other only by a league"?[5] What exactly happened when the Articles of Confederation were replaced by a Constitution for We the People? There is, for example, little doubt that the states retained a degree of "sovereignty" that the federal government is bound to respect.[6] But, as Chief Justice Marshall also stresses, with ratification "the whole character in which the States appear, underwent a change, the extent of which must be determined by a fair consideration of the instrument by which the change was effected."[7] In our "more perfect Union," then, within which the powers of the federal government are few, but of necessity both complete and supreme, what is the nature of that residual state sovereignty? What limits does it impose on federal authority? More specifically, when We the People speak through our elected representatives in Congress assembled, to what extent are the states required to accept those pronouncements? And what does the Tenth Amendment, a measure described initially by James Madison as "superfluous" and whose addition to the text he characterized as "harmless," add to this analytic process?[8]

---

[3]*New York,* 505 U.S. at 149.

[4]U.S. Const. Art. VI, cl. 2.

[5]*Gibbons v. Ogden,* 9 Wheat. 1, 187 (1824).

[6]Like Jack Rakove, I have reservations about how the current Court majority defines and treats the concept of sovereignty, at least as a historical matter. For the purposes of this essay, I will generally use the term as the Court does, as a shorthand for a concept that focuses on the constitutional status of the "states as states." For an alternate view, see Jack N. Rakove, Making a Hash of Sovereignty, Parts I & II, 2 The Green Bag 35 (1998) and 3 The Green Bag 51 (1999).

[7]*Gibbons,* 9 Wheat. at 187.

[8]In his remarks explaining what would eventually become the Tenth Amendment, Madison observed: "Perhaps words which may define this more precisely than the whole of the instrument now does, may be considered as superfluous. I admit they may be deemed unnecessary; but there can be no harm in making such a declaration." 1 Annals of Congress 458 (1789).

These questions come before the United States Supreme Court in a variety contexts, and it has in recent years displayed an increasing inclination to favor the states in the rulings it issues. As Chief Judge J. Harvie Wilkinson III—himself a practitioner of the new, old federalism from his seat on the United States Court of Appeals for the Fourth Circuit—has noted, "the future smiles upon the states."[9] Not everyone, of course, is pleased with the prospect, and while the drumbeat of the new federalism has not yet reached the point where it dictates fully the ebb and flow of everyday life, there is little doubt that federalism, and its constitutional exemplar, the Tenth Amendment, are becoming increasingly import aspects of the current political and legal landscape.

The Court itself is bitterly divided over the meaning and import of the both the Tenth Amendment and the unique theory of government it describes. In virtually every decision of interest, an unwavering bloc of five justices have cast their votes in favor of a view of federal-state relations within which it feels compelled to invalidate federal measures that are not simply unconstitutional. Rather, they "*utterly* fail to adhere to the design and structure of our constitutional scheme."[10] The triumphant majority, consisting of Chief Justice Rehnquist and Justices O'Connor, Kennedy, Scalia, and Thomas, argue that they are simply restoring the "federal balance the Framers designed . . . that this Court is obliged to enforce."[11] Justices Stevens, Souter, Breyer, and Ginsburg, in turn, labor in increasingly gloomy dissent, characterizing these results as "unprecedented,"[12] "formalistically contrived," and a replication of a "nearly disastrous experiment."[13] They maintain, accordingly, that these decisions are "so profoundly mistaken and fundamentally inconsistent with the Framers' conception of the constitutional order that [they] have foresaken any claim to the usual def-

---

[9]J. Harvie Wilkinson III, Fear of Federalism, Wash. Post., Nov. 26, 1999, at A45. For an example of Judge Wilkinson's take of these matters, see his concurring opinion in the 4th Circuit *en banc* decision that would become *United States v. Morrison,* Brzonkala v. Virginia Polytechnic Institute and State University, 169 F.3d 820 (4th Cir. 1999), where he observes that "the present jurisprudence of federalism is purely allocative, standing for the simple proposition that the Constitution does not cast states as mere marionettes of the central government." Id. at 895 (Wilkinson concurring).

[10]Printz v. United States, 521 U.S. 898, 936 (1997) (O'Connor concurring) (emphasis added).

[11]United States v. Lopez, 514 U.S. 549, 583 (1995) (Kennedy concurring). The group has voted together, albeit at times with varying views, in each of the cases that prompted the development of this volume but one, where Justice Kennedy's defection provided the critical fifth vote to strike state-imposed term limits on United States senators and representatives. See United States Term Limits, Inc. v. Thornton, 514 US 779 (1995).

[12]*Printz,* 521 U.S. at 941 (Stevens dissenting).

[13]United States v. Morrison, 120 S. Ct. 1740, 1767 (2000) (Souter dissenting).

erence or respect owed to decisions of this Court."[14] The positions embraced seem sufficiently calcified that Justice O'Connor has complained that it has become "difficult to engage in additional meaningful debate,"[15] even as Justice Souter signals his belief that the "dialogue" will continue in ways that will reveal that "today's ebb . . . rests on error," such that he "doubt[s] that the majority's view will prove to be enduring law."[16]

We live then in a time within which, depending on one's views, it is entirely appropriate to describe the current process in a variety of conflicting yet complementary ways. Proponents of the shift in emphasis from federal to state regulatory prerogatives describe the justices who pursue this goal as worthy of "a 21-gun salute"[17] and characterize the dissents as "rearguard actions" fought "by justices who seem caught in a time-warp."[18] Critics lament the rulings of "an aggressive 'states' rights' cluster" and praise the dissenters for fashioning "well-reasoned" opinions that "skewer the majority for ignoring 'the importance of respecting the Framers' decision to assign the business of lawmaking to Congress.'"[19] The rhetoric, both in the decisions and the commentaries, is heated. And it is hardly surprising that the recent federalism decisions assumed a prominent place in the attempts to cast the presidential election in the Fall of 2000 as a referendum on the Court itself.[20]

What fuels this movement? The triumphant majority claims that they are simply revealing "truths . . . so basic that, like the air around us, they are easily overlooked."[21] But, at least when divorced from the sometimes murky and abstract principles and history that impel them, many of these newly discovered

---

[14]Kimel v. Florida Board of Regents, 120 S. Ct. 631, 653 (2000) (Stevens dissenting).

[15]Id. at 643.

[16]*Morrison,* 120 S. Ct. at 1773 (Souter dissenting).

[17]Bruce Fein, Arresting Mission Creep, Wash. Times, May 23, 2000, at A18.

[18]Charles Fried, Opponents of Federalism Are Mired in a Time Warp, Wall St. J., May 16, 2000, at A29.

[19]Another Loss on States' Rights, N.Y. Times, Jan. 12, 2000, at A26 (quoting Stevens dissenting in *Kimel*).

[20]See, for example, Bruce Fein, As the Supreme Court Turns, Wash. Times, July 18, 2000, at A16 ("Both the Republican candidate . . . and his Democratic opponent . . . are touting the race as a defining moment in the constitutional law expounded by the U.S. Supreme Court."); Linda Greenhouse, The Court Rules, America Changes, N.Y. Times, July 2, 2000, § 4, at 1 (describing the federalism decisions as part of the "questions that this election-year term has raised about the court's future"). But see Alexander Cockburn, Scaremongering and the Court, The Nation, July 24, 2000, at 8 ("Throughout the nation's history the Supreme Court has generally been a reactionary force, and it will no doubt be so whether Gore or Bush is elected in November, or whether the Democrats or Republicans control Congress.").

[21]*New York,* 505 U.S. at 187.

truths seem startling, fueling beliefs on both left and right that much of what is transpiring is about the Court itself, rather than the rule of law.[22]

The Court has, for example, informed us recently that the federal government may not create a private cause of action in federal court for a woman who has been brutally raped, even when the states themselves seem to be saying that they cannot provide a meaningful remedy,[23] may not enlist the assistance of state officials in the national effort to combat crime by registering firearms,[24] and may not require the states to become the custodians of nuclear waste generated within their borders when these same states have failed to avail themselves of other, less intrusive means for disposing of these highly toxic materials.[25] Nor may Congress, even when exercising what remain, at least for the time being, clearly held plenary powers, require these same sovereign states to submit themselves to the jurisdiction of federal or state courts when called to account for violating a national mandate not to discriminate against the disabled,[26] failing to pay overtime wages mandated by federal law,[27] or appropriating for their own use and benefit the trademarked or copyrighted materials of private citizens.[28]

The decisions articulating these and similar results do not always speak expressly of the Tenth Amendment, a provision the majority describes as "reserv[ing] to [the states] a substantial portion of the Nation's primary sovereignty, together with the dignity and essential attributes adhering to that status."[29] In some instances the emphasis is on newly perceived limits on the power to regulate interstate commerce—in an era in which we had previously assumed that nothing lay beyond its scope.[30] In other decisions the appeal to a

---

[22]See, for example, Robert Nagel, The High (and Mighty) Court, Wall St. J., June 30, 2000, at A 14; Jeremy Rabkin, A Supreme Mess at the Supreme Court, The Weekly Standard, July 17, 2000, at 24; Jeffrey Rosen, And the Verdict Is: Hubris, The New Republic, July 10 & 17, 2000, at 16.

[23]*Morrison,* 120 S. Ct. at 1740.

[24]*Printz,* 521 U.S. at 898.

[25]*New York,* 505 U.S. at 144.

[26]*Kimel,* 120 S. Ct. at 631.

[27]Alden v. Maine, 527 U.S. 706 (1998).

[28]College Savings Bank v. Florida Prepaid Postsecondary Education Expense Board, 527 U.S. 666 (1999); Florida Prepaid Postsecondary Education Expense Board v. College Savings Bank, 527 U.S. 627 (1999).

[29]*Alden,* 527 U.S. at 714.

[30]Compare *Morrison,* 120 S. Ct. at 1748 ("*Lopez* emphasized, however, that even under our modern, expansive interpretation of the Commerce Clause, Congress' regulatory authority is not without effective bounds" (citing United States v. Lopez, 514 U.S. 549, 557 (1995)), with Deborah Jones Merritt, Commerce!, 94. Mich. L. Rev. 674, 674 (1995) ("When I graduated from law school in 1980, my classmates and I believed that Congress could regulate any act—no matter how local—under the Commerce Clause."). Federalism concerns have also been expressed in recent cases involving the Spending

new-found respect for a robust federalism is predicated on the Court's understanding of the lessons imposed by the Eleventh Amendment, a measure that in its current interpretive formulation seems to stand for a virtually limitless proposition that the states are, and must remain, immune from suit in federal court, even where—at least, even where it at least appears to be the case—we are to entertain no doubts about the power of Congress to regulate the conduct at issue. In other opinions the Court speaks neither of the Tenth nor Eleventh Amendments, but instead frets about the implications of the principles for which they stand in cases that focus on matters like preemption,[31] *habeas corpus,*[32] medical decisions,[33] or that most scintillating of constitutional principles, standing.[34]

Whatever the issue, and whatever the constitutional focus, in each of these decisions the Court offers its current take on "[v]arious textual provisions of the Constitution [that] assume the States' continued existence and active participation in the fundamental process of governance."[35] Increasingly, its answers to the questions raised are designed "to underscore the vital role reserved to the States by the constitutional design."[36] In doing so, they pose new and incredibly impor-

---

Clause. See Davis v. Monroe County Board of Education, 526 U.S. 629, 658 (1999) (Kennedy dissenting) ("The Nation's schoolchildren will learn their first lessons about federalism in classrooms where the Federal Government is the ever-present regulator."); Cedar Rapids Community School District v. Garrett, 526 U.S. 66, 84–85 (1999) (Thomas dissenting) (identifying "federalism concerns" as the predicate for an interpretation of the Individuals with Disabilities Education Act).

[31]See Geier v. American Honda Motor Co., Inc., 120 S. Ct. 1913, 1928 (2000) (Stevens dissenting) ("'This is a case about federalism,' Coleman v. Thompson, 501 U.S. 722, 726 (1991), that is, about respect for 'the constitutional role of the States as sovereign entities.' Alden v, Maine, 527 U.S. 706, 713 (1999).").

[32]See Edwards v. Carpenter, 120 S. Ct. 1587, 1591 (2000) ("The procedural default doctrine and its attendant 'cause and prejudice' standard are 'grounded concerns of comity and federalism.'" (quoting Coleman v. Thompson, 501 U.S. 722, 730 (1991)); Smith v. Robins, 120 S. Ct. 746, 757 (2000) (speaking of "our established practices, rooted in federalism, of allowing the States wide discretion, subject to the minimum requirements of the Fourteenth Amendment, to experiment with solutions to difficult problems of social policy").

[33]See Olmstead v. L.C. by Zimring, 527 U.S. 581, 610 (1999) (Kennedy concurring) (noting "the federalism costs inherent in referring state decision regarding the administration of treatment programs and the allocation of resources to the reviewing authority of the federal courts"); id. at 624 (Thomas dissenting) ("Further, I fear that the majority's approach imposes significant federalism costs, directing States how to make decisions about their delivery of public services.").

[34]See City of Chicago v. Morales, 527 U.S. 41, 55 n.22 (1999) (Stevens opinion) (discussing "essential principles of federalism" in the context of standing and a facial challenge).

[35]*Alden,* 527 U.S. at 713.

[36]Id.

tant lines of inquiry for individuals who both applaud and lament the directions in which the Court seems to be taking us.

This collection offers a series of perspectives on the controversies that provoke these decisions, the opinions that articulate the current majority's answers, and the questions that must be answered in the wake of the Court's actions. Its nominal focus is the Tenth Amendment, a constitutional provision that, depending on one's perspective, is either lionized or feared as an embodiment of a newly robust conception of state sovereignty that seems on occasion to hold an almost mystical meaning for those justices who embrace it. It would, however, be a mistake to view these essays simply as meditation on the Tenth Amendment or as useful only in understanding those decisions within which the Court relies expressly on that provision. For, as the Court itself has made clear, the Tenth Amendment now stands for something greater than the text itself. In the current majority's system, it "confirms the promise implicit in the original document," a pledge that the states will "not be relegated to the role of mere provinces or political corporations, but [will instead] retain the dignity, though not the full authority, of sovereignty."[37] As such it has become a vital force in our current constitutional system, a startling transformation for a constitutional provision that was, 60 years ago, derided as a "truism."[38]

## An Overview

The three distinguished authors whose work follows approach their task from different yet intensely complementary perspectives. The first essay, *The Tenth Amendment Over Two Centuries: More than a Truism,*[39] is by Professor William Leuchtenburg, arguably the nation's preeminent authority on the New Deal and the Roosevelt presidency. His perspective on these matters is, not surprisingly, shaped by his intense awareness of the importance of the New Deal and its treatment by the Court. As Leuchtenburg has documented elsewhere, Franklin Delano Roosevelt assumed the presidency in the midst of the "Winter of Despair,"[40] a period during which "[m]any Americans came to despair the whole political process" and had developed "a contempt for Congress, for parties, [and] for democratic institutions."[41] For these individuals and this nation, the New Deal offered a beacon of hope, while the tired formalism of a Supreme Court intent on exterminating the Roosevelt initiatives posed the unacceptable

---

[37]Id. at 714 & 715.

[38]United States v. Darby, 312 U.S. 100, 124 (1941).

[39]See this volume at 41 ("More Than a Truism").

[40]William E. Leuchtenburg, Franklin D. Roosevelt and the New Deal 18–40 (Harper Colophon, 1963).

[41]Id. at 27.

threat of denying "to the Federal Government the powers which exist in every other Nation in the world."[42] The decisions of the Court sustaining myriad New Deal measures in the wake of the Constitutional Revolution of 1937 are, accordingly, both important in themselves and, as precedents called into question by the recent federalism decisions, central to the themes explored in this collection.[43]

Leuchtenburg provides a thorough and intensely human perspective on both the Tenth Amendment's "sordid past" and, at least until recently, its potentially more promising present, within which it was possible to see in the Court's decisions an awareness of the vital role the federal government could play in meeting the nation's most pressing needs. As he demonstrates, the cases explicating the Tenth Amendment and applying the principles for which it supposedly stood provided the unfortunate backdrop for what we now characterize as the Constitutional Revolution of 1937. These decisions had "hovered like a dark cloud over [President Roosevelt's] ambition to get the country out of the Great Depression and create a New Deal."[44] Those that started to emerge in 1937, in turn, freed the nation from the bonds of a Court insensitive to the economic and social problems its previous rulings had countenanced, and provided the Congress, and the people it represented, shelter from both the Court and the forces that sought to use the judicial process as a check on the federal government's capacity to use its powers for the common good.

Leuchtenburg is, accordingly, understandably concerned by the shift in perspective that began to emerge in the 1970s. As he notes, the process of transformation began slowly, emerging initially in often solitary dissents authored by Justice William Rehnquist and eventually solidifying in the series of decisions that have taken us to a case he characterizes as "especially nasty," *United States v. Morrison*.[45] Leuchtenburg paints a vivid portrait of the *Morrison* case, one whose unhappy facts and bitterly contested conclusion mirror many of the characteristics that had marked earlier efforts by the Court to place substantive limits on Congress's power to regulate "commerce." He reminds us, in his treatment of this decision and in his discussion of the Tenth Amendment's historical development, of the close association between the principles for which it supposedly

---

[42]Franklin D. Roosevelt, Press Conference, May 31, 1935, quoted in William E. Leuchtenburg, The Origins of Franklin D. Roosevelt's "Court-packing" Plan, in William E. Leuchtenburg, The Supreme Court Reborn: The Constitutional Revolution in the Age of Roosevelt, at 82, 90 (Oxford University Press, 1995) ("Reborn").

[43]For perspectives on the work of the Roosevelt Court, see Reborn (cited in note 42); Bruce A. Ackerman, 2 We The People: Transformations (Belknap Press, 1998); Barry Cushman, Rethinking the New Deal Court: The Structure of a Constitutional Revolution (Oxford University Press, 1997).

[44]More Than a Truism, at 47 (cited in note 39).

[45]120 S. Ct. 1740 (2000).

stood and the rhetoric of those segments of our society that have historically opposed efforts to secure social justice.

Leuchtenburg is clearly apprehensive about the nature and implications of the Court's recent turn, not simply because he disagrees with the Court's crabbed view of federal power, but because he understands the threats posed by the freedom these decisions give to states and localities that are often wed only to their own narrow, parochial interests. For him, like Justice Souter in recent and forceful dissent, the "lessons of 1937" are real and compelling. And they are written not simply in the dry words of a Supreme Court decision, but in the lives of individuals like Reuben Dagenhart, for whom an earlier celebration of state sovereignty, *Hammer v. Dagenhart,*[46] meant that there was nothing wrong with a system that allowed children to enter the factories at the age of 12 and work 12 hours a day in appalling conditions.

In the second essay of this collection, *American Federalism: Was There an Original Understanding,*[47] Professor Jack Rakove explores a different but no less important question. If, as the current Court majority avers, resolving the issues arising in recent federalism decisions is merely a simple exercise in recognizing and giving force to "truths . . . so basic that, like the air around us, they are easily overlooked,"[48] can one actually identify these historical truths with the degree of precision the Court claims for itself? Rakove, who is rightly regarded as one of the most meticulous and knowledgeable scholars of the founding period, questions whether we can. Indeed, he stresses at the outset of his essay that even attempting to do so "is in some sense anachronistic in that it ascribes to the Founders of the American states and their confederation a clarity of purpose and understanding that they probably did not have; it attempts to impose a false precision that has far more to do with our concerns than with theirs."[49]

That being the case, Rakove believes it appropriate to remind ourselves of the contexts within which the Tenth Amendment was proposed and ratified. He describes a Confederation period during which it was appropriate to regard the states not as fully independent sovereigns, but rather in certain important respects not reflected in the current case law as "administrative auxiliaries of Congress."[50] He concedes that the Constitution contemplated that "most of the mat-

---

[46]247 U.S. 251 (1918).

[47]See this volume at 107 ("Original Understanding"). As he notes, his perspectives in this essay are influenced by his prior work, in particular his Pulitzer Prize-winning examination of the founding period, Original Meanings: Politics and Ideas in the Making of the Constitution 7–11 (Knopf, 1996), and his earlier examination of the period from 1774 to 1787, The Beginnings of National Politics: An Interpretive History of the Continental Congress (Knopf, 1979).

[48]New York v. United States, 505 U.S. 144, 187 (1992).

[49]Original Understanding, at 109–10 (cited in note 47).

[50]Id. at 112.

ters that would affect Americans in the daily conduct of their affairs, would remain with the states."[51] But he also finds in the ebb and flow of opinion between Federalist and Anti-Federalist a recognition that the ultimate goal was an effective national government, and deems especially significant the addition of the phrase "or to the people" to the text of the Tenth Amendment, an act suggesting that there might be "an alternative repository of power to the state governments in which were vested all powers of government delegated elsewhere than the union."[52]

Rakove concedes that "[i]n the absence of debate, one should hesitate, even balk, at ascribing intentionality of any kind to this change."[53] But, as he notes in his essay in this collection and elsewhere,[54] the implications of this concept are important, for it acknowledges, "there is a sense in which the identification of the people as an entity distinct from both state and national governments illuminates the political underpinnings of federalism."[55] And he suggests that it might be appropriate to consider a different reading of the amendment, an approach that tracks James Wilson's understanding that the full text worked "a constitutional allocation of authority" that was malleable rather than static, "an ongoing political process" within which "the Tenth Amendment and the concept of reserved powers are not yet a principle demanding vindication," but rather "merely symbols of the devolutionist side of this struggle."[56]

Finally, in his essay *Federalism and Judicial Review,*[57] Professor John Yoo offers a historically grounded perspective on a central aspect of the Court's current approach to these matters as a *court,* that is, as the coordinate branch of government that exercises "the judicial power of the United States." Yoo is justifiably regarded as one of the most meticulous, insightful, and fair-minded individuals now examining the constitutional issues in a historical context, and the reasons for these judgments are readily apparent in his essay.

For many years, it has been taken as a given that the proper judicial response to questions about the exercise of any given federal sovereign power is to defer to whatever judgments Congress might make, absent evidence that the measure in question either discriminates against a suspect class or burdens a

---

[51]Id. at 115.

[52]Id. at 127.

[53]Id.

[54]See in particular Making a Hash of Sovereignty, Parts I & II, 2 The Green Bag 35 (1998) and 3 The Green Bag 51 (1999), in which he argues that "the concept of sovereignty ha[s] little descriptive use in making sense of the American system," 2 The Green Bag at 44, and maintains that "[s]overeignty is too vague and anachronistic a term to allow us to reason about anything more than our propensity to keep using it." 3 The Green Bag at 59.

[55]Original Understanding, at 127 (cited in note 47).

[56]Id. at 128, 129.

[57]See this volume at 131 ("Judicial Review").

fundamental right. Yoo examines with considerable care the historical predicates for the political safeguards of federalism theory, probing deeply into the words and understandings of the Framer and Founders. He argues that there is simply no historical warrant for this approach, embraced most clearly by the Court in *Garcia v. San Antonio Metropolitan Transit Authority* in which it held that "the political process ensures that laws that unduly burden the States will not be promulgated."[58]

This "political process" doctrine, within which the Court simply steps aside, obviously has profound implications for federalism. Under it, the sole meaningful check on the authority of Congress to override the sovereignty of the states is the discipline of Congress itself. Such restraint has, more often than not, seemed absent in recent years.[59] There are, accordingly, sound reasons to fear that the states will inevitably be relegated to a form of second-class citizenship in a federal system within which their fortunes will be subject to the whims of a Congress that has shown an increasing inclination to "do anything it can get away with and let the Supreme Court worry about the Constitution."[60] Yoo, however, marshals a substantial body of evidence indicating that the Framers and Founders believed "that questions of state and national power were to receive the fullest—if not the primary—attention from the Supreme Court."[61]

This vision of an active and robust Supreme Court role policing the boundaries between nation and state reflected a belief "that the chief role states would play in their relationship with the federal government would be the protection of the people's liberty."[62] In particular, the Framers feared the impulses of "self-interested, ambitious politicians."[63] This reluctance to indulge a Congress in-

---

[58]469 U.S. 528, 556 (1985).

[59]See Michael Grunwald, In Legislative Tide, State Power Ebbs; Federalization Has Few Friends but Many Votes, Wash. Post, Oct. 24, 1999, at A1 (observing that "members of Congress still talk a lot about states' rights, about 'a devolution of power' to their beloved 'laboratories of democracy,' but when it comes to actual legislation, a counterdevolution is well underway" and noting that "the congressional push to dictate state policies has been a bipartisan effort").

[60]Justice Antonin Scalia, quoted in A Shot from Justice Scalia, Wash. Post, May 2, 2000, at A22. The observation came in a speech delivered at Michigan State University. See also Ted Gest, Taking Congress Down Three Pegs, U.S. News & World Report, July 7, 1997, at 33 (observing that the recent "struggle" between Court and Congress "often stems from lawmakers' impulses to do what seems popular, even if they doubt that statute will pass muster with the court"); Jeffrey Rosen, Court Watch: Fed Up, The New Republic, May 22, 1995 at 13, 14 ("The intellectual hypocrisy of the Contract with America has been its tendency, despite anti-Federalist rhetoric, to federalize areas of tort and criminal law that have been traditionally left to the states.").

[61]Judicial Review, at 133 (cited in note 57).

[62]Id. at 179.

[63]Id.

clined to wreak havoc and unchecked by the Court seems especially apt in the light of the legislative impulses prevalent today. More importantly, in Yoo's analytic hands, it becomes an approach driven not by boundless respect for the sovereignty of the states, but rather by a healthy appreciation for the manner in which the Framers intended each of the myriad elements of the system to operate. For, as he describes it, they sought a world in which "[t]he federal courts would prevent the states from frustrating the legitimate exercise of national power, and, on the flip side of the coin, they would block the national government from infringing the independent sovereignty of the states."[64]

Each of these essays offers compelling insights and provides a historical basis for testing our assumptions about the federal system. This latter characteristic is, obviously, of considerable importance given the Court's contention that much of what it is now about is mandated as a matter of history, reflecting the supposedly clear intentions of the Framers and Founders. And while one can do no better than to simply read and savor what they offer, I believe it helpful to approach these matters with a brief overview of the decisions that provoked our interest and, for those readers who will indulge me, some personal observations on certain aspects of what it was the Framers and Founders themselves thought about the text and the states, and about the nature of what I myself find in the methods and conclusions found in these decisions.

## The "New" Federalism: The Decisions

A strong argument could be made that the federalism revival began with the arrival of Associate Justice William H. Rehnquist on the Court on December 15, 1971. Now in his thirtieth year on the Court and fifteenth as chief justice, Rehnquist has been a staunch champion of states' rights throughout his tenure, albeit, in the early years, most often castigating the Court for failing to comprehend the proper limits on federal power and to respect the proper role of the states in the federal system.[65] His solitary dissent in *Fry v. United States* is typical, a paean to states' rights in which he declared, "It is not apparent to me why a State's immunity from the plenary authority of the National Government to tax . . . should [be] thought to be any higher on the scale of constitutional values than is a State's claim to be free from the imposition of Congress' plenary au-

---

[64]Id. at 180.

[65]For examples of this in the specific context of the Commerce Clause, in which he was able to secure the agreement only of then Chief Justice Burger, see Hughes v. Oklahoma, 441 U.S. 322, 345 (1979) (Rehnquist dissenting) ("I simply fail to see how interstate commerce in minnows is impeded"); Philadelphia v. New Jersey, 437 U.S. 617, 345 (1978) (Rehnquist dissenting) ("Because past precedent establishes that the Commerce Clause does not present [the states] with such a Hobson's Choice, I dissent.").

thority under the Commerce Clause."[66] That preliminary skirmish, fought in a case in which the Court affirmed the authority of Congress to bar state employee wage increases in excess of a national norm during the economic crisis of the early 1970s, set the stage for the eventual triumph of the Rehnquist position in *National League of Cities v. Usery,*[67] a decision itself reversed a mere nine years later in *Garcia v. San Antonio Metropolitan Transit Authority.*[68]

In *National League of Cities* Rehnquist wrote for a bare 5–4 majority, stressing that "[A] State is not merely a factor in the 'shifting economic arrangements' of the private sector of the economy, but is itself a coordinate element in the system established by the Framers for governing our Federal Union."[69] The attempt by Congress to use the FLSA to regulate "the States as States" must fail, accordingly, as "there are attributes of sovereignty attaching to every state government which may not be impaired by Congress, not because Congress may lack an affirmative grant of legislative authority to reach the matter, but because the Constitution prohibits it from exercising the authority in that manner."[70] *National League of Cities* required courts to distinguish between "matters that are indisputably 'attribute[s]' of state sovereignty,'"[71] which were exempt from federal regulation, and those that were not "integral operations in areas of traditional government functions,"[72] which remained fair game. That task proved "troublesome," requiring the courts to fashion "constitutional distinctions" that were "elusive at best."[73] The *Garcia* Court, accordingly, abandoned the effort, overruling *National League of Cities* and postulating that "the principal and basic limit on [federal power] is that inherent to all congressional action—the built-in restraints that our system provides through state participation in federal governmental action."[74]

The rhetorical storm unleashed by the dissenting justices in *Garcia* foretold the current trend. The sorts of federal regulations permitted by the *Garcia* majority, Justice Powell complained, constituted "federal overreaching [that] un-

---

[66] 421 U.S. 542, 553–54 (1975) (Rehnquist dissenting).

[67] 426 U.S. 833 (1976). *National League of Cities* itself overruled the earlier decision of Maryland v. Wirtz, 392 U.S. 183 (1968). The principles articulated in *National League of Cities* were, in turn, explained and applied in subsequent cases, including Hodel v. Virginia Surface Mining & Recl. Ass'n, 452 U.S. 264 (1981), Transportation Union v. Long Island Rail Road Co., 455 U.S. 678 (1982), FERC v. Mississippi, 456 U.S. 742 (1982), and EEOC v. Wyoming, 460 U.S. 226 (1983).

[68] 469 U.S. 528 (1985).

[69] *National League of Cities,* 426 U.S. at 849 (quoting Kovacs v. Cooper, 336 U.S. 77, 95 (1949)).

[70] Id. at 845.

[71] *Hodel,* 452 U.S. at 288 (quoting *National League of Cities,* 426 U.S. at 845).

[72] Id.

[73] *Garcia,* 469 U.S. at 538 & 539.

[74] Id. at 556.

dermines the constitutionally mandated balance of power between the States and the Federal Government, a balance designed to protect our fundamental liberties."[75] By "reject[ing] *National League of Cities*," Justice O'Connor railed, the Court "washes its hands of all efforts to protect the States" and violates "[t]he *spirit* of the Tenth Amendment," which guarantees "that the States will retain their integrity in a system in which the laws of the United States are nevertheless supreme."[76] The decision was so inappropriate and such an aberration that the chief justice felt comfortable declaring that he did "not think it incumbent on those of us in dissent to spell out further the fine points of a principle that will, I am confident, in time again command the support of a majority of this Court."[77]

This process of redemption began in 1991, when the Court held, in *Gregory v. Ashcroft*,[78] that a Missouri provision mandating that judges retire at the age of 70 did not violate the federal Age Discrimination in Employment Act. In her opinion for the Court, Justice O'Connor sounded the themes that would permeate the pro-states' rights opinions that followed. "As every schoolchild learns," she lectured, "our Constitution establishes a system of dual sovereignty between the States and the Federal Government."[79] That system afforded the states "substantial sovereign authority," including "the authority of the people of the States to determine the qualifications of their most important government officials."[80] Thus, while the judgment of Congress that individuals should not be discriminated against on account of their age was worthy of respect, Congress's authority did not extend to displacing "the prerogative [of the people of Missouri] as citizens of a sovereign State" to "establish a qualification for those who would be their judges."[81] That did not mean that Congress could not regulate state activities. The problem, Justice O'Connor explained, was not a lack of authority, but rather Congress's failure to make express its judgment that state policy choices must yield to an otherwise valid federal initiative. Application of the federal regulation to what the Court characterized as "a qualification for those who sit as [Missouri's] judges" entered "an area traditionally regulated by the States" and as a result interfered with "decision[s] of the most fundamental sort for a sovereign entity."[82] This required a "plain statement" that such was Congress's intention, which Justice O'Connor characterized as "nothing more than

---

[75]Id. at 572 (Powell dissenting).
[76]Id. at 587 & 585 (O'Connor dissenting).
[77]Id. at 580 (Rehnquist dissenting).
[78]501 U.S. 452 (1991).
[79]Id. at 457.
[80]Id. & id. at 463.
[81]Id. at 473.
[82]Id. at 460.

an acknowledgment that the States retain substantial sovereign powers under our constitutional scheme, powers with which Congress does not readily interfere."[83]

A similar respect for state prerogatives permeated a second major decision, *New York v. United States,* in which Justice O'Connor stressed that, "The Tenth Amendment confirms that the power of the Federal Government is subject to limits that may, in a given instance, reserve power to the States. The Tenth Amendment thus directs us to determine, as in this case, whether an incident of state sovereignty is protected by a limitation on an Article I power."[84] The statute at issue in *New York,* the Low-Level Radioactive Waste Policy Amendments Act of 1985, included a section that required states that had not entered into a regional compact for disposal of low-level radioactive waste to take title and possession of any such waste generated within the borders of that state. This provision, the Court held, went too far. Congress could, constitutionally, use either the spending power or its own direct regulatory authority to preempt state law.[85] It could not, however, "commandeer" the states, for "[w]hile Congress has substantial powers to govern the nation directly, including areas of intimate concern to the States, the Constitution has never been understood to confer upon Congress the ability to require the States to govern according to Congress' instructions."[86] The states, Justice O'Connor concluded, "are not mere political subdivisions of the United States," and "[w]hatever the outer limits of [state] sovereignty may be, one thing is clear: The Federal Government may not compel the States to enact or administer a federal regulatory program."[87]

The full implications of this movement became clear in 1995, when the Court did what many regarded as the unthinkable, holding for the first time since 1937 that a federal statute enacted pursuant to Congress's authority under the Commerce Clause was invalid. The Gun Free School Zones Act of 1990 "made it a federal offense 'for any individual knowingly to possess a firearm at a place that the individual knows, or has reasonable cause to believe, is a school zone.'"[88] Writing for the now predictable five-justice majority in *United States v. Lopez,* the Chief Justice informed a stunned nation that "the possession of a gun in a local school zone is in no sense economic activity that might, through repe-

---

[83]Id. at 461. Justice White filed an opinion concurring in part and dissenting in part, which Justice Stevens joined, and Justice Blackmun filed a dissent in which Justice Marshall joined.

[84]505 U.S. 144, 157 (1992).

[85]Id. at 167.

[86]Id. at 162.

[87]Id. at 188. Both Justice White (joined by Justices Blackmun and Stevens) and Justice Stevens filed opinions concurring in part and dissenting in part.

[88]United States v. Lopez, 514 U.S. 549, 551 (1995) (quoting 18 U.S.C. § 922(q)(1)(A) (1998 Ed., Supp. V)).

tition elsewhere, substantially affect any sort of interstate commerce."[89] Rehnquist and his colleagues were unwilling to indulge a congressional assumption that would erase a constitutionally required "distinction between what is truly national and what is truly local."[90] Sustaining the statute would require the Court "to pile inference upon inference in a manner that would bid fair to convert congressional authority under the Commerce Clause to a general police power of the sort retained by the States."[91] That, the chief justice and his colleagues concluded, "we are unwilling to do."[92]

Two years later, in *Printz v. United States*,[93] the Court reiterated the principle articulated in *New York* and extended it to invalidate certain provisions of the Brady Handgun Violence Prevention Act that would "commandeer" state officials by requiring them to conduct background checks in the period between passage of the act and the implementation of a national "instant background check system." Writing for the Court, Justice Scalia found "no evidence of an assumption that the Federal Government may command the States' executive power in the absence of a particular constitutional authorization,"[94] something he could not find in either the history of the text or "its 'essential postulates.'"[95] Repeating the formulation articulated in the previous cases, Scalia emphasized that the states "retained 'a residuary and inviolable sovereignty'" that is both "reflected" and "implicit" in the text and "rendered express" by the Tenth Amendment.[96]

Then, in the spring of 2000, the Court issued two opinions that, while arguably sending mixed messages, nevertheless made it quite clear that the consis-

---

[89]Id. at 567.

[90]Id. at 567–68.

[91]Id. at 567.

[92]Id. at 568. Justice Kennedy added a concurring opinion describing the holding as "necessary though limited," which Justice O'Connor joined. Id. (Kennedy concurring). Justice Thomas, in one of the opinions that has fueled his reputation as a staunch Commerce Clause revisionist, also concurred in an opinion designed "to show how far we have departed from the original understanding" of that clause and lamenting that "[c]onsiderations of *stare decisis* and reliance interests may convince us that we cannot wipe the slate clean." Id. at 585 & 601 n.8 (Thomas concurring). Justices Stevens and Souter wrote dissenting opinions and Justice Breyer a dissent in which he was joined by Justices Stevens, Souter, and Ginsburg.

[93]521 U.S. 898 (1997).

[94]Id. at 909.

[95]Id. at 918 (quoting Principality of Monaco v. Mississippi, 292 U.S. 313, 322 (1934)).

[96]Id. at 919 (quoting The Federalist No. 39 (Madison)). Justices O'Connor and Thomas contributed concurring opinions, and there were three dissenting opinions by, respectively, Justices Stevens (joined by Souter, Ginsburg, and Breyer), Souter, and Breyer (joined by Stevens).

tent five-justice majority was indeed serious about its desire to place firm restraints on the power of Congress to legislate in areas "traditionally" deemed the prerogatives of the states.

In the first of these, *United States v. Morrison,* the chief justice confirmed that he and his colleagues were deadly serious when they indicated in *Lopez* "that even under our modern, expansive interpretation of the Commerce Clause, Congress' regulatory authority is not without effective bounds."[97] The focus was on a section of the Violence Against Women Act of 1994 that created a private cause of action in federal court for victims of a "crime of violence motivated by gender."[98] Christy Brzonkala, then a student at Virginia Polytechnic Institute, alleged that she had been assaulted and repeatedly raped by two members of the Tech football team and brought suit against them and the university. The chief justice and his colleagues stressed that "[i]f the allegations here are true, no civilized system of justice could fail to provide [Brzonkala] a remedy."[99] But, in an opinion that hewed closely to the reasoning of *Lopez,* they concluded that "[g]ender-motivated crimes are not, in any sense of the phrase, economic activity."[100] As such, they lay beyond the reach of Congress's power to regulate commerce.[101]

As in the prior cases, the dominant theme in the majority opinion was on the threat to state autonomy posed by any contrary holding. The chief justice emphasized that the "Constitution requires a distinction between what is truly national and what is truly local."[102] Stressing his belief that the Court's decision "preserve[s] one of the few principles that has been consistent since the [Commerce] Clause was adopted," Rehnquist declared that "[t]he regulation and punishment of intrastate violence that is not directed at the instrumentalities, channels, or goods involved in interstate commerce has always been the province of the States."[103] To hold otherwise would be to suggest that Congress could regulate virtually any crime, a prospect that would "undermine [a] central premise of our constitutional system."[104]

---

[97]120 S. Ct. 1740, 1748 (citing Lopez).

[98]42 U.S.C. § 13981(b) (1994).

[99]*Morrison,* 120 S. Ct. at 1759.

[100]Id. at 1751.

[101]The majority also rejected an attempt to justify the measure as an expression of Congress' authority under section 5 of the 14th Amendment, finding that it "is directed not at any State or state actor, but at individuals who have committed criminal acts motivated by gender bias." Id. at 1758.

[102]Id. at 1754.

[103]Id. (citing Cohens v. Virginia, 6 Wheat. 264 (1821)).

[104]Id. at 1752–53 & 1753 n.7. Justice Thomas concurred, but again signaled his belief that "the very notion of a 'substantial effect' test under the Commerce Clause is inconsistent with the original understanding of Congress' powers and this Court's early Commerce Clause cases." Id. at 1759 (Thomas concurring). Justice Souter wrote a scath-

An arguably different result obtained in a decision handed down just one week later, *Jones v. United States*.[105] Dewey Jones threw a Molotov cocktail into the a house owned and occupied by his cousin, producing both considerable damage and an indictment for violation of a federal statute that made it a crime to "maliciously damage or destroy . . . by means of fire . . . property used in interstate or foreign commerce of in any activity affecting interstate or foreign commerce."[106] The Court had previously held that the statute in question was an appropriate exercise of the commerce power when enforced against an individual who had torched a building "used as rental property," an activity the Court found "affect[ed] commerce within the meaning of" the statute.[107] The issue in *Jones* was whether the same measure "cover[ed] property occupied and used by its owner not for any commercial venture, but as a private residence."[108]

Writing for a unanimous Court, Justice Ginsburg found that it did not. This was not a case, she stressed early in her opinion, where the unqualified phrase "'affecting commerce' . . . signal[ed] Congress' intent to invoke its full authority under the Commerce Clause."[109] Rather, Section 844(i) required that the property be "used" in an activity affecting commerce, a "qualification . . . most sensibly read to mean active employment for commercial purposes, and not merely a passive, passing, or past connection to commerce."[110] The Court rejected the government's broad reading of the phrase "affecting commerce" in language that tracked closely the approach employed by the chief justice in *Morrison*. "Were we to adopt the Government's expansive interpretation of Section 844(i)," she warned, "hardly a building in the land would fall outside the federal statute's domain."[111] More tellingly, *Lopez* compelled this result, for "arson is a paradigmatic common-law state crime,"[112] one whose prosecution, absent a more direct connection with interstate commerce, properly remained with the states.[113]

---

ing dissent, joined by Justices Stevens, Ginsburg, and Breyer. Justice Breyer also dissented, in an opinion joined by the other three, but whose defense of the measure under the 14th Amendment drew the support of only Justice Stevens.

[105] 120 S. Ct. 1904 (2000).

[106] 18 U.S.C. § 844(1) (1994).

[107] Russell v. United States, 471 U.S. 858, 862 (1985).

[108] *Jones*, 120 S. Ct. at 1909.

[109] Id.

[110] Id. at 1910.

[111] Id. at 1911.

[112] Id. at 1912.

[113] Justice Stevens, joined by Justice Thomas, wrote a concurring opinion expressing his belief that a narrow reading was called for in the light of the danger that a contrary holding would preempt state authority without a clear expression of congressional intent to do so. Id. at 1912–13 (Stevens concurring). Justice Thomas, joined by Justice Scalia, also concurred, reserving judgment on whether the measure "as . . . construed, is constitu-

Taken together, these opinions reflect one side of the current interpretive coin, on which we find engraved a vision of the federal system within which the states must be afforded substantial independence and respect. A second series of decisions, in turn, focuses on a constitutionally distinct but, as the Court has recently emphasized, intellectually indistinguishable question: To what extent does the Constitution—in particular the Eleventh Amendment—shield the states, absent their consent, from suits against them filed by private citizens?

The Eleventh Amendment, ratified in 1798, was an immediate, and in the minds of the five justices currently intent on protecting state sovereignty, crystal clear response to *Chisolm v. Georgia,*[114] in which the Court held that the state of Georgia could be held accountable in federal court in an action brought by the executor of the estate of South Carolina merchant when the state failed to pay for war supplies purchased in 1777. Four of the participating justices believed the action proper, with only Justice Iredell in dissent. The outcry provoked by the decision was immediate and intense,[115] and Congress responded with a measure declaring that "[t]he Judicial power of the United States shall not be construed to extend to any suit in law or equity, commenced or prosecuted against one of the United States by Citizens of another State, or by Citizens or Subjects of any Foreign State."[116]

While arguably much more limited in scope if one avers simply to its text, the Court subsequently read the Eleventh Amendment as a general grant of sovereign immunity. In *Hans v. Louisiana,*[117] it held that the Eleventh Amendment does not simply bar suits against an unconsenting state by the citizen of another state. Rather, it embodies a general principle of immunity. Writing for the Court, Justice Bradley observed that "[t]he suability of a State without its consent was a thing unknown to the law."[118] And he argued that the ratification of the Eleventh Amendment represented more than a simple political rejection of *Chisolm.* It was, rather, a vindication of Justice Iredell's arguments in dissent, a verification that "[a]ny such power as that of authorizing the federal judiciary to entertain suits by individuals against the States, had been expressly disclaimed, and even

---

tional in its application to all buildings used for commercial activities." Id. at 1913 (Thomas concurring).

[114]2 Dall. 419 (1793).

[115]Many of the reactions and comments may be found in Maeva Marcus, ed., 5 The Documentary History of the Supreme Court of the United States, 1789–1800, at 217–73 (Columbia University Press, 1994). For a general discussion of the Amendment, see Clyde E. Jacobs, The Eleventh Amendment and Sovereign Immunity (Greenwood Press, 1972).

[116]U.S. Const. Amend. XI.

[117]134 U.S. 1 (1890).

[118]Id. at 16.

resented, by the great defenders of the Constitution while it was on its trial before the American people."[119]

Since *Hans,* Justice Scalia maintained in 1991, the Court has "understood the Eleventh Amendment to stand not so much for what it says, but for the presupposition of our constitutional structure which it confirms: that the States entered the federal system with their sovereignty intact; that the judicial authority in Article III is limited by this sovereignty."[120] It has, however, carved out two exceptions to this general rule.[121] One, subsequently recognized as the fiction it is,[122] was articulated in 1908 in *Ex parte Young,* in which the Court announced that "[i]f the act which [a state official] seeks to enforce be a violation of the Federal Constitution, the officer in proceeding under such enactment comes into conflict with the superior authority of that Constitution, and he is in that case stripped of his official or representative character and is subject in his person to the consequences of his individual conduct."[123] The second, announced in 1976, recognized that "the Eleventh Amendment, and the principle of sovereign immunity which it embodies, are necessarily limited by the enforcement provisions of Section 5 of the Fourteenth Amendment."[124] That being the case, "Congress may, in determining what is 'appropriate legislation' for the purpose of enforcing the provisions of the Fourteenth Amendment, provide for private suits against States or state officials which are constitutionally impermissible in other contexts."[125] The only limitation on this power, articulated in *Atascadero State Hospital v. Scanlon,* was that Congress must "unequivocally express this intention in statutory language [that] ensures . . . certainty."[126]

The current cycle of decisions began in 1989, when the Court extended the logic of *Fitzpatrick* and held in *Pennsylvania v. Union Gas Company* that Con-

---

[119]Id at 12.

[120]Blatchford v. Native Village of Noatak, 501 U.S. 775, 779 (1991).

[121]There was arguably a third exception, the "constructive waiver" theory articulated in Parden v. Terminal Railway Company, 377 U.S. 184 (1964), under which a voluntary state decision to engage in a commercial activity regulated by Congress constitutes "consent" to suit. The Court expressly overruled *Parden* in College Savings Bank v. Florida Prepaid Postsecondary Education Expense Board, 527 U.S. 666, 676–83 (1999). In addition, the Court has held that the prohibition does not extend to suits by the United States, see United States v. Texas, 143 U.S. 621 (1892), or by another state, see South Dakota v. North Carolina, 192 U.S. 286 (1904), and that political subdivisions are not the state for these purposes. See Mt. Healthy City Board of Education v. Doyle, 429 U.S. 274 (1977).

[122]See Pennhurst State School & Hospital v. Halderman, 465 U.S. 89, 105 (1984).

[123]209 U.S. 123, 159–60 (1908).

[124]Fitzpatrick v. Bitzer, 427 U.S. 445, 457 (1976). The opinion was written by then Justice Rehnquist for a unanimous Court, albeit with concurring opinions by Justices Brennan and Stevens.

[125]Id.

[126]473 U.S. 234, 243 (1985).

gress's plenary authority under the Commerce Clause included the power to permit suits in federal court against the states for money damages.[127] Writing for himself and Justices Marshall, Blackmun, and Stevens, Justice Brennan argued that "[l]ike the Fourteenth Amendment, the Commerce Clause with one hand gives power to Congress while, with the other, it takes power away from the States."[128] Believing that "the congressional power thus conferred would be incomplete without the authority to render States liable in damages," Justice Brennan concluded that "it must be that, to the extent that the States gave Congress the authority to regulate commerce, they also relinquished their immunity where Congress found it necessary, in exercising this authority, to render them liable."[129] Justice White, in turn, provided the necessary fifth vote in an opinion in which he wrote, enigmatically:

> This brings me to the question whether Congress has the constitutional power to abrogate the States' immunity. In that respect, I agree with the conclusion reached by Justice Brennan in Part III of his opinion, that Congress has the authority under Article I to abrogate the Eleventh Amendment immunity of the States, although I do not agree with much of his reasoning.[130]

*Union Gas* proved to be an exceedingly short-lived decision. Seven years later, Chief Justice Rehnquist announced the demise of a rule that had been characterized as an "unhappy" and "unstable" victory by those who viewed "state sovereign immunity as . . . constitutionally insignificant."[131] Writing for the now familiar federalism five in *Seminole Tribe of Florida v. Florida,* the chief justice observed that the *Union Gas* rationale "deviated sharply from our established federalism jurisprudence and essentially eviscerated our decision in *Hans.*"[132] He emphasized that "the background principle of state sovereign immunity embodied in the Eleventh Amendment is not so ephemeral as to dissipate

---

[127]491 U.S. 1 (1989).

[128]Id. at 16.

[129]Id. at 19–20.

[130]Id. at 57 (White concurring and dissenting). In his masterful biography of Justice White, Dennis Hutchinson characterized this passage as perhaps the "most damning example" of "White's opaque writing style and occasionally flip concurring opinions." Dennis J. Hutchinson, The Man Who Once Was Whizzer White: A Portrait of Justice Byron R. White 441 (The Free Pres, 1998). Justice White presumably wrote the opinion primarily to express his disagreement with the plurality's conclusion that the legislation at issue made the intent to abrogate "unmistakably clear," and that portion of his opinion was joined by Chief Justice Rehnquist and Justices O'Connor and Kennedy. Justice Scalia concurred and dissented in an opinion joined by Rehnquist, O'Connor, and Kennedy, and Justice O'Connor filed a separate dissent.

[131]*Union Gas,* 491 U.S. at 44–45 (Scalia concurring and dissenting).

[132]517 U.S. 44, 64 (1996).

when the subject of the suit is an area, like the regulation of . . . commerce, that is under the exclusive control of the Federal Government."[133] The logic of *Fitzpatrick* did not extend to a congressional waiver pursuant to an Article I power: "[T]he Fourteenth Amendment, adopted well after the adoption of the Eleventh Amendment and the ratification of the Constitution, operated to alter the pre-existing balance between state and federal power achieved by Article III and the Eleventh Amendment."[134] The Eleventh Amendment, the chief justice concluded, "restricts the judicial power under Article III, and Article I cannot be used to circumvent the constitutional limitations placed upon federal jurisdiction."[135]

One year later, in *Idaho v. Couer d'Alene Tribe of Idaho,* the Court calmed post-*Seminole Tribe* fears that the *Young* exception might be at risk, declaring that it must "ensure that the doctrine of sovereign immunity remains meaningful, while also giving recognition to the need to prevent violations of federal law."[136] Then, on the last day of its October 1998 term, it issued three separate rulings that both reaffirmed its vision of the Eleventh Amendment as a blanket grant of immunity and, in the process, arguably transformed the amendment itself.

Two of the decisions involved actions by a Florida agency that had allegedly appropriated for its own use a process for which a private entity, College Savings Bank, had secured patent and trademark protection. In the first case, the chief justice rejected College Savings' attempt to seek redress in a suit against the state authorized by a federal statute that, consistent with the rule announced in *Atascadero,* had signaled Congress's desire to include "States, instrumentalities of States, and officers and employees of States acting in their official capacity . . . subject to suit in Federal court by any person for infringement of patents and plant variety protections."[137] Relying on *Seminole Tribe,* the chief justice emphasized that neither the Commerce nor Patent Clauses, both Article I provisions, provided a basis for abrogation. He then rejected the argument that the act was an "appropriate" exercise of Congress's powers under Section 5 of the Fourteenth Amendment, applying the Court's holding in *City of Boerne v. Flores,*[138] which "emphasized that Congress' enforcement power is 'remedial' in nature."[139] This meant "that for Congress to invoke Section 5, it must identify

---

[133]Id. at 72.

[134]Id. at 65–66.

[135]Id. at 72–73. Justice Stevens filed a lengthy dissent, as did Justice Souter, who was joined by Justice Ginsburg and Breyer.

[136]521 U.S. 261, 269 (1997).

[137]Florida Prepaid Postsecondary Education Expense Board v. College Savings Bank, 527 U.S. 627, 632 (1999) (quoting the Patent and Plant Variety Protection Remedy Clarification Act, P.L. 102–560 (1990) (codified at 35 U.S.C. § 271 (a) (1998)).

[138]521 U.S. 507 (1997).

[139]*Florida Prepaid,* 527 U.S. 638 (citing *City of Boerne,* 521 U.S. at 519).

conduct transgressing the Fourteenth Amendment's substantive provisions, and it must tailor its legislative scheme to remedying or preventing such conduct."[140] But "[i]n enacting the Patent Remedy Act . . . Congress identified no pattern of patent infringement by the States, let alone a pattern of constitutional violations."[141] Congress had not, accordingly, met its burden, and its attempt to subject the states to suit in federal court could not be sustained.[142]

In the companion case, Justice Scalia rejected College Savings trademark claim in a decision that produced the same 5–4 alignment.[143] He first rejected the suggestion the interests alleged by College Savings constituted property rights protected by the Due Process Clause, in language that tracked closely fears expressed in prior cases that a broad reading of federal power would inappropriately encroach on areas reserved to the states: "To sweep within the Fourteenth Amendment the elusive property interests that are 'by definition' protected by unfair-competition law would violate our frequent admonition that the Due Process Clause is not merely a 'font of tort law.'"[144] He then rejected the suggestion that Florida had waived its immunity by voluntarily engaging in an activity regulated by federal law, declaring that "the constructive-waiver experiment of *Parden* was ill conceived, and [we] see no merit in attempting to salvage any remnant of it."[145]

The third decision, *Alden v. Maine*,[146] dealt with a previously unanswered question, whether the immunity doctrines would also bar a suit filed against an unconsenting state in its own courts. The state of Maine had failed to pay overtime to certain probation officers, and their initial suit in federal court, which was pending when *Seminole Tribe* was decided, was dismissed. The officers then filed the same action in state court, relying on a provision of the Fair Labor Standards Act "purporting to authorize private actions against States in their own courts without regard for consent."[147] The Court rejected this attempt, finding that the state had not consented and that Article I did not authorize a suit in state court absent that consent.

Writing for the Court, Justice Kennedy offered an extended vision of the full nature of the majority's notions of sovereignty, stressing that "immunity

---

[140]Id. at 639.

[141]Id. at 640.

[142]Justice Stevens dissented, writing for himself and Justices Souter, Ginsburg, and Breyer.

[143]College Savings Bank v. Florida Prepaid Postsecondary Education Expense Board, 527 U.S. 666 (1999). Once again, Justice Stevens filed a solitary dissent and then joined the remaining four in a dissent written by Justice Breyer.

[144]Id. at 674 (quoting Paul v. Davis, 424 U.S. 693, 701 (1976)).

[145]Id. at 680 (discussing and overruling Parden v. Terminal Railway Company, 377 U.S. 184 (1964)).

[146]527 U.S. 706 (1999).

[147]Id. at 712 (citing 29 U.S.C. §§ 216(b) & 203(x) (1998)).

from private suits" is "central to sovereign dignity."[148] He declared that "Congress has vast power but not all power," and that "[w]hen Congress legislates in matters affecting the States, it may not treat these sovereign entities as mere prefectures or corporations."[149] Regarding the specific issue in the case, compliance with the overtime provisions of the Fair Labor Standards Act, he observed that "[t]he State of Maine has not questioned Congress' power to prescribe substantive rules of federal law to which it must comply."[150] Such compliance must, however, come from either the voluntary actions of the state—which, in this instance, were eventually secured—or from "a suit by the United States on behalf of the employees,"[151] a form of redress long understood to be permissible.[152]

Justice Kennedy emphasized, however, that for the majority this reflected more than a simple application of the Eleventh Amendment:

> We have . . . sometimes referred to the States' immunity from suit as "Eleventh Amendment immunity." The phrase is a convenient shorthand but something of a misnomer, for the sovereign immunity of the States neither derives from, nor is limited by, the terms of the Eleventh Amendment. Rather, as the Constitution's structure, its history, and the authoritative interpretations by this Court make clear, the States' immunity from suit is a fundamental aspect of the sovereignty which the States enjoyed before the ratification of the Constitution, and which they retain today (either literally or by virtue of their admission to the Union upon an equal footing with the other States) except as altered by the plan of the Convention of certain constitutional amendments.[153]

He then stressed that "[a]lthough the Constitution establishes a National Government with broad, often plenary authority over matters within its recognized competence, the founding document 'specifically recognizes the States as sovereign entities.'"[154] And, in language that tied his opinion directly to the principles articulated in the Court's Tenth Amendment decisions, he declared that "[a]ny doubt regarding the constitutional role of the States as sovereign entities is removed by the Tenth Amendment, which, like the other provisions of the Bill

---

[148]Id. at 715.

[149]Id. at 758.

[150]Id. at 759.

[151]Id.

[152]"In ratifying the Constitution, the States consented to suits brought by other States or by the Federal Government." Id. at 755 (citing Principality of Monaco v. Mississippi, 292 U.S. 313 (1934)).

[153]Id. at 713.

[154]Id. (quoting *Seminole Tribe,* 517 U.S. at 71 n.15).

of Rights, was enacted to allay lingering concerns about the extent of the national power."[155]

Then, in a decision parsing the Age Discrimination in Employment Act, the Court held in *Kimel v. Florida Board of Regents* that while the Act did contain a "clear statement of Congress' intent to abrogate the States' immunity, . . . that abrogation exceeded Congress' authority under Section 5 of the Fourteenth Amendment."[156] Once again, the majority applied the rule articulated in *City of Boerne*, finding that the ADEA was not "appropriate" legislation, in that it failed to evidence "a congruence and proportionality between the injury to prevented or remedied and the means adopted to that end."[157] The Court had consistently held, Justice O'Connor observed, that discrimination on the basis of age warranted only rational basis scrutiny, which "permits States to draw lines on the basis of age when they have a rational basis for doing so at a class-based level, even if it 'is probably not true' that those reasons are valid in the majority of cases."[158] That meant, as a practical matter, that there was very little state conduct that would be deemed unconstitutional for the purposes of supporting abrogation. In addition, she emphasized that the "legislative record as a whole . . . reveals that Congress had virtually no reason to believe that state and local governments were unconstitutionally discriminating on the basis of age."[159] While not dispositive, that reality meant that "Congress had no reason to believe that broad prophylactic legislation was necessary in this field,"[160] especially where, as was the case here, the constitutional "presupposition" of state immunity provided "substantial reasons for adhering to that constitutional design."[161]

These same themes emerged during the Court's October 2000 term. In an entirely predictable reprise of both the issues and the Court's continuing alignment, Chief Justice Rehnquist announced on February 21, 2001, that the provision of the Americans with Disabilities Act that authorized a private cause of action for damages by state employees was invalid.[162] In each important respect the opinion was a reprise of *Kimel*. Congress may not, the chief justice reminded us, "base its abrogation of the States' Eleventh Amendment immunity upon the powers enumerated in Article I."[163] Any attempt to invoke Section 5 of the Four-

---

[155]Id. at 713–14. Justice Souter filed a lengthy dissent, in which he was joined by Justice Stevens, Ginsburg, and Breyer.

[156]120 S. Ct. 631, 637 (2000).

[157]Id. at 644 (quoting *City of Boerne*, 521 U.S. at 520).

[158]Id. at 647.

[159]Id. at 649.

[160]Id. at 650.

[161]Id. at 643. Justice Thomas, joined by Justice Kennedy, concurred in part and dissented in part, maintaining that the congressional intent to abrogate was not clear. Justice Stevens wrote a full dissent in which Justices Souter, Ginsburg, and Breyer joined.

[162]Board of Trustees of the University of Alabama v. Garrett, 121 S. Ct. 955 (2001).

[163]Id. at 962 (citing *Kimel*).

teenth Amendment, in turn, required that the Court "identify with some precision the scope of the constitutional right at issue" and "examine the limitations § 1 of the Fourteenth Amendment places on States' treatment of the disabled."[164] Relying largely on its discussion of the applicable equal protection principles in *Cleburne v. Cleburne Living Center, Inc.*,[165] the majority invoked rational basis review and held that "where a group possesses 'distinguishing characteristics relevant to interests the State has the authority to implement,' a State's decision to act on the basis of those differences does not give rise to a constitutional violation."[166] The legislative record, in turn, revealed "only . . . minimal evidence of unconstitutional state discrimination against the disabled."[167] The measure was, accordingly, neither "congruent" nor "proportional" within the meaning of *Boerne* and *Kimel*, and the admittedly express congressional waiver of state immunity was invalid.[168]

These decisions, in which the Court has fashioned its current understanding of the relationship between nation and states, are obviously infinitely more complex than this terse summary indicates. More importantly, the issues they pose for individual citizens are profound, a reality eloquently expressed in Professor Leuchtenburg's deft hands. Before turning the reader over to him and his colleagues, however, I add the following observations of my own about the nature and implications of what the Court is about and how it has proceeded.

## Why *This* Constitution?

It seems almost silly to ask why we have a Constitution, and that is not the purpose of this discussion. The question is rather why we have the particular text we do, and what judgments we should draw about the reasons for its enactment and the manner in which those who wrote and debated the text viewed that instrument. My reading of the history and the cases suggests that there is an important perspective regarding "the states as states" that is absent from the Court's opinions. I also believe it important to recognize the full significance of the fact that the Framers and Founders understood that the structure they created was indeed new and radical, and that this reality counsels a slightly different interpretive approach than the one commonly embraced. These perspectives strike me as especially important given the manner in which the Court has pro-

---

[164]Id. at 963.

[165]473 U.S. 432 (1985).

[166]*Garrett,* 121 S. Ct. at 963 (quoting *Cleburne,* 473 U.S. at 441).

[167]Id. at 965–66.

[168]Justice Kennedy, joined by Justice O'Connor, concurred. Justice Breyer, joined by Justices Stevens, Souter, and Ginsburg, dissented.

ceeded, both as a reflection on the soundness of the history they profess to explore and the manner in which they do it.

It is above all else worth recalling that the pre-Constitution Confederation was, in perhaps the most apt turn of phrase embraced by Publius, one marked by an "incurable disorder and imbecility in the government."[169] As James Wilson stressed, "[t]he commencement of peace was likewise the commencement of our distress and disgrace."[170] It is then hardly surprising that thoughtful individuals like George Washington, on the eve of the Convention from which the Constitution would emerge, would postulate the need for "thorough reform[s]," not the least of which would be a means by which the nation would be able to secure "obedience to the Ordinances of a Genl. Government" from individual states whose "non-compliance" with national policies and needs had become the rule rather than the exception.[171] The problem, Madison observed, was clear: "[T]he articles of confederation have inconsiderately endeavored to accomplish impossibilities; to reconcile a partial sovereignty in the Union, with compleat sovereignty in the States."[172]

Simply put, the Framers and Founders recognized that the states were not the solution, and that state sovereignty was not the unalloyed blessing that much of the current rhetoric ascribes to it. The states were, rather, the primary source of the problems that plagued the Confederation. And it was in notions of sovereignty, in particular in the express declaration in the Articles of Confederation that each of the 13 states "retains its sovereignty, freedom and independence," that the seeds that presaged the Confederation's doom were sown.[173]

In his important, and regretfully, not-often referenced pre-Convention essay the *Vices of the Political System of the United States,*[174] for example, Madison identified 12 specific categories of concern that described "the mortal diseases of the existing constitution."[175] Each documented, albeit some more forcefully than others, difficulties caused by a structure that was "in fact nothing more than a treaty of amity of commerce and of alliance, between so many independent

---

[169]Federalist 9 (Hamilton), at 55, in Jacob E. Cooke, ed., The Federalist (Weslyan University Press, 1961).

[170]Speech of James Wilson, Pennsylvania Convention, 24 Nov. 1787, in Merrill Jensen, ed., 2 Documentary History of the Ratification of the Constitution, at 340, 347 (State Historical Society of Wisconsin, 1976) ("Documentary History").

[171]Letter from George Washington to James Madison, Mar. 31, 1787, in Robert A. Rutland & William M. E. Rachal, eds., 9 The Papers of James Madison, at 242, 243 (University Press of Virginia, 1973) ("Madison's Papers").

[172]Federalist 42 (Madison), at 284–85 (cited in note 169).

[173]Act of Confederation of the United States of America, 15 Nov. 1777, Art. II, 1 Documentary History, at 86 (cited in note 170).

[174]Vices of the Political system of the U. States, April, 1787, in 9 Madison's Papers, at 348 (cited in note 171).

[175]James Madison to Thomas Jefferson, Mar. 19, 1787, in id. at 317, 318.

and Sovereign States."[176] The problems posed by the states were "numerous," and "repetitions may be foreseen in almost every case where any favorite object of a State shall present a temptation."[177] Madison would continue to support the existence and prerogatives of the states. In a letter to Edmund Randolph, he conceded that "I think with you that it will be well to retain as much as possible of the old Confederation, tho' I doubt whether it may not be best to work the valuable articles into the new System, instead of engrafting the latter on the former."[178] But he understood the problems inherent in a system in which the nation was answerable to the states, and the Constitution he help draft and supported carved out a "middle ground" between full sovereignty for either party.

Madison and his colleagues recognized that if the states were the problem, then a strong national government, supreme when it operated within its proper sphere, was the solution. That sphere would be a limited one. As Madison emphasized in *The Federalist:*

> The powers delegated by the proposed Constitution to the federal government are few and defined. Those which are to remain in the State governments are numerous and indefinite. The former will be exercised principally on external objects, as war, peace, negotiation, and foreign commerce; with which the last the power of taxation will, for the most part, be connected. The powers reserved to the several states will extend to all objects which, in the ordinary course of affairs concern the lives, liberties, and properties of the people, and the internal order, improvement, and prosperity of the State.[179]

But, where the federal government was to act, it needed to act effectively. The Framers and Founders understood that "[i]f Congress have not the power it is annihilated for the nation."[180] Recognizing that one of the primary virtues of congressional action was the ability to fashion a "uniform & practical sanction" in the face of dangers posed by competing or contradictory state regimes,[181] they

---

[176]Id. at 351.

[177]Id. at 348. The same, obviously, seems true today, with the Congress as the too often tempted sinner.

[178]James Madison to Edmund Randolph, April 8, 1787, in 9 Madison's Papers, at 368, 369 (cited in note 171). It is worth noting, given current questions about the scope of the Commerce Clause, and in particular Justices Thomas' views on that provision, that Randolph had written Madison in December, agreeing that "Congress want additional powers," but indicating that "[I] can't suppress my fears of giving that of regulating commerce." Letter from Edmund Randolph, Dec 9, 1786, id. at 201, 202.

[179]Federalist 45 (Madison), at 313 (cited in note 169).

[180]Letter to Joseph C. Cabell, Sept. 18, 1828, in Gaillard Hunt, ed., 9 The Writings of James Madison 316, 330 (G. P. Putnam's Sons, 1908) ("Madison's Writings").

[181]Id. at 332–33. See also id. at 334–35 (position consistent with the holding in Brown v. Maryland 12 Wheat 419 (1827)).

believed it would be foolish to "refer a State therefore to the exercise of a power reserved to her by the Constitution, the impossibility of exercising which was an inducement to adopt the Constitution is, of all remedial devices the last that ought to be brought forward."[182] In that respect, as Madison noted, the states, as states, would properly be viewed as "subordinately useful,"[183] subject to a "national Government armed with a positive and compleat authority in all cases where uniform measures are necessary."[184]

It was against this backdrop, one within which the Framers and Founders recognized a fundamental tension between state and national sovereignty, that the Constitution was ratified and the 10 amendments that became known as the Bill of Rights were proposed and accepted. There were, obviously, a substantial number of individuals who disagreed with the approach taken and, in particular, harbored fears about the extent to which a federal leviathan would swallow putatively helpless states.[185] Indeed, as I have argued at greater length elsewhere, the individuals to whom the text was presented understood that the proposal before them in fact had substantial implications for the independence of the states.[186] The text of the letter transmitting the Constitution to the Confederation Congress noted expressly that "[i]t is obviously impracticable in the federal government of these States; to secure all rights of independent sovereignty to each, and yet provide for the interest and safety of all—Individuals entering into society, must give up a share of liberty to preserve the rest."[187] The powers of "the general

---

[182]Id. at 336. See also id. at 337 (quoting Virginia resolutions stressing "uniformity in their commercial regulations as the *only* effectual policy").

[183]Letter to Randolph, id. at 369.

[184]Id. at 370. He repeated this observation, virtually verbatim, in a subsequent letter to Washington, stressing that "the national Government should be armed with positive and compleat authority in all cases which require uniformity; such as the regulation of trade, including the right of taxing both exports and imports, the fixing the terms and forms of naturalization, &c &c." Letter to George Washington, April 16, 1787, in 9 id. at 383, 383.

[185]For a discussion of the opponents of the Constitution and their views, see Saul Cornell, The Other Founders: Anti-Federalism & the Dissenting Tradition in America, 1788–1828 (University of North Carolina Press, 1999), and Christopher M. Duncan, The Anti-Federalists and Early American Political Thought (Northern Illinois University Press, 1995).

[186]See Mark R. Killenbeck, Pursuing the Great Experiment: Reserved Powers in a Post-Ratification, Compound Republic, 1999 The Supreme Court Review 81 ("Pursuing").

[187]Letter from the President of the Convention to the President of Congress, Sept. 17, 1787 ("President's Letter"), in 1 Documentary History, at 305, 305 (cited in note 170). For a more extended discussion of the letter and its significance, see also Daniel A. Farber, The Constitution's Forgotten Cover Letter: An Essay on the New Federalism and the Original Understanding, 94 Mich. L. Rev. 615 (1995).

government of the Union" were, accordingly, to be "fully and effectively vested" in that entity, consistent with "that which appears to us the greatest interest of every true American, the consolidation of our Union, in which is involved our prosperity, felicity, safety, perhaps our national existence."[188] And individual state interests that might prove "particularly disagreeable or injurious to others" were deemed expendable in light of "our most ardent wish" to promote "the lasting welfare of that country so dear to us all, and secure her freedom and happiness."[189]

As indicated, these express assurances regarding the existence of certain supreme federal powers and their implications for the states animated much of the opposition to the Constitution. But that instrument was ratified by the people, and with that act they accepted the notion that what was now required was "a more perfect Union" within which the powers of the central government would be expanded in ways that made its primacy in matters national both obvious and enforceable. Indeed, the Supremacy Clause, which made this change clear, reflected "the very nature of the Constitution."[190] For if the people were going to be successful in their quest "to establish a national government, that government ought, to the extent of its powers and rights, to be supreme."[191] Any other course of action—any approach that, in the words of the current majority, "preserve[d] the sovereign status of the states"[192]—would, by attributing totemic significance to notions of state sovereignty, run the risk of replicating the mistakes of the Confederation, creating "a mere treaty, dependent upon the good faith of the parties, and not a government, which is only another name for political power and supremacy."[193]

This does not mean that the document forwarded to the people for their consideration answered every possible question with absolute clarity and precision. Which brings me to a second general reservation about the current judicial methodology, the extent to which the Court would have us believe that the understandings of 1787 are definitive.

Virtually everyone at that time understood that the Constitution was imprecise in the manner in which it described things and would be used to structure a government and union that would function in radically altered circumstances.

---

[188]President's Letter, at 305 (cited in note 187).

[189]Id. at 306.

[190]Joseph Story, 3 Commentaries on the Constitution of the United States § 1831 (Hilliard, Gray & Co, 1833) ("Story").

[191]Id.

[192]*Alden,* 527 U.S. at 714. In fairness, Justice Kennedy stresses that the states "retain the dignity, though not the *full* authority, of sovereignty." Id. at 715 (emphasis added). Given the nature of the rhetoric found in *Alden* and elsewhere, however, it is difficult to sense what the principled limits of the concept might be.

[193]3 Story, at 1831 (cited in note 183).

The *President's Letter,* for example, conceded that it had been "difficult to draw with precision the line between those rights which must be surrendered, and those which may be reserved," and emphasized that this task had been made especially difficult "by a difference among the several states as to their situation, extent, habits, and particular interests."[194] It stressed that any initial understandings would be subject to interpretive change, "depend[ent] as well on situation and circumstance, as on the object to be obtained."[195] As James Wilson observed when he responded to concerns expressed during the Pennsylvania Convention about the scope of the powers granted:

> They have asserted that these powers are unlimited and undefined. These words are as easily pronounced as limited and defined. . . . [I]t is not pretended that the line is drawn with mathematical precision; the inaccuracy of language must, to a certain degree, prevent the accomplishment of such a desire. Whoever views the matter in a true light will see that the powers are as minutely enumerated and defined as was possible, and will also discover that the general clause [Article I, Section 8] . . . is nothing more than what was necessary to render effectual the particular powers that are granted.[196]

The Framers and Founders drafted and ratified a constitution, a document that did not "partake of the prolixity of a legal code."[197] This meant that it would be necessary for the political process and, in particular, Congress to "liquidate and ascertain" its meaning as they developed an understanding of what it meant, for example, to regulate commerce.[198] As Representative Theodore Sedgwick observed early on, "the Constitution had expressly declared the ends of Legislation; but in almost every instance had left the means to the honest and sober discretion of the Legislature."[199] This would not be an easy task. Madison, for example, lamented early in the first session that "[a]mong other difficulties, the

---

[194]President's Letter at 305 (cited in note 187).

[195]Id.

[196]James Wilson (Dec 4, 1787), in Merrill Jensen, ed., in 2 Documentary History, at 493, 496 (cited in note 163). See also President's Letter, at 305, 305 ("It is at all times difficult to draw with precision the line between those rights which must be surrendered and those which may be reserved.") (cited in note 187).

[197]M'Culloch v. Maryland, 4 Wheat. 316, 407 (1819).

[198]I draw the allusion from Madison, who observed that the proper delineation of the respective authority of nation and states was a matter deliberately left "more or less obscure and equivocal, until [its] meaning be liquidated and ascertained by a series of particular discussions and adjudications." Federalist 37 (Madison), at 236 (cited in note 169).

[199]2 Annals of Congress 1962 (1789).

exposition of the Constitution is frequently a copious source, and must continue so until its meaning on all great points shall have been settled by precedents."[200]

Ironically, Justice Kennedy comes closest to understanding the true nature of the situation when he observes that "[f]ederalism was our Nation's own discovery. The Framers split the atom of sovereignty," and "[t]he resulting Constitution created a legal system unprecedented in form and design."[201] The allusion has a certain rhetorical appeal. But, like the scientific feat accomplished in 1945 that introduced the nuclear age, it points us toward the uncertainties attendant to what the Framers and Founders themselves would refer to, repeatedly, as a "great experiment."[202] We sometimes forget that many of the individuals who fashioned the atomic bomb harbored substantial doubts about what would happen when the first of their devices was triggered. For them, splitting the atom posed vast opportunities. But it was also an occasion for uncertainty, prompted by the recognition that the world would, quite literally, never again be the same. This was, I believe, also true for the Framer and Founders. As Madison would observe, "[i]t ought to have occurred that the Govt. of the U.S. being a novelty & a compound, had no technical terms or phrases appropriate to it, and that old terms were to be used in new senses, explained by the context or by the facts of the case."[203]

---

[200]Letter to Samuel Johnston, June 21, 1789, in 12 Madison's Papers at 250 (cited in note 171). For a discussion of how Congress handled these issues, and the significance of what it accomplished, see David P. Currie, The Constitution in Congress: The Federalist Period 1789–1801 (University of Chicago Press, 1997); Joseph M. Lynch, Negotiating the Constitution: The Earliest Debates Over Original Intent (Cornell University Press, 1999); Kent Greenfield, Original Penumbras: Constitutional Interpretation in the First Year of Congress, 26 Conn. L. Rev. 79 (1993).

[201]United States Term Limits, Inc. v. Thornton, 514 U.S. 779, 838 (1995) (Kennedy concurring).

[202]See Thomas Jefferson, The solemn Declaration and Protest of the commonwealth of Virginia on the principles of the constitution of the U.S. of America and the violations of them, in 3 James Morton Smith, ed., The Republic of Letters: The Correspondence between Thomas Jefferson and James Madison 1776–1826, at 1944, 1946 (Norton, 1995) (characterizing complex and evolving questions of governance as matters to be "pursue[d] with temper and perseverance" as the nation struggles continuously to perfect "the great experiment which shall prove that man is capable of living in society, governing itself by laws self-imposed, and securing to its members the enjoyment of life, liberty, property and peace"). For other uses of this metaphor, see George Washington, Farewell Address, Sept. 17, 1796, in 1 James D. Richardson, ed., A Compilation of the Messages and Papers of the Presidents, at 213, 216 (Government Printing Office, 1897) ("It is well worth a fair and full experiment."); Letter to John Adams, May 22, 1817, in 8 Madison's Writings at 390, 391 (cited in note 180) (the "proper division and distribution of power among different bodies" is a "great question" and "experiment").

[203]Letter to N. P. Trist, Dec 1831, in 9 Madison's Writings at 471, 475 (cited in note 180).

It is then essential that we recognize that concepts of sovereignty, and especially of the sovereignty of states that were about to enter into a union in which the national government was by intent supreme, were exemplars of the old terms that were about to be used in new senses. It is also important to understand that the Tenth Amendment recognized an important aspect of this transformation by speaking expressly of "the people" and their role as one of the principal and quite possibly the preeminent repositories of sovereignty. That is a point quite properly emphasized by Rakove,[204] and worth repeating, as it is a perspective largely absent from the opinions of those justices expounding on "the benefits of this federal structure" in ways that celebrate the role of the states and minimize that of Congress.[205] In essence, the majority speaks of a Tenth Amendment whose only apparent contribution to text and nation is its affirmation of the primacy of state government. Simply put, they assign institutional autonomy the preeminent role. In *New York v. United States,* for example, Justice O'Connor describes a division of power "among sovereigns and among branches of government" in ways that seem to treat the "residuary and inviolable sovereignty" of the states as beyond the reach of even the people themselves.[206] But this view Bowdlerizes the amendment, reading "the people" out of the text, or at least relegating them to a role inconsistent with the understanding that in our constitutional system, it is the people themselves who are sovereign, for "the supreme power . . . *resides* in the People, as the fountain of government."[207]

Finally, I believe it important to recognize the extent to which the majority glosses over certain matters, treating them in ways that provoke the suspicion they are more interested in results than rationales. This is not to say that the dissenting justices have always comported themselves with complete perfection. But the majority leads us to believe that theirs is purely a quest for "principles" dictated by history and constitutional design. This is especially evident in the more recent Eleventh Amendment cases, within which we are now informed that the results are driven not by the text of that amendment, but rather by the belief that "[t]he generation that designed and adopted our federal system considered immunity from private suits central to sovereign dignity."[208] And while the issues posed by the amendment are complex, and their appropriate resolution far

---

[204]See Original Understanding, at 124–26 (cited in note 47).

[205]*New York,* 505 U.S. at 157.

[206]Id. at 187 & 188 (quoting Federalist 39 (Madison)).

[207]James Wilson, Speech of Dec. 4, 1787, in 2 Documentary History, at 474 (cited in note 170). Wilson would repeat this point in *Chisolm:* "To the Constitution of the United States, the term SOVEREIGN, is totally unknown." *Chisolm,* 2 Dall. at 454. "A *State,*" Wilson stressed, might be a useful and valuable . . . contrivance," but it was also "the *inferior* contrivance of *man;* and from his *native* dignity derives all its *acquired* importance." Id. at 455.

[208]*Alden,* 527 U.S. at 715.

from clear, there are reasons to harbor some reservations about how we have reached this point.

For example, the reaction to *Chisolm* by the individuals who sought and ratified the Eleventh Amendment was certainly consistent with a principled belief that suits against the states posed substantial constitutional difficulties in and of themselves. It is, however, equally plausible that the act of drafting and ratification reflected a more fundamental impulse, the fear that the Court's ruling meant that several deeply indebted states would now actually be required to honor their financial obligations. As Chief Justice Marshall subsequently observed:

> It is a part of our history, that, at the adoption of the constitution, all the States were greatly indebted; and the apprehension that these debts might be prosecuted in the federal Courts, formed a very serious objection to that instrument. Suits were instituted; and the Court maintained its jurisdiction. The alarm was general; and, to quiet the apprehensions that were so extensively entertained, this amendment was proposed in Congress, and adopted by the State legislatures. That its motive was not to maintain the sovereignty of a State from the degradation supposed to attend compulsory appearance before the tribunal of the nation, may be inferred from the terms of the amendment. . . . We must ascribe the amendment, then, to some other cause than the dignity of a State. There is no difficulty in finding this cause. . . . Those who were inhibited from commencing a suit against a State, or from prosecuting one which might be commenced before the adoption of the amendment, were persons who might be its creditors.[209]

Marshall's is but one perspective on these issues, and even his own thoughts on the matter are arguably conflicted.[210] But the majority insists that it is appropriate to ignore the fact that the amendment speaks expressly of only one type of federal jurisdiction, relying in large measure on the holding in *Hans*. That might be an appropriate inference, but it is surely one that is much more equivocal than the majority would lead us to believe, especially when these same individuals

---

[209]Cohens v. Virginia, 6 Wheat. 264, 406 (1821). This passage does not rule out a doctrine of sovereign immunity, as Marshall concludes with the observation that "[t]he amendment, therefore, extended to suits commenced or prosecuted by individuals, but not to those brought by States." Id. at 407. It does, however, touch on and call into question one central aspect of the current majority's take on these matters, the extent to which the 11th Amendment reflects a commitment to an essential founding principle, rather than simply a pragmatic attempt on the part of the states to avoid their debts.

[210]In the Virginia convention, for example, Marshall indicated that he saw "a difficulty making a state defendant, which does not prevent its being plaintiff," Jonathan Elliot, ed., 3 The Debates in the Several State Conventions on the Adoption of the Federal Constitution, at 533 (2d ed., J. B. Lippincott Co., 1896), a fact noted by Justice Kennedy in his opinion for the Court in *Alden*. See *Alden*, 527 U.S. at 715–16.

express today the same fear that may have motivated the passage of the amendment to begin with, that "[p]rivate suits against nonconsenting States—especially suits for money damages—may threaten the financial integrity of the States."[211] I am troubled, accordingly, by opinions that treat sovereignty as ineluctably an expression of concerns for dignity, rather than recognizing, as often seems to be the case, that it may then have been, and remains now, a convenient construct behind which states may lurk while evading their responsibilities. And I have reservations about the extent to which it is appropriate to rely on the judgments of Justice Iredell and the *Hans* Court when there is every reason to believe that their vision of sovereignty is grounded in preratification understandings that may well not easily transfer to a postratification arrangement that, by "splitting the atom of sovereignty," fundamentally transformed both political theory and this nation.

I am also concerned about the manner in which the Court has treated *Union Gas*. As noted, the primary opinion in that case represented the views of a plurality that achieved the status of decision by virtue of Justice White's concurring opinion. And while he did not explain himself, when speaking of the specific question, "the constitutional power to abrogate the States' immunity," Justice White's response regarding the power itself could not have been clearer: "I agree with the conclusion reached by Justice Brennan . . . that Congress has the authority under Article I to abrogate the Eleventh Amendment immunity of the States, although I do not agree with much of his reasoning."[212]

In *Seminole Tribe,* however, Justice White is described as writing separately in *Union Gas* "in order to express that he '[d]id not agree with much of [the plurality's] reasoning'" and as writing "separately in order to indicate his disagreement with the plurality's rationale."[213] These are both accurate statements, as far as they go. But both ignore a fact of some consequence, that the rule in *Union Gas* commanded five firm votes, even if the manner in which Justice Brennan reasoned toward that conclusion does not. Does this matter? Probably not. But it is important to recognize that *Seminole Tribe* is at least as much *coup d'etat* as it is reasoned evolution in judicial reasoning, a matter of no small importance for a majority that itself now complains of the "refusal" of the dissenting justices to "engage in meaningful debate on the place of state sovereign immunity in the Constitution."[214]

---

[211]*Alden,* 527 U.S. at 750. I am not insensitive to the financial implications attendant to many suits against the states, but I find reprehensible the notion that states should be released from obligations imposed by the people writ large simply because they are unwilling to meet their financial responsibilities.

[212]*Union Gas,* 491 U.S. at 57 (White concurring and dissenting).

[213]*Seminole Tribe,* 517 U.S. at 59–60 & 64 (quoting *Union Gas,* 491 U.S. at 57 (White concurring and dissenting).

[214]*Kimel,* 120 S. Ct. at 643.

Ultimately, a proper understanding of the role of the states requires that their powers and prerogatives be assessed in context, not as inquiries into the nature and import of sovereignty per se, but rather in the light of the manner in which the Framers and Founders intended the system to operate over time. That is a difficult task in its own right, and has been compounded over the years by the transformation of the federal government's role in response to the realities posed by a substantially changed nation, a transformation that occurred as part of a process of "liquidating and ascertaining" the meaning of an inherently imprecise and dynamic text.

It is, for example, clear beyond doubt that the founding generation did not envision a society in which the Commerce Clause would serve as the constitutional predicate for a system in which the federal government would regulate vast swaths of our economic and social life.[215] Opponents of an expansive federal presence may, quite properly, lament decisions like *Wickard v. Filburn,*[216] and seek their demise. But it is important to recognize that there is another side to the *Wickard* coin, one that contemplates the necessity of federal intervention in those circumstances where it is obvious that any attempt to rely on the states would truly and tragically be misplaced. The Court's decisions sustaining an expansive reading of the commerce power in the various Civil Rights Acts, for example, strike me as appropriate decisions of a Court that recognized the truly serious problems the nation faced.[217] And the consequences of repudiation are, I suspect, far more than those castigating the "original sin" of *Wickard* would be willing to pay.

Proponents of the various measures struck down in *Lopez* and *Morrison* will surely disagree, but there is nevertheless an abiding sense that neither of the statutes at issue in those cases reflected the sort of circumstances that offered the social and political foundations for much of the legislation sustained as part of the Roosevelt Revolution. The Gun Free Schools Zone Act offers a compelling example. In his lengthy dissent, Justice Breyer offers an impassioned defense of

---

[215]This does not necessarily mean that they would find many modern measures inconsistent with their own understanding of that clause. As I have noted in another forum, Congress early on enacted statutes that did not appear to proceed on the assumption that the Commerce Power, for example, was confined to the regulation of "selling, buying, and bartering, as well as transporting for these purposes," *Lopez,* 514 U.S. 549, 585 (1995) (Thomas concurring), but were rather constitutionally proper exercises of the enumerated power because it seemed to believe that the objects of regulation had what is now referred to as a "'substantial effect' on [interstate] commerce." One of these measures was an act for the government and regulation of seamen in the merchants service, Act of July 20, 1790, Ch. 29, 1 Stat. 131. I discuss the act, and its significance, in Pursuing, at 93–95 (cited in note 186).

[216]317 U.S. 111 (1942).

[217]See, for example, Katzenbach v. McClung, 379 U.S. 294 (1964); Heart of Atlanta Motel, Inc. v. United States, 379 U.S. 241 (1964).

the measure, speculating that "Congress *could* have found that gun-related violence near the classroom poses a serious economic threat."[218] And he marshals
an imposing array of materials in support of this proposition.[219] Unfortunately,
there is no real reason to believe that Congress, collectively, viewed the measure
as anything other than a politically popular quick fix for problems that may or
may not have existed and that it may or may not have understood.

The fate of the Violence Against Women Act is more troubling, especially
in the light of that measure's substantial legislative record "regarding the serious
impact that gender-motivated violence has on victims and their families" and its
"substantial adverse effect on interstate commerce."[220] This is especially the case
given that "Attorneys General from 38 States urged Congress to enact the Civil
Rights Remedy, representing that 'the current system for dealing with violence
against women is inadequate'" and that "[t]hirty six of [the states] and the
Commonwealth of Puerto Rico . . . filed an *amicus* brief in support" of the
measure, "while only one state has taken" the opposite side.[221] There is, nevertheless, something to be said for the notion that Congress should treat the federalization of crimes and civil causes of action traditionally understood to be the
prerogative of the states more seriously than it has of late. And while I believe
that the fears of the "slippery slope" postulated by the *Morrison* majority are
overstated, I have substantial reservations about a regime within which the assumption is that a state enforcement default perforce justifies federal intervention in circumstances where the primary activities are so clearly divorced from
traditional notions of commerce.[222]

The point is not that Congress may act only when the nation finds itself in
extremis. That sort of limitation offers, at best, precisely the kind of imprecise
inquire that plagues the Court in so many other instances. It is, rather, that these
sorts of judgments require more than simple invocation of the "spirit" of the
Tenth Amendment and the "background principles" for which the Eleventh
Amendment stands. I agree with Yoo that the Court cannot, and should not, ab-
dicate its responsibility to review the actions of Congress. But I also believe it
owes the considered judgments of Congress more deference than it has displayed in recent decisions.

---

[218]*Lopez,* 514 U.S. at 623 (Breyer dissenting) (emphasis added).

[219]See id. at 631–44.

[220]*Morrison,* 120 S. Ct. at 1752 & id. at 1763 (quoting H.R. Rep. No 103–711, at
385 (1994)).

[221]Id. at 1773 (Souter dissenting) (quoting Crimes of Violence Motivated by Gender,
Hearing before the Subcommittee on Civil and Constitutional Rights, House Committee
on the Judiciary, 103d Cong., 1st Sess., at 34–36 (1993).

[222]The same cannot be said of the Civil Rights Act measures at stake in *McLung* and
*Heart of Atlanta,* which attacked state and private bias against African Americans in activities that were undeniably commercial in nature.

The question is not simply, as the majority seemingly would have us believe, what is the constitutional predicate for what Congress has done and what are the implications of this action for the states, with a special emphasis on the latter. It is, rather, two-fold. On what substantial and plausible basis does Congress justify its intrusions into matters normally reserved for the states? In particular, has Congress taken seriously its obligation to legislate for the nation, and usurped the prerogatives of the states only because it is absolutely necessary? And for what principled reasons should the Court discard a settled understanding that most decisions are properly left almost exclusively to the political branches, no matter how unjustified or even perhaps silly their judgments might be about what matters the national government should properly be concerned with?

The Federalism Five answer these questions in the light of their belief that state sovereignty must assume near totemic stature in our Compound Republic, and their contention that this belief is mandated by any reasoned reading of the thoughts and intentions of the Framers and Founders. And in one respect, I sense that they are correct, for it is unlikely at best that the statesmen who wrote, ratified, and implemented the Constitution would have believed it either necessary or proper to enact many of the measures now contested. Their assumption was that such matters were quite properly the purview of the states, and that, to the extent that any of the conduct complained of posed a problem for the social order, it would be at the state level that such dislocations would be identified and addressed.

But there was, at the same time, an abiding sense that the meaning of the document had not been fixed in 1787, and that if the decision was made by the people's representatives that a national response was in order, that national response would be both appropriate and supreme. That does not mean that the Court has no role in policing the transgressions of both the Congress and the states. Madison, for example, understood both the danger of the "General Govt." undertaking "subversive encroachments on the rights & authorities of the States" and the extent to which the states themselves posed problems.[223] But he stressed that "[n]or do I think that Congress, even seconded by the Judicial Power, can, without some change in the character of the nation, succeed in *durable* violations of the rights & authorities of the States."[224] And his primary criticism of the Marshall Court in the years after *M'Culloch* and *Cohens* was not for its ac-

---

[223]Letter to Spencer Roane, May 6, 1821, in 9 Madison's Writings, at 55, 56–57 (cited in note 180). See also id. at 57–58, where he states

encroachments of the [National Legislature] are more to be apprehended from impulses given to it by a majority of the States seduced by expected advantages, than from the love of Power in the Body itself, controuled as it is *now* by its responsibility to the Constituent Body.

[224]Id. at 58.

ceptance of the Hamiltonian view of implied powers he had contested in his earlier assaults on the power to create a Bank. Rather, he feared the consequences of judicial rhetoric that seemed to indicate that the Court was washing its hands of its responsibility to police the boundaries of the federal system. Consistent with his posture during ratification, Madison sensed that the real threat to "sovereignty" lay not in the pronouncements of the Court *per se,* but in "the latitude of power which it has assigned to the National Legislature[.]"[225] In language that anticipated *Garcia,* Madison observed:

> But what is to controul Congress when backed and even pushed on by a majority of their Constituents, as was the case in the late contest relative to Missouri, and as may again happen in the constructive power relating to Roads & Canals? Nothing within the pale of the Constitution but sound arguments & conciliatory expostulations addressed both to Congress & to their Constituents.[226]

It is worth noting that Madison did not equate threats to sovereignty with overreaching in favor of purely national objectives. The evils of "latitude" lay, rather, in the "impulses given to it by a majority of the States seduced by expected advantages, than from the love of Power in the Body itself, countrouled as it *now* is by its responsibility to the Constituent Body."[227]

## Conclusion

The authors whose work appears in these pages remind us of the necessary elements and dynamics of the founding dialogue and of the two centuries of interpretive debate that have followed. They offer essential insights and perspectives, and while the conclusions they derive are not consistent, they enrich the dialogue far beyond what one can find in the pages of the United States Reports. These remain difficult questions, with new chapters in the story forthcoming from a Court that will continue to examine these issues and refine its holdings. As part of that process, both the Court and those interested in its work would do well to reflect on the perspectives found in the pages that follow.

---

[225] Id. 57.

[226] Id. at 56–57.

[227] Id. at 57–58. This language tracks closely the dominant fear in Madison and Jefferson's opposition to a program of internal improvements, the apprehension that such projects would become highly politicized appeals to purely local interests. See also Letter from James Madison to Henry St. George Tucker (Dec. 23, 1817), in 8 id. at 406 ("Another & perhaps a greater danger is to be apprehended from the influence which the usefulness & popularity of measures may have on questions of their Constitutionality.").

CHAPTER TWO

# The Tenth Amendment over Two Centuries:
More than a Truism

## William E. Leuchtenburg

Recently, we have heard repeatedly that we are, or may be, "living in a Constitutional moment"[1]—that the U.S. Supreme Court opinions that began with the resuscitation of the Tenth Amendment in 1976 and are now reaching some sort of apogee represent a new paradigm—that, in sum, 2001 is 1937, but 1937 undone. Scholars who have spent a lifetime studying the scope of the freedom of speech guarantee or the reach of the Equal Protection Clause are astonished to find themselves hotly debating the pertinence of the Tenth Amendment. "Remember when federalism was something dimly recalled as a sleep-inducing segment of a high school civics class?" one writer asked. "Now it is not only the subject of a lead story in *The New York Times* . . . but a prominent topic on the Washington cocktail circuit."[2]

---

[1]Mark Tushnet, Living in a Constitutional Moment?: Lopez and Constitutional Theory, Address at the Law School of the College of William and Mary, October 3, 1995. The paper, which I heard delivered, was subsequently published at 46 Case W. Res. L. Rev. 845 (1996). The term "constitutional moment" was popularized by Bruce Ackerman.

[2]Rochelle L. Stanfield, Look at the Numbers, Nat'l J., Jan. 9, 1982, at 75. The former Tennessee Governor, Lamar Alexander, noted that "[f]or the last thirty years, most of the talk about New Federalism has been . . . the kind of thing that one-tenth of 1 percent

41

Yet to anyone newly arrived at the study of the Constitution, the hullabaloo must seem puzzling. When the national government was forbidden to set wages and hours standards of state employees, most Americans went their daily rounds unaware that anything had happened. The same could be said of *United States v. Lopez,*[3] the 1995 decision that evoked such an outcry within the narrow circle of avid Court watchers. I was once referred to in *The Nation* as the patron of the "born-again liberal."[4] (The term was not meant kindly.) But not even to a born-again liberal is it self-evident that when a high school senior comes to school with a gun, he is engaged in interstate commerce. Why then has the ruling sent such reverberations through the legal universe? That is a question that can be answered only when these events, especially the revival of the Tenth Amendment, are placed in a historical context.

## From Pariah to Truism

Alone of the 10 amendments that, by some reckonings, the Bill of Rights comprises,[5] the Tenth Amendment has a sordid past. In the mid-nineteenth century, it served to shield the institution of slavery, and on the eve of secession Senator Jefferson Davis of Mississippi rested his defense of the rights of the slave states on the Tenth Amendment.[6] When, in the aftermath of the Civil War, Congress

---

of the people were interested in." Rochelle L. Stanfield, The New Federalism, Nat'l J., Jan. 28, 1995, at 226 ("New Federalism").

[3] 514 U.S. 549 (1995).

[4] "Like several other students drawn to and influenced by Prof. William Leuchtenburg at Columbia University, Sitkoff apparently emerged from his immersion in research a born-again liberal." John S. Rosenberg, review of Harvard Sitkoff, A New Deal for Blacks (Oxford University Press, 1978), in The Nation, Feb. 17, 1979, at 185.

[5] Many commentators limit the term "Bill of Rights" to the first eight amendments, and often not all of those. William E. Leuchtenburg, The Supreme Court Reborn: The Constitutional Revolution in the Age of Roosevelt 321–32 (Oxford University Press, 1995) ("Court Reborn"); Sanford Levinson, The Embarrassing Second Amendment, 90 Yale L. J. 637 (1989).

[6] Jefferson Davis, 1 The Rise and Fall of the Confederate Government 67 (Appleton, 1981). One exception to this generalization is Salmon P. Chase's efforts to employ the Tenth Amendment as a weapon against the Fugitive Slave Act. Harold M. Hyman & William M. Wiecek, Equal Justice Under Law: Constitutional Development, 1835–1875, at 110–11 (Harper and Row, 1982). For developments in this period, see Stanley I. Kutler, Judicial Power and Reconstruction Politics 163–66 (University of Chicago Press, 1968); Burt Neuborne, The Myth of Parity, 90 Harv. L. Rev. 1111 (1977). In his concurrence in Dred Scott, Justice John Campbell cited the Tenth Amendment as a refutation of the "radical error . . . that the Federal Government may lawfully do whatever is not directly prohibited by the Constitution." Dred Scott v. Sandford, 19 How. 393, 506 (1857).

sought to safeguard the liberties of the freedmen, the Supreme Court struck down the Civil Rights Act of 1875 as "repugnant to the Tenth Amendment."[7] By these holdings, as Jesse Choper has pointed out, the Court "largely thwarted the political branches' efforts to insure racial freedom and to advance the civil liberties of the politically underprivileged. These causes, as a consequence, were blocked for nearly seventy-five years."[8]

In more recent times, the Tenth Amendment became the mainstay of racists seeking to preserve Jim Crow. A Texas Democrat charged that Franklin D. Roosevelt's World War II edict on fair employment practices violated the Tenth Amendment,[9] and the Mississippi governor, Fielding Wright, who was Strom Thurmond's running mate on the Dixiecrat ticket in 1948, grounded his opposition to Harry Truman's civil rights program on the Tenth Amendment.[10] In 1960, the president of the Southern States Industrial Council, calling attention to "its opposition to the encroachment of the Federal Government into the area of authority reserved to the States by the Tenth Amendment," singled out the attempt "now being made to enact a so-called 'Civil Rights' bill" as "the culminating effort to denude the States of all power."[11] During the mobilization of

---

[7] Civil Rights Cases, 109 U.S. 3 (1883).

[8] Jesse H. Choper, The Scope of National Power Vis-à-Vis the States: The Dispensability of Judicial Review, 86 Yale L. J. 1582 (1977) ("Scope of National Power"). See also Eugene Gressman, The Unhappy History of Civil Rights Legislation, 50 Mich. L. Rev. 1340–41 (1952).

[9] Lloyd E. Price to Wright Morrow and Arch Rowan (June 1, 1948), Palmer Bradley Papers, Box 1 (Houston Metropolitan Research Center, Houston Public Library).

[10] Houston Post, Oct. 22, 1948, clipping, Id. Box 2. See also National Economic Council, What About Those "Civil Rights"?, Economic Council Letter, Mar. 15, 1948, copy in William Langer Papers, Box 211 (University of North Dakota).

[11] J. Clifford Miller, Jr., to J. William Fulbright (Feb. 29, 1960), Fulbright Papers, BCN 145, F43 (University of Arkansas, Fayetteville). See also Eugene Peacock, "Why Are the Dixiecrats?," Christian Century, Sept. 22, 1948, at 975. A North Carolina Congressman grumbled, "[i]t seems to me that the Court is paying very little attention to the 10th Amendment in its zeal to enforce other amendments, namely the 5th, 14th, and 15th." Charles Raper Jonas to W. B. Simons, July 26, 1957, Jonas Papers, Folder 50 (University of North Carolina at Chapel Hill). At a press conference in Fayetteville, North Carolina in 1964, Barry Goldwater, who voted against civil rights legislation, extolled the Tenth Amendment as a safeguard to constitutional government. Notes, Robert Macneil Papers, Box 11 (State Historical Society of Wisconsin). In sum, the cry of states' rights has long been "primarily a refuge for scoundrels." D. Bruce La Pierre, The Political Safeguards of Federalism Redux: Intergovernmental Immunity and the States as Agents of the Nation, 60 Wash. U. L. J. 782 (1982) ("Political Safeguards"). For lucid, powerful refutations of the constitutional arguments of the segregationists, see William P. Murphy, review of James Jackson Kilpatrick, The Sovereign States, 29 Miss. L. J. 110 (1957), and review of Charles J. Bloch, States' Rights—The Law of the Land, 8 J. Pub. L. 284 (1959).

Freedom Summer in 1964, southern white students, led by six Delta State College undergraduates, formed the Association of Tenth Amendment Conservatives to defend "the time-honored and history-proven custom" of racial segregation against the "impending invasion" of Mississippi by northern college students.[12] In like manner a year later, Congressman John Bell Williams of Mississippi, a white supremacist firebrand, told a Natchez constituent that he favored legislation "reaffirming the limitation of powers imposed on the Federal government by the Tenth Amendment."[13]

The Supreme Court relied on the Tenth Amendment to turn back the initiatives of the federal government to achieve social justice, especially by humanizing the factory system.[14] In the early years of this century, reformers such as Florence Kelley had become increasingly distraught at the ordeal of nearly two million children employed in brutalizing slaughter houses ankle deep in blood, water, and refuse, or as "glass house boys" taken from orphan asylums to labor "as blower dogs, working by night or day, at any age they might be."[15] In 1916 Congress finally responded with a Child Labor Act. But the textile interests persuaded the Dagenharts, a father and two sons employed in a small cotton factory in Charlotte, to file suit against the United States district attorney for western North Carolina, William Hammer, asking that the law be struck down so that the elder Dagenhart could continue to enjoy the benefits of his children's toil.[16]

In 1918, by a 5–4 vote, the Supreme Court ruled that the Child Labor Act was unconstitutional in *Hammer v. Dagenhart.*[17] In an opinion that has gone

---

[12]Jackson Daily News, May 1, 1964, clipping, Jackson Movement Papers (Tougaloo College). See also Harry A. B. Robinson to O. C. Fisher, Aug. 4, 1964, Fisher Papers, Box 387 (Baylor Collection of Political Materials).

[13]John Bell Williams to Amos J. Barron, May 24, 1965, John Bell Williams Papers, R033–B017–S3–10382 (Miss. Dept. Archives and History). A writer sympathetic to the recent reinvigoration of the Tenth Amendment by the Court has acknowledged "federalism's unfortunate past affinity with bad causes like slavery and racial segregation." Wilfred M. McClay, A More Perfect Union?: Toward a New Federalism, Commentary, Sept. 1995, at 30 ("More Perfect Union").

[14]Pollock v. Farmers Loan and Trust Co., 157 U.S. 429, 584 (1895). In the late nineteenth and early twentieth centuries, corporation attorneys and publicists such as John Randolph Tucker and William D. Guthrie sought to erect the Tenth Amendment as a barrier against federal control, and when the Court struck down the income tax, it drew in part on the Tenth Amendment. Benjamin R. Twiss, Lawyers and the Constitution: How Laissez Faire Came to the Supreme Court 159–60, 217–18 (Princeton University Press, 1942).

[15]Josephine Goldmark, Impatient Crusader: Florence Kelley's Life Story 39–41 (University of Illinois Press, 1953).

[16]Stephen B. Wood, Constitutional Politics in the Progressive Era: Child Labor and the Law 81–99 (University of Chicago Press, 1968).

[17]247 U.S. 251 (1918).

down with *Dred Scott* as one of the most infamous in our history,[18] Justice William Rufus Day declared that "the grant of authority over a purely federal matter was not intended to destroy the local power always existing and carefully reserved to the States in the Tenth Amendment," and warned that "it must never be forgotten that . . . to [the states] and to the people the powers not expressly delegated to the National Government are reserved."[19] In an unusually strongly worded dissent, Oliver Wendell Holmes denounced Day's opinion as wretched law, and that has been the judgment of commentators ever since. Holmes observed, "I should have thought that the most conspicuous decisions of this Court had made it clear that the power to regulate commerce and other constitutional powers could not be cut down or qualified by the fact that it might interfere with the carrying out of the domestic policy of any State."[20] In truth, as early as 1871, in employing the Tenth Amendment to circumscribe Congress's power to tax, the Court had announced that the federal government and state governments "are upon an equality." With respect to the reserved powers, "the State is as independent of the general government as that government is independent of the States."[21] Now in *Hammer* this conception of dual federalism—that Congress may not exercise its delegated powers if they trench upon powers reserved by the Tenth Amendment to the states—was applied to the Commerce Clause.[22]

Justice Day achieved this feat by deliberately misreading the Constitution, injecting the word "expressly" into the Tenth Amendment despite a lengthy re-

---

[18]As William Van Alstyne has written drolly, *Hammer* is "an unadmired decision." William W. Van Alstyne, The Second Death of Federalism, 83 Mich. L. Rev. 1709 (1985) ("Second Death"). See, in particular, Edward S. Corwin, The Twilight of the Supreme Court: A History of Our Constitutional Theory 33 (Yale University Press, 1934). For a rare exception, a commentator who believes that "on balance, *Hammer* was correctly decided," see Richard A. Epstein, The Proper Scope of the Commerce Power, 73 Va. L. Rev. 1427 (1987) ("Proper Scope"). Epstein, it should be noted, views child labor laws with "suspicion," on the assumption that "the only proper grounds for government intervention in family relations are abuse or neglect." Id. at 1430.

[19]*Hammer,* 247 U.S. at 274–75.

[20]Id. at 278 (Holmes dissenting).

[21]Collector v. Day, 11 Wall. 113, 126 (1871). In 1907, the Court advanced the view that the "principal purpose" of the Tenth Amendment "was not the distribution of power between the United States and the States, but a reservation to the people of all powers not granted." Kansas v. Colorado, 206 U.S. 46. 90 (1907).

[22]E. S. Corwin, the main purveyor of the term, has defined the "postulates" of "what I mean by Dual Federalism" as "l. The national government is one of enumerated powers only; 2. Also the purposes which it may constitutionally promote are few; 3. Within their respective spheres the two centers of government are 'sovereign' and hence 'equal'; 4. The relation of the two centers with each other is one of tension rather than collaboration." E. S. Corwin, The Passing of Dual Federalism, 36 Va. L. Rev. 4 (1950) ("Passing").

cord of admonitions against doing so. In *M'Culloch v. Maryland,* John Marshall, noting that the Tenth Amendment did not include the adverb "expressly," commented: "The men who drew and adopted this instrument had experienced the embarrassment resulting from the insertion of this word in the articles of confederation, and probably omitted it to avoid those embarrassments."[23]

Not long after Chief Justice Marshall's opinion, Joseph Story, in his *Commentaries on the Constitution,* pointed out:

> When this amendment was before congress, a proposition was moved to insert the word "expressly" before "delegated," so as to read "the powers not *expressly* delegated to the United States by the constitution," etc. On that occasion it was remarked that it is impossible to confine a government to the exercise of express powers. There must necessarily be powers admitted by implication, unless the constitution should descend to the most minute details. It is a general principle that all corporate bodies possess all powers incident to a corporate capacity, without being absolutely expressed. The motion was accordingly negatived. Indeed, one of the great defects of the confederation was . . . that it contained a clause prohibiting the exercise of any power, jurisdiction, or right not *expressly delegated.* The consequence was that congress were crippled at every step of their progress; and were often compelled by the very necessities of the times to usurp powers.[24]

Justice Story then set down what many scholars came to accept as the definitive explication of the Tenth Amendment:

> It is plain . . . that it could not have been the intention of the framers of this amendment to give it effect as an abridgment of any of the powers granted under the constitution, whether they are express or implied, direct or incidental. Its sole design is to exclude any interpretation by which other powers should be assumed beyond those which are granted. . . . The attempts, then, which have been made from time to time to force upon this language an abridging or restrictive influence are utterly unfounded in any just rules of interpreting the words or the sense of the instrument. Stripped of the ingenious disguises in which they are clothed, they are neither more nor less than attempts to foist into the text the word "expressly"; to qualify what is general, and obscure what is

---

[23]M'Culloch v. Maryland, 4 Wheat. 316, 476 (1819). Day was not the first justice to import the adverb "expressly" into an opinion. See Salmon P. Chase in Lane County v. Oregon, 7 Wall. 71, 76 (1868).

[24]Joseph Story, 3 Commentaries on the Constitution of the United States § 1900 (Hilliard, Gray, and Company, 1833). For greater clarity, I have excised some of Story's intrusive commas.

clear and defined. They make the sense of the passage bend to the wishes and prejudices of the interpreter.[25]

By importing "expressly" into *Hammer v. Dagenhart,* Justice Day was, in effect, amending the Constitution.

*Hammer* caused such consternation not merely because of its faulty reasoning, but probably even more because it denied the United States government any capacity to end the plague of child labor and similar injustices. Six years after the decision was handed down, a journalist asked Reuben Dagenhart, who had been 14 at the time of the case, what benefit he had gotten from it. He replied,

> I don't see that I got any benefit. I guess I'd been a lot better off if they hadn't won it. Look at me! A hundred and five pounds, a grown man and no education. I may be mistaken, but I think the years I've put in the cotton mills have stunted my growth. They kept me from getting any schooling. I had to stop school after the third grade and now I need the education I didn't get.[26]

After hearing Reuben tell of how he had gone into the mill at 12 and labored 12 hours a day, sometimes working nights as well, "lifting a hundred pounds and I only weighed sixty-five pounds myself," the reporter persisted, "Just what did you and John get out of that suit, then?" Reuben answered: "Why, we got some automobile rides when them big lawyers from the North was down here. Oh, yes, and they bought both of us a Coca-Cola. That's all we got out of it."[27]

When Franklin D. Roosevelt took office in 1933, *Hammer* hovered like a dark cloud over his ambition to get the country out of the Great Depression and create a New Deal. FDR's choice for Secretary of Labor, Frances Perkins, was told that, given the *Hammer* legacy, she might have to give up on her plans to institute a Welfare State.[28] Fear of how the Supreme Court might apply the

---

[25]Id. § 1901. Walter Berns has pointed out that the Tenth Amendment "is not a rule of the law of the Constitution" on which a "court can base its holding." Litigants may cite the amendment, but to decide a case the Court must turn to some specific clause of the Constitution to determine whether the exercise of power is legitimate. Walter Berns, The Meaning of the Tenth Amendment, in Robert A. Goldwin, ed., A Nation of States: Essays on the American Federal System 131–32 (Rand McNally, 1963).

[26]Lowell Mellett, How Sharper than a Serpent's Tooth to Have a Thankless Child, Labor, Nov. 17, 1923, reprinted in Wallace Mendelson, ed., The Constitution and the Supreme Court 106 (Dodd, Mead, 1965).

[27]Id. Congress sought to overcome the *Hammer* barrier by resorting to the taxing power, but the Supreme Court closed off that route too. Bailey v. Drexel Furniture Co., 259 U.S. 20 (1922).

[28]Frances Perkins, The Roosevelt I Knew 250 (Viking, 1946). During the interim since *Hammer,* the Court had not always given a broad reading to the Tenth Amendment,

Tenth Amendment beset the architects of both of the major mobilization pro-
grams—the National Industrial Recovery Act and the Agricultural Adjustment
Act—and, as it turned out, not without reason. In 1935, in his opinion for the
Court in the *Schechter* "sick chicken" case striking down the NRA, Chief Justice
Charles Evans Hughes said that "assertions of extra-constitutional authority
were . . . precluded by the explicit terms of the Tenth Amendment."[29] Not many
months later, in the Hoosac Mills case, *United States v. Butler,* Justice Owen
Roberts declared that a "principle embodied in our Constitution prohibits the
enforcement of the Agricultural Adjustment Act. The act invades the reserved
rights of the states." Roberts added: "From the accepted doctrine that the United
States is a government of delegated powers, it follows that those not *expressly*
granted, or reasonably to be implied . . . , are reserved to the states or to the people. To forestall any suggestion to the contrary, the Tenth Amendment was
adopted."[30]

Roberts's opinion in *Butler* drew about as many barbs as Day's in *Hammer.*
Of law journals that expressed a view on *Butler,* the formidable total of 27 were

---

however. In 1919 the Court unanimously rejected a Tenth Amendment argument in vali-
dating wartime prohibition. "That the United States lacks the police power, and that this
was reserved to the States by the Tenth Amendment, is true," observed Justice Louis
Brandeis. "But it is nonetheless true that when the United States exerts any of the powers
conferred upon it by the Constitution, no valid objection can be based upon the fact that
such exercise may be attended by the same incidents which attend the exercise by a State
of its police power." Hamilton v. Kentucky Distilleries Co., 251 U.S. 146, 156 (1919). In
1920, in turning back a challenge to the Migratory Bird Treaty Act and regulations issued
by the Secretary of Agriculture under its authority, the Court, in an opinion by Oliver
Wendell Holmes, declared that federal action was not "forbidden by some invisible radia-
tion from the general terms of the Tenth Amendment." Missouri v. Holland, 252 U.S.
416, 434 (1920). See Charles A. Lofgren, *Missouri v. Holland* in Historical Perspective,
1975 Sup. Ct. Rev. 77. (Significantly, one of the two dissenters was Willis Van Devanter,
who would join in striking down New Deal legislation.) In 1931, Owen Roberts, who
would be a pivotal figure in the FDR era, said of the Tenth Amendment: "It added nothing to the instrument as originally ratified and has no limited and special operation . . .
upon the people's delegation . . . of certain functions to the Congress." United States v.
Sprague, 282 U.S. 716, 733–34 (1931).

[29]Schechter Poultry Corp. v. United States, 295 U.S. 495, 528–29 (1935). In a little-
noted case that same year, the Court said of a provision of the Home Owners Loan Act,
adopted in the First Hundred Days of 1933: "There is an invasion of the sovereignty or
quasi-sovereignty of Wisconsin and an impairment of its public policy which the State is
privileged to redress as a suitor in the courts so long as the Tenth Amendment preserves a
field of autonomy against federal encroachment." Hopkins Federal Savings Ass'n v.
Cleary, 296 U.S. 315, 337 (1935). For the pleasure of conservative lawyers in that decision, see James M. Beck to John W. Davis, Dec. 9, 1935; Davis to Beck, Dec. 13, 1935,
Beck Papers (Princeton University).

[30]United States v. Butler, 297 U.S. 1, 68 (1936) (emphasis added).

unfavorable. Only three were approving, and two of these just mildly.[31] The widely read historian Charles A. Beard remarked that "Roberts talks like Calhoun and Jefferson Davis,"[32] and Senator Morris Sheppard of Texas castigated the "ridiculous" reasoning in the AAA case as representing the "epitome of obsolescence." *Butler,* he maintained, "is the opinion of a mind that has ceased to live, and that can ruminate only on a dim recalled past."[33] The prominent Columbia professor Howard Lee McBain confided:

> I have always been a believer in, and a defender of, the institution of judicial supremacy. I must say, however, that this monstrous opinion of Roberts shakes my faith to its very foundations. . . . Roberts has by this decision done his muddled utmost to expand the numbers and intensify the zeal of those who would abolish or severely cripple judicial supremacy as an institution.[34]

With the twin agencies of the New Deal mobilization destroyed, the Four Horsemen—Pierce Butler, James McReynolds, George Sutherland, Willis Van Devanter—and their allies continued to employ the Tenth Amendment as a weapon against Roosevelt's programs. In his opinion for the Court in *Carter* in 1936 terminating government regulation of the coal industry, Justice George Sutherland warned that:

> [e]very journey to a forbidden end begins with the first step; and . . . the end of the journey may find the states so despoiled of their powers . . . as to reduce them to little more than geographical subdivisions of the national domain. It is safe to say that if, when the Constitution was under consideration, it had been thought that any such danger lurked behind its plain words, it would never have been ratified.[35]

---

[31]Charles E. Clark to Thomas Corcoran, April 26, 1937, Corcoran Papers, Box 192 (Library of Congress).

[32]Charles A. Beard to Harlan Fiske Stone, April 19, 1936, Stone Papers, Box 6 (Library of Congress) ("Stone Papers").

[33]Escal Franklin Duke, The Political Career of Morris Sheppard, 1875–1941 436–37 (Ph.D. Dissertation, University of Texas, 1958).

[34]Howard Lee McBain to Harlan Fiske Stone, Jan. 9, 1936, Stone Papers, Box 82 (cited in note 32). "I think Roberts' opinion in the AAA case is not equal to the occasion," former Supreme Court Justice John H. Clarke observed. It could only be explained, he believed, by the need "to alter his original writing in order to hold his majority. I may be mistaken in this, but it seems to me the joints are quite apparent." John H. Clarke to Newton D. Baker, Feb. 11, 1936, Clarke Papers, File 3, Folder 24 (Western Reserve Historical Society).

[35]Carter v. Carter Coal Co., 298 U.S. 238, 295–96 (1936). One commentator has said that Sutherland was "doubtlessly correct" in making that statement about the intent of the Framers. Charles A. Lofgren, The Origins of the Tenth Amendment: History, Sovereignty, and the Problem of Constitutional Intention ("Origins"), in Ronald K. L.

*William E. Leuchtenburg*

A year later, Sutherland wrote that provisions of the Social Security Act "invade the . . . powers of the several states reserved by the Tenth Amendment," and Justice Pierce Butler agreed that "the statutory scheme is repugnant to the Tenth Amendment."[36] But by then—the spring of 1937—the Court had ruled on *Parrish*[37] and *Jones and Laughlin*,[38] and the Four Horsemen were in a minority. Indeed, in his opinion in one of the *Social Security Cases*, Benjamin Cardozo announced flatly, "[t]he excise is not void as involving the coercion of the States in contravention of the Tenth Amendment."[39]

Even the Constitutional Revolution of 1937, though, did not immediately liberate the Court from the thralldom of *Hammer v. Dagenhart*.[40] As a Yale Law School professor observed in 1941,

> Strange to contemplate, is the hold which the doctrine of the independent operation of the Tenth Amendment has acquired over members of the Court in so short a time. . . . Powerful minds on the Court could not rid themselves of the spell and found it necessary, after holding that particular enactments were within the Federal power, to go on to a consideration of the supposedly inde-

---

ereignty, and the Problem of Constitutional Intention ("Origins"), in Ronald K. L. Collins, ed., Constitutional Government in America: Essays and Proceedings from Southwestern University Law Review's First West Coast Conference on Constitutional Law 349 (Carolina Academic Press, 1980) "Constitutional Government"). In neither *Schechter* nor *Carter* was the Tenth Amendment the main reliance of the holding. For criticism of *Carter*, see 81 Harv. L. Rev. 13 (1967); 5 Brooklyn L. Rev. 468–69 (1936); Stanley High MS. Diary, May 18, 1937 (Franklin D. Roosevelt Library).

[36]Steward Machine Co. v. Davis, 301 U.S. 548, 610 & 616 (1937). The totality of the dissent in two of the Social Security cases was only one sentence long: "Mr. Justice McReynolds and Mr. Justice Butler are of the opinion that the provisions of the Act here challenged are repugnant to the Tenth Amendment." Id. at 598; Helvering v. Davis, 301 U.S. 619, 646 (1937).

[37]West Coast Hotel Co. v. Parrish, 300 U.S. 379 (1937).

[38]NLRB v. Jones & Laughlin Steel Corp., 301 U.S. 1 (1937).

[39]Steward Machine Co. v. Davis, 301 U.S. 548, 585 (1937).

[40]In the most important of the Wagner Act opinions, Charles Evans Hughes said that the "distinction between what is national and what is local in the activities of commerce is vital to the maintenance of our federal system." NLRB v. Jones and Laughlin, 301 U.S. 1, 30 (1937). When the government argued *Mulford v. Smith*, it claimed that *Hammer* could be distinguished but also asserted, according to the terse notes prepared for argument, "Hammer vs. Dagenhart sign board pointing up abandoned highway." Handwritten notes for argument, *Mulford v. Smith*, Robert H. Jackson Papers, Box 82 (Library of Congress).

pendent question of whether the enactment was also free of invalidity under the Tenth Amendment.[41]

In case after case, the Department of Justice implored the Court to repudiate the illogic of *Hammer,* but for several years without success.

In 1941, however, the Supreme Court, in a unanimous decision in *United States v. Darby,*[42] reversed the ruling of a district court quashing the indictment of a Georgia lumber manufacturer for violating the wages and hours provisions of the Fair Labor Standards Act. Hughes assigned the opinion to Harlan Fiske Stone, who in the spring of 1936 had written Charles Beard:

> I have always held that the framers of the Constitution intended to create a strong government, adequate to deal with every situation. I think they would have been surprised, even after the Tenth Amendment, to learn that the Constitution reserved a legislative field to the states. It granted power to the national government and, in the vernacular of the farmer, "the tail goes with the hide."[43]

Speaking for the Court, Stone called *Hammer* both an "aberration" and "a departure" from sound principles; whatever "vitality" it once had, he declared, "has long since been exhausted."[44] "Our conclusion," he went on, "is unaffected by the Tenth Amendment," for in a long line of cases starting with *Martin v. Hunter's Lessee,*[45] that amendment had been "construed as not depriving the national government of authority to resort to all means for the exercise of a granted power which are appropriate and plainly adopted to the permitted end."[46] In the most memorable passage, Stone asserted: "The amendment states but a truism that all is retained which has not been surrendered. There is nothing in the history of its adoption to suggest that it was more than declaratory of the relationship between the national and state governments as it had been established by the Constitution before the amendment. . . ."[47]

---

[41]A. H. Feller, The Tenth Amendment Retires, 27 A.B.A. Journal (April, 1941), at 227.

[42]312 U.S. 100 (1941).

[43]Harlan Fiske Stone to Charles Beard, April 16, 1936, Stone Papers, Box 6 (cited in note 32).

[44]*Darby,* 312 U.S. at 116–17.

[45]Martin v. Hunter's Lessee, 1 Wheat. 304, 325 (1816).

[46]*Darby,* 312 U.S. at 123–24.

[47]Id. at 124. Stone later remarked that his *Darby* opinion had been "deliberately fashioned on the model of Justice Holmes' dissent in *Hammer v. Dagenhart*." Alpheus Thomas Mason, Harlan Fiske Stone: Pillar of the Law 552 (Viking, 1946) ("Stone"). One of his former law clerks wrote Stone: "It must be a great source of satisfaction to you to have the full court accept today the views which you, flanked by Holmes and Brandeis, fought so valiantly for in the years gone by." Milton Handler to Harlan Fiske Stone, Feb.

When *Darby* reached conference on December 21, 1940, the Roosevelt appointees, recognizing that jurisprudence had come to a great divide, were jubilant. After Stone's draft was circulated, Felix Frankfurter scrawled on it: "I especially rejoice over (1) the way you buried *Hammer v. Dagenhart* and (2) your definitive exposure of the empty hobgoblin of the 10th Amendment. It's a superb job."[48] In like manner, Stanley Reed wrote on the draft: "I agree. It has been a long journey but the end is here. We should have overturned *Hammer* years ago."[49]

For a generation after *Darby,* it became commonplace for commentators to say that the Tenth Amendment was a relic of the past. A southern editor conceded regretfully that, after *Darby,* states' rights were dead, "as dead as the gallant boys from North Carolina who fell on the scarred slopes of Gettysburg,"[50] and a former law school dean who had become a federal judge told the Princeton political scientist E. S. Corwin:

> I have been meaning to write you for some time to commiserate with you for the way in which the Supreme Court is now taking away all the . . . business of constitutional law teachers. . . . When I remember the amount of time I used to spend in demonstrating how awful *Hammer v. Dagenhart* was I am wondering what you who remained in the business are finding to do.[51]

---

14, 1941, Handler Papers (Columbia University Law School). Stone chose *Darby* as the vehicle to express his views on exegesis of the Constitution despite the fact that he disliked minimum wage statutes. "The truth is," he said, "that I feel obliged to uphold some laws which make me gag." Stone, at 555–56.

[48]Felix Frankfurter to Harlan Fiske Stone, n.d., Stone Papers, Box 66 (cited in note 32).

[49]Stanley Reed to Harlan Fiske Stone, n.d., id. On the other hand, early in 1941, very likely with *Darby* in mind, a former Hoover official commented on his fellow Republican, Justice Stone: "I feel the extreme radicalness of some of his recent decisions have gone beyond his own principles." William R. Castle, Jr. MS. Diary, Feb. 28, 1941, Castle Papers (Houghton Library, Harvard University). In conference, Hughes, as well as McReynolds, passed. "You have written a strong opinion, again setting forth with suitable elaboration the general principles which we have held should govern the exercise of the commerce power," the chief justice wrote Stone. But he quickly added: "Of course, there is much that could be said with respect to the indefiniteness of the present statute, as a criminal statute. . . . Even with the best possible test, the statute is a highly unsatisfactory one, but as it is a border line case I should prefer not to write." William O. Douglas Papers, Box 51 (Library of Congress); Charles Evans Hughes to Harlan Fiske Stone, Jan. 27, 1941, Stone Papers, Box 66 (cited in note 32).

[50]Stone, at 555 (cited in note 47).

[51]Charles E. Clark to Edward S. Corwin, Feb. 10, 1941, Corwin Papers, Box 1 (Princeton University).

In 1950, Corwin, reviewing "a long period of approximately a hundred years" from the Taney Court through Sutherland's opinion in 1936 "when the foes of national power in this country" prevailed "through their interpretation of the Tenth Amendment," concluded: "This entire system of constitutional interpretation touching the Federal System is today in ruins." Corwin, who had cheered the Constitutional Revolution of 1937 as it was happening, expressed alarm that "today the question faces us whether the constituent States of the System can be saved for any useful purpose, and thereby saved as the vital cells that they have been heretofore of democratic sentiment, impulse, and action."[52]

Litigants abandoned hope that the Supreme Court would any longer be open to the contention that the Tenth Amendment served as a brake on the power of the federal government to discipline private enterprise. Insofar as the Tenth Amendment survived at all, it was in a different realm: In the claim that it should deter the federal government from interfering with the operations of state governments.

That avenue did not seem very promising either. As far back as 1936, in the heyday of the Four Horsemen, the Court had validated a penalty levied on the State Belt Railroad, which ran along the San Francisco waterfront, for violating the federal Safety Appliance Act despite the state's plea that it was discharging a sovereign function. In a unanimous opinion in *United States v. California,* Stone declared: "The sovereign power of the states is necessarily diminished to the extent of the grants of power to the federal government in the Constitution."[53] Not even James McReynolds dissented. The Court reaffirmed this conception a decade later when it sustained an edict of the federal price administrator forbidding the state of Washington to sell timber on school lands at a figure above that set by the national government. In *Case v. Bowles,* Justice Black cited a number of precedents in support of the proposition "that the Tenth Amendment 'does not operate as a limitation upon the powers, express or implied, delegated to the national government.'"[54]

The issue arose again in 1968 when the Court turned away an attempt by Maryland, supported by 27 other states, to enjoin application of the Fair Labor Standards Act to state institutions such as schools and hospitals. Though by the terms of the 1938 statute until amended in 1966, the states had been exempt from its provisions, Justice John Marshall Harlan, speaking in a 6–2 ruling in

---

[52]Passing, at 17, 23 (cited in note 22). One critic has protested that "Darby's view of the [commerce] clause makes hash of the reserved powers clause of the tenth amendment." Proper Scope, at 1407 (cited in note 18).

[53]297 U.S. 175, 184 (1936).

[54]Case v. Bowles, 327 U.S. 92, 102 (1946). For drafts of Black's opinion, see Hugo Black Papers, Box 280 (Library of Congress). Note, too, Charles A. Lofgren, National League of Cities v. Usery: Dual Federalism Reborn, 4 Claremont J. Pub. Affairs 23–24 (Spring 1977).

*Maryland v. Wirtz,* announced, "[i]f a State is engaging in economic activities that are validly regulated by the Federal Government when engaged in by private persons, the State too may be forced to conform its activities to federal regulation."[55] It was striking that these words came from Harlan, one of the most forthright champions of federalism on the bench.

Once the Maryland case had been resolved, the next challenge proved easy. In 1970 alarm about runaway inflation led Congress to authorize temporary wage and price controls. The state of Ohio, defying federal authority, granted wage increases to its 65,000 employees at nearly double the rate set by the national government. But in 1975, in *Fry v. United States,*[56] the Court, in an opinion by Thurgood Marshall (one of the U.S. government's lawyers in this case was Robert Bork), validated the action of a federal pay board under authority of the Economic Stabilization Act of 1970 in requiring Ohio to rescind the pay raise. The Court, noting that state and local employees composed 14 percent of the country's work force, found the regulation reasonable and denied that it invaded rights of the states protected by the Tenth Amendment.

Only William Rehnquist remained unconvinced. After quoting from a nineteenth-century opinion proclaiming that the Constitution envisioned "an indestructible Union, composed of indestructible States,"[57] he observed that "the Court's opinion in this case is the latest in a series of decisions which casts some doubts upon whether those States are indeed 'indestructible.'"[58] He fretted especially about "how much meaning is left to" the Tenth Amendment "and the basic constitutional principles which it illumines."[59] Still, he went on, it was "not the Tenth Amendment by its terms that prohibits congressional action which set a mandatory ceiling on the wages of all state employees." Both the Tenth and the Eleventh Amendments were "simply examples of the understanding of those who drafted and ratified the Constitution that the States were sovereign in many respects" and "Congress was . . . not free to deal with a State as if it were just another individual or business enterprise subject to regulation."[60]

---

[55]Maryland v. Wirtz, 392 U.S. 183, 197 (1968). For correspondence among the justices on the case, see Earl Warren Papers, Box 553 (Library of Congress).

[56]421 U.S. 542 (1975). Douglas did not join in the opinion of the Court, for he thought that since the act had expired, the writ of certiorari had been improvidently granted.

[57]Id. at 549 (quoting Chief Justice Salmon P. Chase's opinion in Texas v. White, 7 Wall. 700, 725 (1869)).

[58]Id.

[59]Id. at 550.

[60]Id. at 557. "Justice Marshall sustained a poorly drafted and politically inspired law against claims of an invasion of state sovereignty," one critic wrote. Stanley H. Friedelbaum, Reprise or Denouement: Deference and the New Dissonance in the Burger Court, 26 Emory L. J. 369 (1977).

Though Rehnquist's tone was mournful, *Fry* gave him a glimmer of hope. As Jeff Powell has pointed out: "Justice Marshall's opinion was remarkable not for its pro-federal holding but for its apparent willingness to consider Ohio's Tenth Amendment argument. Earlier decisions had given much shorter shrift to invocations of state sovereignty."[61] Moreover, unlike Stone in *Darby,* who saw no limits to the plenary power of Congress over commerce, Marshall said, in a much-cited footnote in which, curiously, he employed the baneful adverb "expressly": "While the Tenth Amendment has been characterized as a 'truism,' . . . it is not without significance. The Amendment expressly declares the constitutional policy that Congress may not exercise power in a fashion that impairs States' integrity or their ability to function effectively in a federal system."[62] One commentary responded:

> Of course the amendment, by its own words at least, declares no such thing, no more at any rate than it implies a narrow definition of national powers when they collide with matters traditionally of state concern. So even as the modern Supreme Court was embracing Marshall's doctrine of political checks, it has been reluctant to let go entirely of the counterprinciple of nation-state equality.[63]

## The Tenth Amendment Reborn?

This was the situation as the country celebrated the bicentennial of independence in 1976. Not for 40 years, not since *Carter Coal,* had the Supreme Court struck down any act of Congress as beyond the reach of the commerce power.[64] Not since well before *Darby* had the Tenth Amendment stood as an obstacle to federal regulation of corporations. Moreover, the series of cases culminating in the lopsided vote in *Fry* in 1975 had made clear that the Tenth Amendment could not impede federal regulation of the activities of state governments either. In the wake of *Fry,* one scholar wrote: "The tenth amendment seems largely a limit without content. Its contours are vague; its force is uncertain; its significance more reassuring than real," for it had "proved to be a flimsy aid in with-

---

[61]H. Jefferson Powell, The Compleat Jeffersonian: Justice Rehnquist and Federalism, 91 Yale L. J. 1323 (1982) ("Compleat").

[62]*Fry,* 421 U.S. at 547 n.7.

[63]D. Grier Stephenson, Jr., & Barry Michael Levine, Vicarious Federalism: The Modern Supreme Court and the Tenth Amendment, 19 Urban Lawyer 690 (1987).

[64]The only other ruling since 1936 to invalidate an act of Congress on federalist grounds was Oregon v. Mitchell, 400 U.S. 112 (1970), a decision striking down a statute imposing a federal voting age requirement on the states.

standing federal power."[65] Hence, when in 1976 the Supreme Court handed down a decision that broke abruptly with this pattern, it sent shock waves through the legal community. Once again the focus was on the Fair Labor Standards Act.

In *National League of Cities v. Usery,*[66] a suit brought by a coalition of urban interests against the Secretary of Labor, the Court struck down 1974 amendments to the Fair Labor Standards Act that had removed the exemption of most employees of state and local governments. "This Court has never doubted that there are limits upon the power of Congress to override state sovereignty, even when exercising its otherwise plenary powers to tax or to regulate commerce,"[67] Justice Rehnquist asserted, a claim that astonished dissenters. "It is one thing to recognize the authority of Congress to enact laws regulating individual businesses," he said. "It is quite another to uphold a similar exercise of congressional authority directed, not to private citizens, but to the States as States."[68] Legitimating the 1974 amendments, Rehnquist contended, would "significantly alter or displace the States' abilities to structure employer-employee relationships in such areas as fire prevention [and] police protection. . . . If Congress may withdraw from the States the authority to make . . . fundamental employment decisions . . . , there would be little left of the States' 'separate and independent existence.'"[69] Congress, he maintained, exceeds its power when it acts in ways that "directly displace the States' freedom to structure integral operations in areas of traditional governmental functions."[70] *National League of*

---

[65]David D. Salmon, The Federalist Principle: The Interaction of the Commerce Clause and the Tenth Amendment in the Clean Air Act, 2 Col. J. Envt'l L. 343 (1976). "In modern times," one of the foremost commentators observed, "generations of law students have been taught that there appeared to be no limits to Congress' commerce power—certainly none that the Court would declare." A. E. Dick Howard, The States and the Supreme Court, 31 Cath. U. L. Rev. 432 (1982).

[66]426 U.S. 833 (1976).

[67]Id. at 842.

[68]Id. at 845.

[69]Id. at 851 (quoting Coyle v. Oklahoma, 221 U.S. 559, 580 (1911)).

[70]Id. at 852. Rehnquist distinguished *Fry* and *Case v. Bowles;* maintained that what he insisted were dicta in *United States v. California* were "simply wrong"; and overruled *Wirtz.* Rehnquist, who professed to believe in judicial restraint, made an exception when he thought that the rights of the states needed safeguarding. Sue Davis, Justice William H. Rehnquist: Right-Wing Ideologue or Majoritarian Democrat?, in Charles M. Lamb & Stephen C. Halpern, eds., The Burger Court: Political and Judicial Profiles 323, 336 (University of Illinois Press, 1991) ("Burger Court"); Sue Davis, Justice Rehnquist and the Constitution 36 (Princeton University Press, 1989). Chief Justice Warren Earl Burger also expressed solicitude for the values of federalism. In a subsequent opinion, he remarked, "[o]nly last week, in *National League of Cities v. Usery* . . . we took steps to

*Cities* has been called "an even clearer statement of dual federalism than *Hammer.*"[71] Since there could be no doubt that Congress, under the commerce power, had adequate authority to enact such a law, the statute had fallen simply because the Court held that Congress could not use this power when it transgressed the rights of the states.

Not without serious misgivings did Harry Blackmun agree to go along with Rehnquist in a 5–4 ruling. He felt perturbed enough to file a concurrence in which he admitted that he was "not untroubled by certain possible implications of the Court's opinion," adding: "I may misinterpret the Court's opinion, but it seems to me that it adopts a balancing approach, and does not outlaw federal power in areas such as environmental protection, where the federal interest is demonstrably greater and where state facility compliance with imposed federal standards would be essential." Only because he had that understanding, and because he did not "read the opinion so despairingly" as did the minority, was Blackmun willing to consent.[72] Stunning though the decision was, Blackmun's concurrence served to diffuse the impact of Rehnquist's words and to give federal judges grounds for concluding that *National League of Cities* had less force than Rehnquist intended.

Rehnquist had encountered a devil of a time finding four justices to go along with him to create the five-man majority. In conference the vote had initially gone the other way, because Potter Stewart, who had been a dissenter in the Maryland case, was such a stickler for *stare decisis* that he would not join Rehnquist even though he thought the amendments were unconstitutional. Moreover, he did not want to be the fifth vote for a bloc of Nixon appointees. Accordingly, Chief Justice Warren Burger assigned the task of writing the opinion upholding the amendments to William Brennan. But at this juncture, according to one account, Byron White, who was in agreement with Brennan, turned toward Stewart and said softly, "I understand why you're voting that way, Potter, but I think it is a kind of chickenshit position. It keeps the jurisprudence of the Court tied up for reasons that are not on the public records." Nettled, Stewart changed his vote, and Burger then assigned the opinion to Rehnquist. Afterward,

---

arrest the downgrading of States to a role comparable to the departments of France, governed entirely out of the national capital." Elrod v. Burns, 427 U.S. 347, 375 (1976).

[71]Sotirios A. Barber, Tenth Amendment, in Leonard W. Levy, ed., 4 Encyclopedia of the American Constitution 1876 (Macmillan, 1986).

[72]*National League of Cities,* 426 U.S. at 856 (Blackmun concurring). Blackmun approached issues of federalism in a temperate, nonideological manner. Stephen L. Wasby, Justice Harry A. Blackmun: Transformation from "Minnesota Twin" to Independent Voice, in Burger Court, at 118 (cited in note 70).

Brennan, in a fury, told his clerks, "White should have kept his mouth shut!"[73] This melodrama may well have contributed to the acerbity of Brennan's dissent.

Rarely in the history of the Supreme Court has an opinion drawn so blistering an assault as the one that Justice Brennan visited upon Rehnquist's effort. Brennan's dissent, one commentator has written, "is remarkable for its depth of feeling, its sense of occasion, of foreboding, of fatal and momentous choice."[74] Brennan began by expressing surprise "that my Brethren should choose this bicentennial year of our independence to repudiate principles governing judicial interpretation of our Constitution settled since the time of Chief Justice Marshall."[75] He went on to charge that "[m]y Brethren . . . have today manufactured an abstraction without substance, founded neither in the words of the Constitution nor on precedent,"[76] and to accuse the majority of "sophistry," of "absurd" ratiocination, of "paucity of legal reasoning or principle" with "profoundly pernicious consequences," of "cavalier" disregard for even the most recent precedents—in sum, of fostering notions "so ominous for our constitutional jurisprudence as to leave one incredulous."

Though Rehnquist had mentioned the Tenth Amendment only once, and then merely to quote from an earlier opinion, Brennan reckoned, not unreasonably, that Tenth Amendment assumptions underlay the decision, and he flailed the majority mercilessly for this departure. "The reliance of my Brethren upon the Tenth Amendment . . . must astound scholars of the Constitution," he declared.[77] "The only analysis even remotely resembling that adopted today is found in a line of opinions . . . that ultimately provoked a constitutional crisis for the Court in the 1930's."[78] After citing *Hammer v. Dagenhart, Butler,* and *Carter Coal,* he remarked: "It may have been the eventual abandonment of that overly restrictive construction . . . that spelled defeat for the Court-packing plan, and preserved the integrity of this institution."[79] The attitude of the majority in

---

[73]Bob Woodward & Scott Armstrong, The Brethren: Inside the Supreme Court 482–84 (Avon, 1979). This account strikes me as credible, though, as one reviewer remarked, every assertion in the book has to be read "with the caveat 'if true.'" Renata Adler, review of The Brethren, in N.Y. Times Book Rev., Dec. 16, 1979, at 1. On the controversy over the reliability of The Brethren as a source, see Laura Krugman Ray, Judicial Fictions: Images of Supreme Court Justices in the Novel, Drama, and Film, 39 Ariz. L. Rev. 191, 249 (1997).

[74]Frank I. Michelman, States' Rights and States' Roles: Permutations of Sovereignty in *National League of Cities v. Usery,* 86 Yale L. J. 1165 (1977). On Michelman's approach, see Laura Kalman, The Strange Career of Legal Liberalism 65 & 280 (Yale University Press, 1996).

[75]*National League of Cities,* 426 U.S. at 857 (Brennan dissenting).

[76]Id. at 860.

[77]Id. at 861–62.

[78]Id. at 867–68.

[79]Id. at 868.

*National League of Cities,* he maintained, was "not far different from the dissenting opinions" in the Constitutional Revolution of 1937, though even the Four Horsemen "were more faithful to the Constitution than is today's decision."[80] Brennan alleged that:

> [t]oday's repudiation of [an] unbroken line of precedents that firmly reject my Brethren's ill-conceived abstraction can only be regarded as a transparent cover for invalidating a congressional judgment with which they disagree. . . . I cannot recall another instance in the Court's history when the reasoning of so many decisions covering so long a span of time has been discarded in such a roughshod manner. That this is done without any justification not already often advanced and consistently rejected clearly renders today's decision an *ipse dixit* reflecting nothing but displeasure with a congressional judgment.[81]

Brennan's sharp differences with the majority ran deeper than a disagreement over statutory construction. He protested:

> My Brethren do more than turn aside longstanding constitutional jurisprudence that emphatically rejects today's conclusion. More alarming is the startling restructuring of our federal system, and the role they create therein for the federal judiciary. This Court is simply not at liberty to erect a mirror of its own conception of a desirable governmental structure.[82]

Brennan took issue not only with Rehnquist's opinion but also with the concurrence, for Blackmun's notion of balancing was no more than "a thinly veiled rationalization for judicial supervision of a policy judgment that our system of government reserves to Congress."[83] The attempt of the Court to control the relationship of the national government to the states violated "the fundamental tenet of our federalism that the extent of federal intervention into the States' affairs . . . shall be determined by the States' exercise of political power through their representatives in Congress" who were "*elected from the States.*"[84] Brennan concluded: "We are left then with a catastrophic judicial blow at Congress' power" and with "an ominous portent of disruption of our constitutional structure implicit in today's mischievous decision."[85]

---

[80]Id. at 868 n.9.

[81]Id. at 867 & 871–72.

[82]Id. at 875.

[83]Id. at 876.

[84]Id. at 876–77.

[85]Id. at 880. White and Marshall joined in Brennan's opinion. Brennan cited Herbert Wechsler, The Political Safeguards of Federalism: The Role of the States in the Composition and Selection of the National Government, 54 Colum. L. Rev. 543 (1954). Stevens filed a separate dissent in which he observed sardonically, "[t]he Court holds that the

In the law journals, both the holding and Rehnquist's opinion took a brutal drubbing, criticism that, as a commentator observed, "was extraordinary both for its breadth and severity." With scarcely a suggestion of collegial deference, a United States Circuit Court of Appeals judge asserted:

> I know, as well as I know my name, that the tenth amendment does not mean what, in *National League of Cities,* Justice Rehnquist said it means. Indeed I would be willing to make a small wager that if a poll were taken among courts of appeals judges, all federal judges, all state supreme court judges, or all judges, *National League of Cities* would lose in each category.[86]

Dean Alfange, Jr., accused Rehnquist of "unwarranted hyperbole" and of being "wholly unreasonable,"[87] and Archibald Cox thought it "unnecessary and unwise to have five Justices undo a deliberate legislative judgment by the Congress for no other reason than that the Justices as members of Congress would have voted not to bring the wages and hours of state, county, and municipal employees within the coverage of the federal law."[88] While acknowledging that there were "rare instances" when judicial intervention was justifiable to protect the states because "the political safeguards of federalism" could not always be counted upon, Laurence Tribe denied that such a consideration supported "the result in *National League of Cities,* for in that case no claim was or could have been made that the imposition of wage and hour regulations on the states would threaten their meaningful existence."[89]

The intensity of the response derived in good part from the suspicion that a majority dominated by four Nixon appointees had resolved to return to the dark

---

Federal Government may not interfere with a sovereign State's inherent right to pay a substandard wage to the janitor at the state capitol. The principle on which the holding rests is difficult to perceive." Though he considered wages and hours legislation "unwise," he also believed that it was a valid exercise of congressional power. *National League of Cities,* 426 U.S. at 880–81 (Stevens dissenting). See also Bryan H. Wildenthal, Judicial Philosophies in Collision: Justice Blackmun, *Garcia,* and the Tenth Amendment, 32 Ariz. L. Rev. 753 (1990) ("Judicial Philosophies").

[86]John J. Gibbons, Keynote Address—Symposium: Constitutional Adjudication and Democratic Theory, 56 N.Y.U. L. Rev. 269 (1981).

[87]Dean Alfange, Jr., Congressional Regulation of the 'States Qua States': From *National League of Cities* to *EEOC v. Wyoming,* 1983 Sup. Ct. Rev. 230–31 ("Congressional Regulation").

[88]Archibald Cox, Federalism and Individual Rights Under the Burger Court, 73 Nw. U. L. Rev. 25 (1978) ("Federalism and Individual Rights").

[89]Laurence H. Tribe, Unraveling *National League of Cities:* The New Federalism and Affirmative Rights to Essential Government Services, 90 Harv. L. Rev. 1072 (1977). See also, Choper, Scope of National Power, at 1552–1621 (cited in note 8). Robert F. Nagel, Federalism as a Fundamental Value: *National League of Cities* in Perspective, 1982 Sup. Ct. Rev. 81–82 ("Fundamental Value").

ages before 1937. *National League of Cities,* one commentator wrote, "represented a counter-insurgency of the former ideas, an attempt to reestablish the old ideology in a limited sphere of doctrine." He added: "*National League of Cities,* then, was part of the Burger Court's holy war against the lingering forces of bankrupt liberalism and big government. It is not an exaggeration to compare the decision to the opening salvo in a war."[90] Another writer concluded, "[o]ne can see in *National League of Cities* the seeds of a doctrinal development not unlike the *Lochner* jurisprudence. . . . Despite obvious differences, *National League of Cities'* immunity for states against federal regulation bears haunting similarities to the Court's earlier immunity for business against state and federal regulation."[91]

Not everyone, though, joined in the chorus of condemnation. Stanley Friedelbaum thought that "Justice Brennan's irate reaction to the majority opinion in *National League of Cities* almost defied credibility,"[92] while William Van Alstyne contended that the ruling "represented only the most modest sort of federalism restraint on Congress, a point often overlooked in the general academic rush to condemn it." It was "quite arguable," he said, "that the majority's opinion was unduly modest rather than too sweeping."[93] Even when charging that Rehnquist had departed "from the expressed terms of the Constitution," Sotirios Barber reflected, "[s]omething does seem wrong with the theory that the Tenth Amendment counts for nothing."[94]

In an extended dissection of the dispute, Robert Nagel attributed the hostile reaction to the preoccupation of jurists and scholars with rights and their indifference to "judicial protection of principles that allocate decision-making responsibility among governmental units." He observed:

> Modern judges work diligently at redesigning local educational programs and at defining the acceptable number of square feet in a prison cell. They void a multiplicity of laws relating to hair length, sexual preference, and abortion. But they deal rarely and, for the most part, gingerly with the great issues of power distribution that were faced so ambitiously and successfully by the framers.

Nagel went on to say that scholars indulge "almost any amount of philosophical or psychological vagueness and complexity when the goal is defining rights,"

---

[90] J. M. Balkin, Ideology and Counter-Ideology from *Lochner* to *Garcia,* 54 UMKC L. Rev. 175, 194 (1986) ("Ideology").

[91] Martha A. Field, *Garcia v. San Antonio Metropolitan Transit Authority:* The Demise of a Misguided Doctrine, 99 Harv. L. Rev. 89–90 (1985) ("Demise").

[92] Stanley H. Friedelbaum, The Rehnquist Court: In Pursuit of Judicial Conservatism 6 (Greenwood Press, 1994).

[93] Second Death, at 1713, 1716–17 (cited in note 18).

[94] Sotirios A. Barber, *National League of Cities v. Usery:* New Meaning for the Tenth Amendment, 1976 Sup. Ct. Rev. 164.

but "often exhibit a kind of intellectual crabbedness when structural claims are made."[95]

Neither champion nor critic, though, found Rehnquist's formulation satisfactory. One writer noted the "widely deplored theoretical inadequacy,"[96] and even a commentator who applauded the Court's "renewed interest in protecting the states' independent status," Lewis Kaden, admitted that the effects of the decision "puzzle legislators, executive officials, and judges," and faulted Rehnquist's opinion because it "makes light of precedent and . . . articulates no principle of sufficient generality to aid lawmakers or lower federal courts in testing federal regulation of state activity. The constitutional roots of the judicial protection afforded state autonomy remain ambiguous."[97]

Martin Shapiro, too, regretted the conundrum Rehnquist had created. *National League of Cities,* he wrote,

> rests on no more elegant logic than "too much is too much." Just as pushing the equal protection clause to its logical extreme can destroy all independent state decision-making, so pushing the commerce power to that extreme could do so. Aside from using the words "integral" and "traditionally" over and over again, Justice Rehnquist does not, and cannot, draw the boundaries of state sovereignty. All he can say is that if federalism is to mean anything, it must mean that state governments must have power over their own employees.

Noting "the fundamental absurdity of two sovereignties operating in the same territory and on the same persons," Shapiro called *National League of Cities* "a perfect example of the absurdity."[98]

Yet another commentator, Jeff Powell, traced Rehnquist's tribulations to his resolve to eschew reliance on the Tenth Amendment. As he had done in *Fry,* in *National League of Cities* Rehnquist viewed the Tenth Amendment as an expression of state sovereignty but not its source, "possibly," Powell surmised, "because of the historical difficulties" of rooting his argument in the text of the Constitution. "But," Powell added, "in avoiding the historical pitfalls associated with linking his state sovereignty doctrine too closely to the Tenth Amendment, Justice Rehnquist left the doctrine floating in mid-air, without a visible constitutional foundation other than his theory of federalism."[99]

A final group thought that too much notice was being paid to *National League of Cities,* either because Rehnquist had hedged his opinion with so many

---

[95]Fundamental Value, at 86–87 (cited in note 89).

[96]Political Safeguards, at 784 (cited in note 11).

[97]Lewis B. Kaden, Politics, Money, and State Sovereignty: The Judicial Role, 89 Col. L. Rev. 848–49 (1979).

[98]Martin Shapiro, American Federalism, in Constitutional Government, at 367–68 (cited in note 35).

[99]Compleat, at 1329 (cited in note 61).

qualifiers and conceded so much to national prerogative or because the centripetal forces were too potent to resist. Noting that, historically, the principal issue in federalism has been "the extent to which the basic charter mandates a clear division of powers, one that both protects and *confines* the central and state governments in their respective spheres," Henry P. Monaghan remarked:

> That issue is devoid of current significance. The radical transformation that has occurred in the structure of "Our Federalism" in the nearly two centuries of our existence has emptied the concept of nearly all legal content and replaced it with a frank recognition of the legal hegemony of the national government.

Writing in 1980, he added that *National League of Cities* "has, as yet, shown no generative power and, in any event, is by its own terms not a barrier to national control over the private sector."[100] In like manner, Archibald Cox concluded:

> Perhaps the new revival of the old philosophy will prevail, but the main current of constitutional history and the ever-closer interrelationship of public and private activities make it more likely that *National League of Cities* will come to be seen as no more than an unprincipled exception to the general rule of federal supremacy.[101]

## Retrenchment: The Road to *Garcia*

Cox proved to be prescient, for over the next nine years, the Court found difficulty in agreeing on what the apparently momentous ruling entailed and proved reluctant to adhere to it. The issue reached the justices again in 1981 when a district court, relying upon *National League of Cities,* invalidated the Surface Mining Act of 1977 for violating the Tenth Amendment and other provisions of

---

[100]Henry P. Monaghan, The Burger Court and "Our Federalism," 43 L. & Contemp. Probs. 40, 42 (1980).

[101]Federalism and Individual Rights, at 22 (cited in note 88). One commentator has suggested that the Court was not intent on laying out new doctrine but was exercising a "cuing function" to prompt Congress to remember that it should "renew its traditional role as protector of the states." Philip Bobbitt, Constitutional Fate: Theory of the Constitution 191–95 (Oxford University Press, 1982). David O'Brien has characterized Rehnquist's conception of state sovereignty as "modest," for he has confined the exercise of federal authority only under the Commerce Clause, while sustaining the application of national power to the states under the Fourteenth Amendment and the taxing and spending power. Federalism as a Metaphor in the Constitutional Politics of Public Administration, 49 Pub. Ad. Rev. 412 (Sept./Oct. 1989). Indeed, O'Brien notes, Rehnquist validated the imposition of the Civil Rights Act of 1964 on state and local governments "within a week of *National League of Cities*." See Fitzpatrick v. Bitzer, 427 U.S. 445 (1976).

the Constitution. In *Hodel v. Virginia Surface Mining & Reclamation Association*,[102] the Supreme Court reversed. *National League of Cities,* Justice Marshall pointed out, stipulated that any challenge to the exercise of national power had to meet "*each* of three requirements," and in this instance the strip coal interests had failed to demonstrate that the environmental efforts of the federal government affected the "States as States."[103] Marshall continued:

> Contrary to the assumption by both the District Court and appellees, nothing in *National League of Cities* suggests that the Tenth Amendment shields the States from pre-emptive federal regulation of *private* activities affecting interstate commerce. . . . It would . . . be a radical departure from long-established precedent for this Court to hold that the Tenth Amendment prohibits Congress from displacing state police power laws regulating private activity. Nothing in *National League of Cities* compels or even hints at such a departure.[104]

Burger, Powell, and Rehnquist each saw fit to compose separate, grudging concurrences, though Powell regretted that the statute had "been written with little comprehension of its potential effect on this rugged area" in western Virginia,[105] and though Rehnquist believed there was "no doubt that Congress . . . has stretched its authority to the 'nth degree.'"[106]

In 1982, the Court raised eyebrows when, in an opinion by Chief Justice Burger in *United Transportation Union v. Long Island Rail Road,* it turned down a Tenth Amendment claim in ruling that the Railway Labor Act of 1926 superseded state law on labor relations.[107] Commentators found it difficult to understand how the justices who had composed the majority in *National League of Cities* were unpersuaded by a Court of Appeals' conviction that "there is now no reasoned basis for finding that the operation of an intrastate passenger service

---

[102]452 U.S. 264 (1981).

[103]Id. at 287.

[104]Id. at 290–91 & 292.

[105]Id. at 307 (Powell concurring).

[106]Id. at 311 (Rehnquist concurring). In a footnote, Marshall added that meeting these three requirements did not "guarantee that a Tenth Amendment challenge to congressional commerce power will succeed. There are situations in which the nature of the federal interest advanced may be such that it justifies state submission." Id. at 288 n.29. *Hodel,* it has been observed, "actually involved the older, easier problem of federal regulation aimed at private activity, rather than at the states as such." Paul J. Mishkin, The Current Understanding of the Tenth Amendment, in Harry N. Scheiber, ed., Federalism and the Judicial Mind: Essays on American Constitutional Law and Politics 151 (Institute of Governmental Studies Press, 1992) ("Federalism and the Judicial Mind"). Another commentator called the three-prong test in *Hodel* "an intellectual sham" because it did not resolve the ambiguities in *National League of Cities.* Political Safeguards, at 895 (cited in note 11).

[107]United Transportation Union v. Long Island Rail Road Co., 455 U.S. 678 (1982).

which transports tens of thousands to and from their jobs every day is any less a governmental function than are sanitation or public parks and recreation,"[108] especially since, because the line was unprofitable, the state had been compelled to take it over or leave the citizenry without service.[109]

Though that decision was unanimous, the Court revealed not many weeks later how fragmented it had become in endeavoring to apply the principles of *National League of Cities* and how much ill feeling the effort was generating. In *Federal Energy Regulatory Commission v. Mississippi*,[110] four justices joined Blackmun's opinion for the Court, while Powell concurred in part and dissented in part, and Sandra Day O'Connor filed a separate opinion concurring in part and dissenting in part in which Burger and Rehnquist joined. The Public Utility Regulatory Policies Act of 1978 was a valid statute, Blackmun said, even though "the Federal Government attempts to use state regulatory machinery to advance federal goals,"[111] a procedure that Justice O'Connor denounced as "conscript[ing] state utility commissions into the national bureaucratic army."[112]

In what she has called "the battle of the footnotes," O'Connor, in Phillip Cooper's words, "went after Blackmun,"[113] charging him with allowing Congress "to kidnap state utility commissions into the national regulatory family," fostering "dismemberment of state government," reaching a conclusion "antithetical to the values of federalism and inconsistent with our constitutional history," engaging in "somewhat disingenuous" and "irrelevant reasoning," and indulging "an absurdity."[114] Unlike other "freshmen" justices who initially played a subdued role, O'Connor "came out swinging," perhaps because during the confirmation process questions were raised about whether the first woman on the bench could stand the gaff, though, in fact, she had already demonstrated, as Cooper makes clear, that "she was and is a tough-minded person who gives as well as she gets."[115] One commentator noted:

> The impression left by the opinions in *FERC* is less one of retreat from *National League of Cities* by the majority than of a renewed enthusiasm for that precedent on the part of the Burger-Rehnquist-O'Connor bloc. Justice Rehn-

---

[108]United Transportation Union v. Long Island Rail Road Co., 634 F.2d 19, 26–27 (2d Cir. 1980).

[109]Congressional Regulation, at 253 (cited in note 87).

[110]456 U.S. 742 (1982).

[111]Id. at 759.

[112]Id. at 775 (O'Connor concurring and dissenting). For Blackmun's approach to preemption, see Karen H. Flax, In the Wake of *National League of Cities v. Usery:* A "Derelict" Makes Waves, 34 S.C. L. Rev. 679 (1983).

[113]Phillip J. Cooper, Battles on the Bench: Conflict Inside the Supreme Court 61 (University Press of Kansas, 1995) ("Battles").

[114]*FERC*, 456 U.S. at 775, 781–82, 785 n.15, 792.

[115]Battles, at 61 (cited in note 113).

quist clearly gained an articulate and vociferous ally in his drive to limit power with President Reagan's appointment of his erstwhile Stanford Law School classmate.[116]

In a television interview in which she alluded to "the battle of the footnotes," Bill Moyers asked her, "[d]o you have another justice in mind when you write?" The colloquy continued:

O'CONNOR: Absolutely, sometimes you do. . . .
MOYERS: Do you frame your language with him in mind? . . .
O'CONNOR: Sometimes.
MOYERS: But they sometimes antagonize some of your colleagues, don't they?
O'CONNOR: That can happen too.
MOYERS: One of your brethren scolded you a little bit for some of your language.
O'CONNOR: That can happen too.[117]

Blackmun had, indeed, responded to O'Connor in kind. He had told an interviewer that if "someone is going to play hardball with me, I'm going to play hardball back,"[118] and in his *FERC* opinion he characterized the new justice's views as "demonstrably incorrect," "peculiar," "curious," and "absurd."[119] In an especially sharp rejoinder, Blackmun declared: "While these rhetorical devices make for absorbing reading, they unfortunately are substituted for useful constitutional analysis. For while Justice O'Connor articulates a view of state sovereignty that is almost mystical, she entirely fails to address our central point."[120]

In 1983 the Court decided on a suit brought by the Equal Employment Opportunity Commission against the state of Wyoming on behalf of Bill Crump, a supervisor in the Wyoming Game and Fish Department who had been dismissed at age 55 as too old despite the provisions of the Age Discrimination in Employment Act of 1967, which in 1974 had been extended to state and local employees. A district court had ruled against the federal government, but in a 5–4 vote the Supreme Court reversed, though not a few observers found it difficult to discern any difference in principle between this case and *National League of Cities*. In his opinion for the Court, Justice Brennan asserted that a rubric in *National League of Cities* was murky at the time, and "our subsequent cases applying the . . . test have had little occasion to amplify on our understanding of the

---

[116]Judicial Philosophies, at 762 (cited in note 85).
[117]Battles, at 63 (cited in note 113).
[118]Id. at 61–62.
[119]*FERC*, 456 U.S. at 762 n.25, 763 n.27, 765 n.29.
[120]Id. at 767 n.30.

concept."[121] In *EEOC v. Wyoming,* a commentator has remarked, "Justice Brennan prepared an adroit, if not always a convincing, revision of *National League of Cities'* teachings. . . . Perhaps the timing for a direct overruling was inappropriate, or perhaps more was required to convince Justice Blackmun of his errant conduct seven years earlier."[122] John Paul Stevens, though, let it be known that he was ready to go much farther. Concurring, he stated:

> I think it so plain that *National League of Cities* not only was incorrectly decided, but also is inconsistent with the central purpose of the Constitution itself, that it is not entitled to the deference that the doctrine of *stare decisis* ordinarily commands for this Court's precedents. Notwithstanding my respect for that doctrine, I believe that the law would be well served by a prompt rejection of *National League of Cities'* modern embodiment of the spirit of the Articles of Confederation.[123]

*EEOC v. Wyoming* demonstrated once again how badly in disarray the Court was on these issues. Stevens offered his concurrence; Burger filed a dissent, which Powell, Rehnquist, and O'Connor joined; and Powell contributed another dissent, to which O'Connor added her name. The case also provided a battleground for two diametrically opposed conceptions of the nature of the Constitution. Justice Stevens, drawing on a 1947 exploration by Wiley Rutledge, claimed that the main intent of the Founding Fathers was "to secure freedom of trade" and hence that the commerce power was at the heart of the Constitution. "Neither the Tenth Amendment, nor any other provision of the constitution, affords any support," he said, for the "limitation on the scope of . . . federal power" imposed by "pure judicial fiat" in *National League of Cities.*[124] Justice Powell, in rejoinder, was not satisfied merely with endorsing Chief Justice Burger's dissent, which accused the majority of approving usurpation of state authority, "fundamentally alter[ing] our scheme of government," and "forc[ing] the states into a Procrustean national mold."[125] Powell also took exception to Stevens's "novel view of our nation's history" with its "startling" notion that the commerce clause was the *raison d'être* of the Constitution. "One would never know from the concurring opinion that the Constitution formed a federal system, comprising a National Government with delegated powers and state govern-

---

[121]EEOC v. Wyoming, 460 U.S. 226, 238 n.11 (1983).

[122]Stanley H. Friedelbaum, Justice William J. Brennan, Jr.: Policy-Making in the Judicial Thicket, in Burger Court, at 118 (cited in note 70). Since Brennan's opinion in *Wyoming* rested on "a judicial reexamination of what is a purely policy question," wrote Dean Alfange, Jr., "it marks the triumph, not the demise, of the *National League of Cities* approach." Congressional Regulation, at 267 (cited in note 87).

[123]*EEOC v. Wyoming,* 460 U.S. at 249–50 (Stevens concurring).

[124]Id. at 248.

[125]Id. at 265 (Burger dissenting).

ments that retained a significant measure of sovereign authority," Powell objected.[126] Given Stevens's attitude toward *National League of Cities,* he concluded, "it is not easy to think of any state function—however sovereign—that could not be pre-empted."[127]

When *Garcia v. San Antonio Metropolitan Transit Authority* reached the Supreme Court in 1985, Warren Burger did all he could to preserve *National League of Cities,* even if it meant manipulating the Court's procedures. A United States District Court had granted summary judgment to SAMTA, which contended that, in the light of *National League of Cities,* it no longer had to pay overtime to employees such as the San Antonio bus driver Joe Garcia, because a mass transit system was a traditional governmental function and thus exempt from the Fair Labor Standards Act. Not until the rest of the justices had already voted in conference did Burger announce his own position, which provided the fifth vote to avoid a reversal of *National League of Cities* by upholding the District Court. Well aware that Blackmun had been wavering, the chief justice then assigned him the opinion, quite possibly reasoning that a sharply worded draft by a Rehnquist or an O'Connor might push Blackmun into the Brennan-Marshall camp.[128]

Blackmun, however, upset this strategy. He had already revealed his shakiness in conference. Although he believed that municipal mass transit "reeks of localism," he thought that a "good opinion can be written either way," and hence had voted with the Burger majority with some diffidence. Two months later, he surprised his colleagues by circulating a draft opinion in which he reversed the vote he had cast in conference, writing: "I have spent a lot of time on these cases. I have finally decided to come down on the side of reversal. I have been able to find no principled way in which to affirm." Hard pressed, Burger then tried a different tactic. He told Blackmun: "At this stage—almost mid-June—a 30-page opinion coming out contrary to the Conference vote on a very important issue places those who may dissent in a very difficult position. I think we should set the case over for reargument." That démarche not only elicited remonstrances from Brennan and Marshall, but also from Stevens, who composed a long memorandum that, among other contentions, suggested shrewdly that one reason for Burger's maneuver might be "the thought that the membership in the Court might change over the summer and thereby produce a different outcome." He was unmistakably alluding to the prospect that, in light of Ronald Reagan's re-election, Brennan or Marshall might step down. "In my view," Stevens said,

---

[126]Id. at 268–69 (Powell dissenting).
[127]Id. 275.
[128]Battles, at 97–98 (cited in note 113).

"this would not be a proper ground for reargument." Despite these protests, Burger managed to get *Garcia* reargued, but to no avail.[129]

In *Garcia*, the Court, in yet another judgment on the Fair Labor Standards Act, gave up the struggle to delineate a bright line and jettisoned *National League of Cities*. Blackmun, who had been so troubled by the original decision, now joined in a 5–4 ruling in which he wrote the opinion. *National League of Cities,* Blackmun said, had failed to explain "how a 'traditional' function is to be distinguished from a 'nontraditional' one,"[130] and "[a]ttempts by other courts since then to draw guidance from this model have proved it both impracticable and doctrinally barren."[131] The Court's endeavor to summon history to its side in another case had wound up "in line-drawing of the most arbitrary sort,"[132] and "a nonhistorical standard for selecting immune governmental functions is likely to be just as unworkable."[133] Moreover, there was a "more fundamental" difficulty; the determination of the Court to preserve states' rights in a federal system was actually unfaithful to federalism, for it impaired the liberty of the states to act as they chose. "Any rule of state immunity that looks to the 'traditional,' 'integral,' or 'necessary' nature of governmental functions inevitably invites an unelected federal judiciary to make decisions about which state policies it favors and which ones it dislikes,"[134] he maintained. Embracing the perception he had earlier rejected when Brennan had proffered it, Blackmun now agreed that the states' "sovereign interests . . . are more properly protected by procedural safeguards inherent in the structure of the federal system than by judicially created limitations on federal power. . . . The political process ensures that laws that

---

[129]Mark Tushnet, Why the Supreme Court Overruled *National League of Cities,* 47 Vand. L. Rev. 1627–32 (1987); Battles, at 97–98 (cited in note 113). Despite Reagan's fervent advocacy of devolution, his appointee as Solicitor General, Rex Lee, opposed the states in a series of cases climaxing in *Garcia*. The Supreme Court correspondent of Congressional Quarterly observed, "[t]he government . . . is loath to surrender power, no matter who lives in the White House." Yet she also notes that a Solicitor General does not always reflect the views of the president and that Attorney General Edwin Meese denounced *Garcia* as "an inaccurate reading of the text of the Constitution," adding, "[w]e hope for a day when the Court returns to the basic principles of the Constitution as expressed in *Usery*." Elder Witt, A Different Justice: Reagan and the Supreme Court, Cong. Qt., 1986, at 121.

[130]Garcia v. San Antonio Metropolitan Transit Authority, 469 U.S. 528, 530 (1985).

[131]Id. at 557.

[132]Id. at 544.

[133]Id. at 545.

[134]Id. at 546.

unduly burden the States will not be promulgated."[135] In short, he concluded, "in *National League of Cities* the Court tried to repair what did not need repair."[136]

The reason for Blackmun's switch has been the source of considerable conjecture. It may have resulted from nothing more than the maturation of his thinking about the Tenth Amendment. In an article published in the same year as *Garcia,* he stated that "[w]e must avoid the temptation to let 'federalism' become the Natural Law of the 1980's, a brooding omnipresence to which duly enacted statutes are made to pay homage."[137] Some scholars, though, have propounded harsher explanations. "It was almost as if he had joined the majority in *Usery* as a lark, but soon tired of the novelty," Lino Graglia has written, adding as an afterthought, "[p]erhaps he merely enjoyed the demonstration of the potency of his vote."[138] Pursuing a quite different line of speculation, Phillip J. Cooper has hypothesized that Blackmun's switch may have been the consequence of ill-advised "drawing of battle lines" that can "have the perverse effect of pushing a colleague away when his or her vote is sorely needed." In "the war of the footnotes" in *FERC v. Mississippi,* O'Connor had lashed out at Blackmun

> as if he were the declared enemy of federalism, which was certainly not a well-grounded charge. . . . O'Connor's pressure in *FERC* forced Blackmun to defend the other side of the case more vigorously than he might have, given his own ambiguity on the matter. By the time of *Garcia,* Blackmun was still wavering, but he had been pushed hard, and, ultimately, he pushed back, providing the critical vote to reverse *Usery.*[139]

The opinion of the Court elicited a lengthy dissent from Justice Powell, who, perhaps because he was riled by Blackmun's turnaround, taxed Blackmun with waffling, "logical inconsistencies," and "myopic" vision. Rare have been the occasions, Powell said, when "the principle of *stare decisis* and the rationale

---

[135] Id. at 552 & 556.

[136] Id. at 557. Blackmun's shift was decisive; all of the other votes remained unchanged from *National League of Cities,* save that Stewart's replacement, O'Connor, voted as Stewart had earlier.

[137] Harry A. Blackmun, Section 1983 and Federal Protection of Individual Rights— Will the Statute Remain Alive or Fade Away?, 60 N.Y.U. L. Rev. 23 (1985). One scholar has observed, "[t]he Blackmun doctrine about the place of 'federal' features in the constitution of the American national government closely parallels an extended analysis made by James Madison in essay 39 of The Federalist." Vincent Ostrom, The Meaning of American Federalism: Constituting a Self-Governing Society 103 (Institute for Contemporary Studies Press, 1991).

[138] Lino A. Graglia, *United States v. Lopez:* Judicial Review Under the Commerce Clause, 74 Tex. L. Rev. 748 (1996) ("Judicial Review").

[139] Battles, at 135–36 (cited in note 113).

of recent decisions were ignored as abruptly as we now witness,"[140] the very objection that the minority had raised in *National League of Cities,* which upset a precedent only eight years young. The Tenth Amendment, Powell maintained, had been accorded an "integral role . . . in our constitutional theory," but "[d]espite some genuflecting in the Court's opinion to the concept of federalism, today's decision effectively reduces the Tenth Amendment to meaningless rhetoric. . . . Indeed, the Court barely acknowledges that the Tenth Amendment exists."[141] It did "not seem to have occurred to the Court," Powell riposted, "that *it*—an unelected majority of five Justices—today rejects almost 200 years of the understanding of the constitutional status of federalism."[142] Many would view as "naive" the notion that "federal overreaching" would be restrained by "federal political officials" whom the decision would leave "the sole judges of the limits of their own power."[143] The role of the states was "a matter of constitutional law, not of legislative grace," Powell asserted, and instead of permitting "[t]he emasculation of the powers of the States that can result" from *Garcia,* the federal judiciary should make certain that these inalienable rights were respected.[144]

In a briefer, but more impassioned, dissent, Justice O'Connor began by saying, "[t]he Court today surveys the battle scene of federalism and sounds a retreat. Like Justice Powell, I would prefer to hold the field and, at the very least, render a little aid to the wounded."[145] Though she joined Powell's opinion, as did Burger and Rehnquist, she filed a separate dissent in order to voice her indignation at the majority's conception of federalism and the role of the judiciary. She deplored the Court's willingness to "wash . . . its hands of all efforts to protect the States," for "[w]ith the abandonment of *National League of Cities,* all that stands between the remaining essentials of state sovereignty and Congress is," in a nice turn of phrase, "the latter's underdeveloped capacity for self-restraint."[146] In a one-paragraph dissent, Rehnquist had affirmed his continuing commitment to "a principle that will, I am confident, in time again command the support of a majority of this Court,"[147] and O'Connor, quite possibly with an eye on looming vacancies on the bench, ended her statement by letting it be known,

---

[140]*Garcia,* 469 U.S. at 557–58.

[141]Id. at 560.

[142]Id.

[143]Id. at 567.

[144]Id. at 572. One commentator has remarked on *Garcia:* "It is ironic that the Court discovers the total importance of these 'safeguards' now. For it is undoubtedly true that these safeguards were far stronger in prior times, when the Court did not relinquish its role in enforcing constitutional protection of federalism." Paul J. Mishkin, The Current Understanding of the Tenth Amendment, in Federalism and the Judicial Mind, at 155 (cited in note 106).

[145]*Garcia,* 469 U.S. at 580 (O'Connor dissenting).

[146]Id. at 588.

[147]Id. at 580 (Rehnquist dissenting).

"I share Justice Rehnquist's belief that this Court will in time again assume its constitutional responsibility."[148]

Even more than earlier decisions, *Garcia* polarized the legal community. Martha Field suggested the possibility of an "ominous" reading of the Constitution by the Rehnquist bloc. "The *Garcia* dissenters may have regarded their doctrine of state immunity not as a symbol but as a first step," she proposed. "Once decisions immunizing states from direct federal regulation had reinforced the notion of state sovereignty, it would not be a great leap to begin to hold that federal regulation of private conduct traditionally subject to state power likewise infringed upon state authority."[149] Most of the passion spent on the ruling, however, came from those who were saddened by what they regarded as abnegation by the majority.

A number of scholars expressed concern about the implications of *Garcia* both for federalism and for the Court's perception of its function. Though *Garcia* could portend "the 'death-knell' for states' rights—at least for the time being," wrote one commentator, "a far more pressing implication . . . is that it undermines the role of the Supreme Court in reviewing congressional legislation. In relying on the political process, the Court has given Congress carte blanche authority to determine the extent of its power under the commerce clause."[150] Observing that "*Garcia*'s merciless critique of the criterion of tradition seems to evince a desire for watertight, mechanical tests of protected governmental functions that simply cannot be had in an area as complex as that of federalism," another writer reflected:

> The era of weak national governments is clearly behind us. But for this very reason we should think twice before leaving behind us the era of strong local government as well. It is to be hoped that *Garcia* will come to be seen not as the last word on the subject of federalism but as the new and clean slate on which to inscribe the future jurisprudence of state-national relations.[151]

---

[148]Id. at 589 (O'Connor dissenting). In *Garcia*, the liberals, who had been accused of being activists seeking to impose newfound rights, emerged as advocates of judicial restraint and regard for the political process while the conservative dissenters championed activism. Judicial Philosophies, at 768 (cited in note 85).

[149]Demise, at 105–06 (cited in note 91).

[150]Stephen L. Smith, State Autonomy after *Garcia:* Will the Political Process Protect States' Interests?, 71 Iowa L. Rev. 1550 (1986).

[151]Andrzej Rapaczynski, From Sovereignty to Process: The Jurisprudence of Federalism after *Garcia,* 1985 Sup. Ct. Rev. 415, 419. One commentary spoke of "the judicial abdication model of *Garcia.*" Martin Redish & Karen Drizin, Constitutional Federalism and Judicial Review: The Role of Textual Analysis, 62 N.Y.U. L. Rev. 2 (1987). See also Second Death (cited in note 18); A. E. Dick Howard, Garcia: Of Federalism and Constitutional Values, 16 Publius: The Journal of Federalism 33 (Summer 1986).

Yet even those who were outraged by *Garcia* saw no hope of early reconsideration. A writer in the *Harvard Journal of Law and Public Policy,* condemning the majority for "judicial legerdemain," a "squeamish" attitude toward the necessity of defining limits to national authority and "unwarranted confidence" in the political process, groused, "*Garcia* disguises possible capitulation to legislative tyranny as judicial restraint." Still more pointedly, he gibed, "[j]udicial deference is one thing, but judicial cowardice is another." Nonetheless, he concluded:

> Unless there is a change of personnel on the Court, something to which Justices Rehnquist and O'Connor seem to point, it is highly unlikely that the Court will soon again reverse itself; the present Court suffers enough criticism for what is taken as Hamlet-like indecision. Justice Blackmun, whose switch from *National League of Cities* to *Garcia* was decisive, would also not likely switch again. *Garcia* is thus likely to remain law until there is a change in the Court's own constitution.[152]

For a time, Rehnquist and O'Connor waited in vain. As a result of *National League of Cities,* wrote Linda Greenhouse, "the Tenth Amendment was the constitutional frog that turned into a prince. A kiss by the Supreme Court had . . . lifted the amendment from decades of scorn and neglect." *Garcia,* though, had "unceremoniously turned the Tenth Amendment back into a frog."[153] In 1988, speaking for the Court, Justice Brennan announced that "nothing in *Garcia* or the Tenth Amendment authorizes courts to second-guess the substantive basis for congressional legislation."[154] That same year, a law review commentator declared, "[t]he tenth amendment . . . currently rests at its lowest level of influence since this country adopted the Constitution and its first ten amendments two hundred years ago." As a consequence of *Garcia,* he said, "it has returned to a state of dormancy," with some federal courts characterizing it "as a 'dead letter' in constitutional law."[155] Two years later, a survey concluded a chapter on

---

[152]Comment, *Garcia v. San Antonio Metropolitan Transit Authority* and the Manifest Destiny of Congressional Power, 8 Harv. J. L. & Public Policy 753 (1985).

[153]N.Y. Times, Mar. 13, 1983, quoted in Louis Fisher & Neal Devins, Political Dynamics of Constitutional Law 116 (West, 1992).

[154]South Carolina v. Baker, 485 U.S. 505, 513 (1988). Justice O'Connor dissented on behalf of "state autonomy." Id. at 530. In the five years after *Garcia,* the Court twice rejected Tenth Amendment claims. The other case was Missouri v. Jenkins, 495 U.S. 33, 55 (1990).

[155]Michael G. Smith, The Tenth Amendment: A Dead Letter or Just Asleep as a Limitation on Congress in the Area of State Powers?, 37 Kan. L. Rev. 167 (1988).

the Tenth Amendment by saying, "[a]t the moment, it appears to be a truism once again."[156]

## The Tenth Amendment Reborn?

The last had not been heard of Rehnquist and his allies, however. In 1991, in *Gregory v. Ashcroft*,[157] the Court, in a 7–2 ruling, validated a provision of the Missouri constitution terminating the tenure of judges at 70 that was challenged as violating the federal Age Discrimination in Employment Act. To several of the justices, the case called for nothing more than routine statutory construction, but Sandra Day O'Connor went out of her way to elaborate on the Tenth Amendment in a manner that led commentators to wonder whether, since four other justices joined her opinion, the Court might be readying itself to depart from *Garcia*. "As every schoolchild learns," Justice O'Connor lectured her brethren, "our Constitution establishes a system of dual sovereignty between the States and the Federal Government."[158]

The very next year, the Court gave further encouragement to those seeking to invigorate federalism by holding in *New York v. United States* that, although the federal government may preempt a field, it may not, in O'Connor's words, "commandeer state governments into the service of federal regulatory purposes."[159] Hence, it struck down a provision of the Low Level Radioactive Waste Policy Amendments Act of 1985 requiring the states to take title to waste and penalizing them if they failed to do so. "States," O'Connor postulated, "are not mere political subdivisions of the United States."[160] Yet, in alluding to the Tenth Amendment, she acknowledged that "[t]he Court's jurisprudence in this area has traveled an unsteady path."[161] In speaking for a badly fragmented court, she neither sought to upset *Garcia* not rested her opinion squarely on the Tenth Amendment. Hence, David O'Brien asserted, "the Rehnquist Court, in *New York v. United States,* appears to have abandoned altogether the project of reinvigora-

---

[156]Ellen Alderman & Caroline Kennedy, In Our Defense: The Bill of Rights in Action 335 (William Morrow, 1991). It added, though: "But the Supreme Court may decide it represents instead a reservoir of power waiting to be exercised by the states."

[157]501 U.S. 542 (1991).

[158]Id. at 457, 463. See John C. Pittenger, *Garcia* and the Political Safeguards of Federalism: Is There a Better Solution to the Conundrum of the Tenth Amendment?, 22 Publius: The Journal of Federalism 2 (Winter 1992); Robert H. Freilich & David G. Richardson, Returning to a General Theory of Federalism: Framing a New Tenth Amendment United States Supreme Court Case, 26 Urban Lawyer 223 (Spring 1994) ("General Theory").

[159]505 U.S. 144, 175 (1992).

[160]Id. at 188.

[161]Id. at 160.

ting the Tenth Amendment."[162] Though both *Gregory* and *New York* caused mild stirs, they did not begin to create the tempest that was generated by a 1995 ruling involving Alfonso Lopez, an 18-year-old student in Texas.

When on a late winter day in 1992 Lopez arrived at Edison High School in San Antonio packing a .38 and five bullets intended for a gang war, he had no reason to suppose that he was going to have a significant impact on constitutional law. But his action resulted in a hotly disputed 5–4 ruling in April 1995 in which the Supreme Court struck down the Gun-Free School Zones Act of 1990, thereby writing an important new chapter in the history of reserved powers, even though Rehnquist, in finding that Congress had exceeded its authority under the commerce clause, never mentioned the Tenth Amendment. "We start with first principles," he proclaimed. "As James Madison wrote, 'The powers delegated by the proposed Constitution to the federal government are few and defined. Those which are to remain in the State governments are numerous and indefinite.'"[163]

The dissenters presented three opinions, by far the most forceful coming from Justice David Souter, who accused the majority of "ignoring the painful lesson learned in 1937."[164] He declared:

> The distinction between what is patently commercial and what is not looks much like the old distinction between what directly affects commerce and what touches it only indirectly. And the act of calibrating the level of deference by drawing a line between what is patently commercial and what is less purely so will probably resemble the process of deciding how much interference with contractual freedom was fatal. Thus, it seems fair to ask, whether the step taken by the Court today does anything but portend a return to the untenable jurisprudence from which the Court extricated itself almost 60 years ago.[165]

The "chastening experience" of the 1930s, he said, had taught that "nothing about the judiciary as an institution made it a superior source of policy on the subject Congress dealt with. There is no reason to expect the lesson would be different another time."[166] Souter ended his protest against a ruling that, he stated, "tugs the Court off course" by veering toward "the old judicial pretension discredited and abandoned in 1937," with the foreboding observation:

---

[162]David M. O'Brien, "The Supreme Court and Intergovernmental Relations: What Happened to "Our Federalism"?, 9 J. L. & Politics, 618 (1993). See also General Theory (cited in note 156).

[163]United States v. Lopez, 514 U.S. 549, 552 (1995) (quoting The Federalist 45 (Madison)).

[164]Id. at 609 (Souter dissenting).

[165]Id. at 608.

[166]Id. at 611.

Today's decision may be seen as only a misstep, . . . hardly an epochal case. I
would not argue otherwise, but I would raise a caveat. Not every epochal case
has come in epochal trappings. *Jones & Laughlin* did not reject the direct-
indirect standard in so many words. . . . But we know what happened.[167]

Was Souter's apprehension justifiable? Certainly, many thought so at the
time. When the Court announced its holding in *Lopez,* reported the columnist
Edwin Yoder, "one justice peered down from the bench to see a distinguished
lawyer silently mouthing the word, 'Wow.'"[168] *Lopez* came as such a shock because 60 years had gone by since the Court had last invoked the Commerce
Clause to invalidate an act of Congress. For two generations, law students had
been taught that the matter had been settled forever in 1942 by *Wickard v. Filburn,*[169] where the Court, in a unanimous decision, had ruled that an Ohio farmer
growing wheat wholly for consumption on his own farm was in interstate commerce, and hence subject to congressional regulation. *Lopez* put decades of understanding in doubt. Deborah Jones-Merritt, professor of law at Ohio State
University, noting that "the Commerce Clause had become an intellectual joke
among academics and attorneys," asked, "[c]an Farmer Filburn begin raising
marijuana or machine guns on his Ohio farm?"[170]

The *Washington Post* reported that experts were dubbing the ruling "breath-
taking and historic," and Anthony Lewis's column on this "astonishing" holding
ran under the somber headline, *The Court Strides Back to Its Darkest Days.*[171] In
*The New Yorker,* Jeffrey Toobin, reflecting on the Court's Term, commented: "It
appears that Rehnquist and his conservative colleagues don't just want to turn
the clock back to the days before Earl Warren; they're hankering, it seems, for
the Articles of Confederation—and they're just one vote away."[172]

---

[167]Id. at 604, 614 & 614–15.

[168]Raleigh News and Observer, May 3, 1995.

[169]317 U.S. 111 (1942).

[170]Deborah Jones-Merritt, Commerce!, 94 Mich. L. Rev. 691, 675 (1995).

[171]Raleigh News and Observer, April 30 & April 29, 1995.

[172]Jeffrey Toobin, Chicken Supreme, New Yorker, Aug. 14, 1995, at 82 ("Chicken
Supreme"). When *Lopez* was handed down, a new edition of a leading constitutional law
text was in press with the sentence, "[t]he Supreme Court today interprets the commerce
clause as a *complete* grant of power." Questioned about this after *Lopez,* one of the co-
authors, Ronald Rotunda, said "ruefully," "[i]t was right when we wrote it." Subsequently, the sentence was changed to read, "[t]he Supreme Court today interprets the
commerce clause as a *broad* grant of power." (emphasis added). Lynn A. Baker, Condi-
tional Federal Spending after *Lopez,* 95 Colum. L. Rev. 1918–19 (1995) (citing N.Y.
Times, April 30, 1995). Lino Graglia wrote in mock alarm: "For the first time in almost
sixty years, every commentator incredulously noted, the Court had actually found a federal statute to exceed the scope of federal legislative authority. Could it be that six decades after its defeat at the hands of the New Deal, the Court had decided to return to the

These misgivings were in good part based on the perception that the pattern of decisions by the Supreme Court correlated with a trend to the right in American politics. In his first inaugural address, Richard Nixon had spoken of a "New Federalism in which power, funds, and responsibility will flow from Washington to the States and to the people," a theme he returned to in his discussion of federalism in his 1974 State of the Union Message.[173] President Reagan, in his First Inaugural Address, set forth his "intention . . . to demand recognition of the distinction between the powers granted to the Federal Government and those reserved to the States or to the people."[174] Reagan's appointee as head of the Office of Legal Counsel actually had a framed inscription of the Tenth Amendment mounted on his wall.[175] In his first address as Senate Majority Leader in January 1995, Robert Dole declared, "[i]f I have one goal for the 104th Congress, it is this: that we will dust off the 10th Amendment and restore it to its rightful place in our Constitution."[176] "What is remarkable about the Court's 1994 term," observed Toobin, "is how closely the issues raised by the Rehnquist wing hew to the Contract with America."[177]

Predictably, conservative theoreticians and publicists greeted *Lopez* with jubilation. "When some punk carrying a gun near a school becomes 'interstate commerce,'" wrote the economist Thomas Sowell, "then the sky is the limit."[178] An essayist in *The American Spectator* noted that the *Lopez* minority, citing the example of the 1930s, had "warned that the Court cannot afford to set itself against the main tides of public opinion. But it is clearly the dissenters who are out of step with the tide of opinion, still defending the New Deal and the Great

---

fray?" Judicial Review, at 751 (cited in note 138). Erwin Chemerinsky concluded, "[t]he *Lopez* decision opened a door to constitutional challenges that appeared to have been closed almost 60 years ago, and there is no doubt that hundreds of federal laws will be contested." Erwin Chemerinsky, Changing Course, 36 Trial, June 1995, at 89.

[173]Public Papers of the Presidents of the United States: Richard Nixon, 1969, at 638 (Government Printing Office, 1971); Public Papers, 1974, at 92–93 (1975).

[174]Public Papers of the Presidents of the United States: Ronald Reagan, 1981, at 2 (Government Printing Office, 1982).

[175]Douglas W. Kmiec, The Attorney General's Lawyer: Inside the Meese Justice Department 132 (Praeger, 1992) ("Attorney General's Lawyer").

[176]New Federalism, at 227 (cited in note 2).

[177]Chicken Supreme, at 82 (cited in note 172). "Contract with America" was the term the Republican leader in the House of Representatives, Newt Gingrich, gave to a set of conservative propositions the Republican Party had adopted in appealing to voters in 1994. Shortly after *Lopez* was handed down, an editorial writer commented: "If the court does shift in membership to a majority more compatible with Thomas's view and if a Republican Congress is successful in dismantling significant portions of federal regulatory statutes, the 10th Amendment could become the battlefield on which many disputes will be resolved." Boston Globe, June 19, 1995.

[178]Thomas Sowell, Is the Constitution Superfluous?, Forbes, June 5, 1995, at 61.

Society long after those programs have passed out of public favor."[179] Steven G. Calabresi called *Lopez* "a revolution and long overdue revival of the doctrine that the federal government is one of limited and enumerated powers." He added that it "must be recognized as an extraordinary event. Even if *Lopez* produces no progeny and is soon overruled, the opinion has shattered forever the notion that, after fifty years of Commerce Clause precedent, we can never go back to the days of limited national power."[180] And in a column entitled *Rethinking 1937*, George Will, rejoicing that "the Supreme Court steps away from sophistry," speculated that, as a consequence of *Lopez*, "1995 really might be remembered as a year of restoration."[181]

Moreover, Clarence Thomas left no doubt that he would like to turn back the clock. In his concurrence in *Lopez*, Justice Thomas called for a fundamental re-examination of more than half a century of commerce power jurisprudence that he said came "close to turning the Tenth Amendment on its head."[182] Contending that "commerce" differed from manufacturing, he cited with apparent approval such long-rejected precedents as *E. C. Knight, Schechter,* and *Carter Coal.*[183] *Lopez* did not represent a "wrong turn," he insisted. "If anything, the 'wrong turn' was the Court's dramatic departure in the 1930's from a century and a half of precedent."[184] In a footnote, he acknowledged, "[a]lthough I might be willing to return to the original understanding, I recognize that many believe that it is too late in the day . . . to wipe the slate clean."[185] But he wrote this ruefully, for wiping the slate clean was clearly his heart's desire: "At an appropriate juncture, I think we must modify our Commerce Clause jurisprudence."[186] A month later, Thomas reasserted these views when, dissenting in the *Term Limits* case, he spoke of principles "enshrined" in the Tenth Amendment and demanded respect for "reserved powers."[187] "Presumably," wrote Kathleen Sullivan in the

---

[179]Jeremy Rabkin, State Your Business, American Spectator, July, 1995, at 56.

[180]Steven G. Calabresi, "A Government of Limited and Enumerated Powers": In Defense of *United States v. Lopez*, 94 Mich. L. Rev. 752 (1995).

[181]George F. Will, Rethinking 1937, Newsweek, May 15, 1995, at 70.

[182]*Lopez*, 514 U.S. at 589 (Thomas concurring).

[183]United States v. E. C. Knight Co., 156 U.S. 1 (1895); Schechter Poultry Corp. v. United States, 295 U.S. 495 (1935); Carter v. Carter Coal Co., 298 U.S. 238 (1936).

[184]*Lopez*, 514 U.S. at 599 (Thomas concurring).

[185]Id. at 601 n.8.

[186]Id. at 602. Jeffrey Rosen, noting that Thomas spoke "in a comically overconfident tone, combining self-congratulation with sneering attacks on all of his colleagues and predecessors," charged that Thomas's argument was "lifted, almost word for word in places, from a 1987 article by Richard Epstein, 'The Proper Scope of the Commerce Power,' which Thomas mysteriously fails to cite." Jeffrey Rosen, Fed Up, New Republic, May 22, 1995, at 13 ("Fed Up").

[187]United States Term Limits v. Thornton, 514 U.S. 779, 848 (1995) (Thomas dissenting).

*Harvard Law Review,* "Justice Thomas would overrule *United States v. Darby.*"[188]

Other evidence, though, suggested that too much was being made of the ideological and doctrinal significance both of *National League of Cities,* in part because of Brennan's boisterous dissent, and of *Lopez,* and that Thomas was at this time living in a realm of his own. *National League of Cities* had conceded the power of Congress to compel corporations to adhere to wages and hours standards, and Rehnquist had taken part in *Perez,* the loan shark decision that recognized a broad national police power.[189] In his concurrence in *Lopez,* which was joined by O'Connor, Justice Anthony Kennedy—like O'Connor a member of the majority and alert to how the ruling could be interpreted—made a point of affirming:

> *Stare decisis* operates with great force in counseling us not to call in question the essential principles now in place respecting the congressional power to regulate transactions of a commercial nature. That fundamental restraint on our power forecloses us from reverting to an understanding of commerce that would serve only an 18th-century economy, dependent then upon producing and trading practices that had changed but little over the preceding centuries; it also mandates against returning to the time when congressional authority to regulate undoubted commercial activities was limited by a judicial determination that those matters had an insufficient connection to an interstate system. Congress can regulate in the commercial sphere on the assumption that we have a single market and a unified purpose to build a stable national economy.[190]

No less a figure than Laurence Tribe, surely no favorite of the Right, said, with respect to the meager legislative findings in the Gun-Free School Zones Act, that "Congress has pushed the outer edge of the envelope rather carelessly."[191] It had not taken the trouble even to mention the word "commerce" in the statute, nor was any evidence adduced linking guns in school areas to commerce.[192] Accordingly, many commentators thought that in the future Congress

---

[188]Kathleen Sullivan, Dueling Sovereignties: *United States Term Limits, Inc. v. Thornton,* 109 Harv. L. Rev. 80, 106 (1995). Thomas's dissent in *Term Limits,* another scholar has said, was "in some respects . . . nothing less than a paean to democracy grounded in fifty small republics." Cynthia L. Cates, Splitting the Atom of Sovereignty: *Term Limits, Inc.'s* Conflicting Views of Popular Autonomy in a Federal Republic, 26 Publius: The Journal of Federalism, XXVI 135 (Summer 1996).

[189]Perez v. United States, 402 U.S. 146 (1971).

[190]*Lopez,* 514 U.S. at 574 (Kennedy concurring).

[191]Raleigh News and Observer, April 27, 1995. It should be noted, though, that in an earlier case the Court had remarked that "no formal findings were made, which of course are not necessary." Katzenbach v. McClung, 379 U.S. 294, 299 (1964).

[192]Yet, Lino Graglia objected, if Congress had obliged the Court by inserting the "compulsory incantation" about the relevance of the statute to interstate commerce, when

could satisfy the Court simply by inserting verbiage linking legislation more clearly to delegated powers. Indeed, in *Turning Right,* David Savage, the astute Supreme Court correspondent of the *Los Angeles Times,* stressed that the Rehnquist bloc had disappointed the *Wall Street Journal* and Republican officials by being "unwilling to move aggressively to defend private property or big business. . . . Rehnquist and his colleagues are progovernment conservatives, not Chamber of Commerce advocates."[193]

Furthermore, respect for federalism is not a monopoly of conservatives. When in 1946 the Supreme Court validated federal taxes on the sale of mineral waters by the state of New York from its spa in Saratoga Springs, despite the state's claim that it was exercising an "essential governmental function," protest came not from conservative jurists but from William O. Douglas, who had also departed from the majority in *Case v. Bowles.*[194] In a vigorous dissent in *New York v. United States* (not to be confused with the 1992 case bearing the same title), Douglas objected:

---

in fact this was "a patent police power measure," it would only have been continuing "a foolish game" it had been playing with the indulgence of the judiciary for more than half a century. Judicial Review, at 754–55 (cited in note 138).

[193]David G. Savage, Turning Right: The Making of the Rehnquist Supreme Court 474–75 (Wiley, 1993). Rehnquist's theory of federalism, Jeff Powell has stressed, was not "merely a surrogate or disguise for a simple conservative politics," because he has invoked it at times on behalf of holdings that displeased the Right. Compleat, at 1334 (cited in note 61). "Since 1937," Martin Shapiro observed in 1986, "the Court has consistently declared that it simply will not protect business property no matter what." Shapiro, The Supreme Court's "Return" to Economic Regulation, Studies in American Political Development 93 (1986). Shapiro emphasized, however, that the Court continued to employ substantive economic due process, and in the course of doing so created what "were essentially economic rights constituting a 'new property.'" Id. at 93. See also William W. Van Alstyne, The Recrudescence of Property Rights as the Foremost Principle of Civil Liberties: The First Decade of the Burger Court, 43 Law & Contemp. Probs. 66 (1980). Nor have conservatives always been consistent champions of federalism. For all its rhetoric about the Tenth Amendment, the Reagan administration did not hesitate to try to gain Court approval for federal intervention in the "Baby Doe" case, although it was moving into an area long understood to be the domain of the states. Herman Schwartz, Introduction, in Schwartz, ed., The Burger Years: Rights and Wrongs in the Supreme Court, 1969–1986 xix (Viking, 1987). Expanding the scope of the Tenth Amendment "will not please everyone," Ed Meese warned a conservative gathering. "[F]ederalism will give states the freedom to make choices with which we, as conservatives, may very well disagree." Attorney General's Lawyer, at 137 (cited in note 175).

[194]327 U.S. 92 (1946). In a lone dissent in a 1946 case concerning the imposition of federal price control on the sale by an Idaho county of a used tractor, Douglas objected to "substantial intrusions on the sovereignty of the States, involving matters of great delicacy" and "serious constitutional questions." Hulbert v. Twin Falls County, 327 U.S. 103, 105–06 (1946) (Douglas dissenting).

The notion that the sovereign position of the States must find its protection in the will of a transient majority of Congress is foreign to and a negation of our constitutional system. . . . The Constitution is a compact between sovereigns. The power of one sovereign to tax another is an innovation so startling as to require explicit authority if it is to be allowed. If the power of the federal government to tax the States is conceded, the reserved power of the States guaranteed by the Tenth Amendment does not give them the independence which they have always been assumed to have. They are relegated to a more servile status. . . . They must pay the federal government for the privilege of exercising the powers of sovereignty guaranteed them by the Constitution. . . .[195]

Douglas got another opportunity to make known his misgivings in 1968 when, in his dissent in *Maryland v. Wirtz,* he deplored the extension of the Fair Labor Standards Act as a "serious invasion of state sovereignty protected by the Tenth Amendment." Departures of this nature "could devour the essentials of state sovereignty, though that sovereignty is attested by the Tenth Amendment," he admonished, and in this instance the action by Congress served to "disrupt the fiscal policy of the States and threaten their autonomy," with the consequence that "the State as a sovereign power is being seriously tampered with, potentially crippled."[196]

In his final year on the bench, Hugo Black—who had joined Douglas's dissent in *New York v. United States*—wrote an opinion for the Court expressing the conviction that "the National Government will fare best if the States and their institutions are left free to perform their separate functions in their separate ways." He believed that "Our Federalism" works best when the federal government "always endeavors" to act in ways that will not unduly interfere with the legitimate activities of the States."[197] Moreover, during the past generation law professors not usually grouped in the conservative camp have expressed concern about dismissing the Tenth Amendment as a truism. On one occasion, commenting on the assumption that there is no restraint on federal invasion of the prerogatives of the states, Charles Black wrote:

---

[195]New York v. United States, 326 U.S. 572, 594–95 (1946).

[196]Maryland v. Wirtz, 392 U.S. 183, 201–05 (1968) (Douglas dissenting). See Howard Ball & Phillip J. Cooper, Of Power and Right: Hugo Black, William O. Douglas, and America's Constitutional Revolution 273–74 (Oxford University Press, 1992). Justice Stewart joined in Douglas's dissent.

[197]Younger v. Harris, 401 U.S. 37, 44 (1971). For drafts of the opinion and communications among the Justices, see Hugo Black Papers, Boxes 438, 439. For an incisive commentary, see A. E. Dick Howard, The Supreme Court and Federalism, in Annual Chief Justice Earl Warren Conference on Advocacy in the United States, Final Report—The Courts: The Pendulum of Federalism, June 15–16, 1979 (The Roscoe Pound-American Trial Lawyers Foundation, 1979).

But are not its implications startling? Can Congress prohibit the interstate travel of divorced men? Such a law would have no close relation to economic matters, but that is true of the Mann Act, as applied to non-commercialized "immorality." Could Congress bar from interstate shipment goods produced in a factory where employees swear? If not, why not? Some people think swearing is worse than child labor; some think it not as bad.

Unless one is prepared to answer these questions in the affirmative, as a matter of constitutional law, one must conclude that some limits on federal power arise by mere implication from the fact of there being states, with general authority over their own local concerns. There is nothing strange to constitutional discourse about an implied limitation on governmental power; the states are subject to disabilities that are merely inferred from the coexistence of the federal government, and there is no reason why an implication might not run the other way.[198]

Writing in the *New Republic*, Jeffrey Rosen put a different spin on *Lopez*. The decision, he maintained, "is good news for liberal constitutionalists. The mindless impulse to federalize crimes that the states are prosecuting perfectly well on their own has been, in recent years, more of a Republican than a Democratic vice. . . . The obvious losers in the wake of *Lopez* are statist conservatives, whose addiction to passing federal laws for purely symbolic purposes has now been called into question." It was hard to see, he said, how Rehnquist could continue to validate legislation such as the flag burning law, which bore such a tenuous relationship to interstate commerce.[199]

---

[198]Charles L. Black, Jr., Perspectives in Constitutional Law 29–30 (Prentice-Hall, 1963). In like manner, J. M. Balkin has written:

One does not have to agree with the ideological presuppositions of Justices Rehnquist and Powell to acknowledge that democratic processes sometimes do fail us, and that it is certainly possible that they might fail in the area of protecting state and local interests. The simple statement of faith that the processes will never fail to protect state and local interests is as ideological as anything in *National League of Cities* itself. . . .

If it is sometimes necessary for the Court to correct majoritarian processes in order to protect individuals, why should we think it is never necessary to correct those same processes to protect state and local interests? And if we know that somewhere along the line, the process will fail to protect the interests of state and local government, does that not justify judicial supervision and a high level of scrutiny along the line of *Carolene Products*?

Ideology, at 213 (cited in note 90). "Federalism is not a humdrum matter of public administration," wrote Samuel H. Beer in 1993, "but a serious question of political philosophy." Samuel H. Beer, To Make a Nation: The Rediscovery of American Federalism 21 (Harvard University Press, 1993).

[199]Fed Up, at 13–14 (cited in note 186).

## The Tenth Amendment Today: Revolution or Reform?

In the six years that have elapsed since *Lopez* was handed down, the debate over the significance of the decision has remained unresolved. In 1996, Larry Kramer of New York University Law School wrote:

> What should we make of *United States v. Lopez?* Initial reactions were largely of the Chicken Little variety and filled with dire predictions of renewed judicial shackles imposed on a hamstrung federal government. Sober second thoughts have been, well, sober, and many observers now say that *Lopez* may not be such a big deal after all. . . .
>
> So which is it? Is *Lopez* a sport, a judicial shot across the bow to remind Congress to take its responsibilities seriously? Or have the ghosts of Sutherland, Butler, Van Devanter, and McReynolds returned to haunt us after all?[200]

Though commentators differed about how to answer these questions, everyone acknowledged that, surprisingly, federalism had become a hot-button topic. "In 1996," reported one survey, "the political spotlight again focused on federalism," with the Tenth Amendment serving "as a rhetorical rallying point" and "devolution revolution" the new catch phrase.[201] That same year, Senator Ted Stevens of Alaska introduced the Tenth Amendment Enforcement Act, a bill endorsed by the Majority Leader and 22 other Republicans, with an Arizona Republican, John Shadegg, sponsoring a companion measure in the House. A speaker to a Civil War Roundtable at a Georgia country club wound up by saying, "[a]lthough the will to utilize it has long been missing, the Tenth Amendment was not repealed at Appomattox," and the director of Jefferson Davis's estate, Beauvoir, observed, "[t]here's sure a whole lot of talk now about the Tenth Amendment and states' rights and government getting too big and too intrusive and telling folks what to do."[202]

Neo-Confederates and others who favored "systematic weakening of the nanny state" looked to the judiciary to advance their cause.[203] Robert H. Nelson, professor in the School of Public Affairs at the University of Maryland and Senior Fellow of the Competitive Enterprise Institute, wrote: "For decades the left has used the judiciary to enhance the powers of the federal government. The

---

[200]Larry Kramer, What's a Constitution For Anyway? Of History and Theory, Bruce Ackerman and the New Deal, 46 Case W. Res. L. Rev. 885 (1996).

[201]Carol S. Weissert & Sanford F. Schram, The State of American Federalism, 1995–1996, 26 Publius: The Journal of Federalism 1 (Summer 1996). "Devolution revolution" is attributed to Richard Nathan.

[202]Peter Applebome, Dixie Rising: How the South is Shaping American Values, Politics, and Culture 146–47, 317 (Random House, 1996).

[203]More Perfect Union, at 29 (cited in note 13).

time is right for Republican governors to ask the courts to enforce the Constitution in order to roll back federal power-grabbing."[204] Two conservative attorneys rejoiced that *Lopez* marked "a watershed in the Court's jurisprudence," for within two years after that ruling "some outcroppings" of the "vast legal-political regulatory" structure had already been toppled and lower courts were using the decision to circumscribe federal power.[205] Douglas Kmiec, professor of constitutional law at Pepperdine University and former assistant attorney general under Reagan, regretted, though, that the Court had taken only some tentative first steps in undoing the Constitutional Revolution of 1937. "The majority opinion in *Lopez*," he noted, "cites, but neither explains nor overrules, the many prior cases that tolerate sweeping exercises of federal authority." He asked, "[i]s there a Rehnquist-led majority for restoring the Founders' interpretation of commerce as the actual exchange of goods and services?"[206]

The Supreme Court has yet to meet Kmiec's rigorous standard, but in a series of decisions, starting only 11 months after *Lopez* with the *Seminole Tribe* case,[207] it has continued to invalidate acts of Congress on federalist grounds, invariably by the same 5–4 alignment. In *Seminole Tribe* the Court found unconstitutional the provision of the Indian Gaming Regulatory Act of 1988 authorizing tribes to sue states in federal courts to compel them to negotiate in good faith. The Indian Commerce Clause, the Court declared, did not empower Congress "to abrogate the States' sovereign immunity."[208] The same five justices who had constituted the majority in *Lopez* relied upon the Eleventh Amendment, although the litigation had taken place wholly within the borders of a single state. In claiming that the Court had long "understood the Eleventh Amendment to stand not so much for what it says, but for the presupposition . . . which it confirms," Rehnquist was quoting a precedent only five years old.[209] Despite its invocation of the Eleventh Amendment, *Seminole Tribe*, one commentary ob-

---

[204]Robert H. Nelson, Reality Check: Judicial Activism in Reverse, Forbes, Nov. 16, 1998, at 208.

[205]David B. Rivkin, Jr. & Lee A. Casey, Federalism (Cont'd), Commentary, December, 1996, at 47–48.

[206]Douglas W. Kmiec, The Court Rediscovers Federalism, Policy Review, Sept.-Oct. 1997, at 62 ("Rediscovers").

[207]Seminole Tribe of Florida v. Florida, 517 U.S. 44 (1996).

[208]Id. at 47.

[209]Id. at 54 (citing Blatchford v. Native Village of Noatak, 501 U.S. 775, 779 (1991)). The Court, though, rested heavily on Hans v. Louisiana, 134 U.S. 1 (1890). *Seminole Tribe* overruled a decision handed down by the Court just seven years before, Pennsylvania v. Union Gas Co., 491 U.S. 1 (1989).

served, in fact "extended the philosophy of *Lopez*," which had been grounded on the Tenth Amendment.[210]

For the minority, Justice Souter, joined by Justices Ruth Bader Ginsburg and Stephen Breyer, responded to Rehnquist's emphasis on "the States' immunity from suit" by asserting that "the Court today holds for the first time since the founding of the Republic that Congress has no authority to subject a State to the jurisdiction of a federal court at the behest of an individual asserting a federal right,"[211] a holding "fundamentally mistaken."[212] Souter and his allies could not comprehend how the Eleventh Amendment, which deals with diversity of citizenship, could restrict suits entirely within a state. In a separate dissent, Justice Stevens echoed their indignation at this "profoundly misguided" reasoning, but spoke on his own because he believed "the shocking character of the majority's affront to a coequal branch of our Government merits additional comment."[213] In his opinion for the Court, though, Rehnquist had already dismissed the dissent contemptuously as "a theory cobbled together from law review articles and its own version of historic events."[214]

The very next year, the Court, in another 5–4 decision, *Printz v. United States*,[215] once again struck out at Congress. In response to a suit brought by two western sheriffs (one of them Jay Printz of Montana), the Court invalidated the provisions of the Brady Handgun Violence Prevention Act of 1993 requiring local law enforcement officers, temporarily, to conduct background checks on would-be gun purchasers. Instead of pointing to a clause of the Constitution that Congress had allegedly violated, Justice Antonin Scalia asserted that commands issued by the Federal Government to officers of a state were "fundamentally incompatible with our constitutional system."[216] As he rightly said, the ruling "should have come as no surprise,"[217] for the Court had signaled its attitude in *New York v. United States*.[218] He also cited *Gregory v. Ashcroft*,[219] declaring, "[i]t is incontestable that the Constitution established a system of dual sovereignty."[220] While Scalia did allude to the Tenth Amendment, though only in passing, two justices were more direct in their concurring opinions. Sandra Day

---

[210]Kenneth T. Palmer & Edward B. Laverty, The Impact of *United States v. Lopez* on Intergovernmental Relations: A Preliminary Assessment, 26 Publius: The Journal of Federalism 114 (Summer 1996).

[211]*Seminole Tribe*, 517 U.S. at 59 (Souter dissenting).

[212]Id. at 100.

[213]Id. at 78 (Stevens dissenting).

[214]Id. at 68.

[215]521 U.S. 898 (1997).

[216]Id. at 935.

[217]Id. at 926.

[218]505 U.S. 144 (1992).

[219]501 U.S. 452 (1991).

[220]*Printz*, 521 at 918.

O'Connor said bluntly, "[t]he Brady Act violates the Tenth Amendment,"[221] while Clarence Thomas explained, "I write separately to emphasize that the Tenth Amendment affirms the undeniable notion that under our Constitution, the Federal Government is one of enumerated, hence limited, powers."[222] The commerce power, he added, citing his opinion in *Lopez,* did not extend to gun sales within a state.[223]

In dissent, Justice Stevens, joined by Justices Breyer, Ginsburg, and Souter, declared, "[w]hen Congress exercises the powers delegated to it by the Constitution, it may impose affirmative obligations on executive and judicial officers of state and local governments as well as ordinary citizens."[224] Stevens saw nothing in the Tenth Amendment that would be inhibiting. Indeed, he maintained, "[t]here is not a clause, sentence, or paragraph in the entire text of the Constitution of the United States that supports the proposition that a local police officer can ignore a command contained in a statute enacted by Congress pursuant to an express delegation of powers enumerated in Article I."[225] The Framers, he went on, sought "to enhance the power of the national government, not to provide some new, unmentioned immunity for state officers."[226] The majority, he objected, indulged in "judicial inferences drawn from a silent text."[227] Moreover, "perversely," the Rehnquist bloc, in preventing the federal government from enlisting state officials, was leaving Washington with no alternative save to "create vast national bureaucracies."[228]

The same 5–4 alignment held again in 1999 when, in *Alden v. Maine,*[229] the Court ruled that Congress did not have the power to subject nonconsenting states to private suits in state courts. The litigation had arisen when 65 parole officers and juvenile case workers, having found the federal courts closed to them by the *Seminole Tribe* decision, sought to sue Maine in state court for failing to abide by the overtime provisions of the Fair Labor Standards Act, the New Deal law that once again had become a bone of contention. During oral argument, United States Deputy Solicitor General Seth Waxman had asserted that if Maine was permitted to set aside an act of Congress, the country's statutes might as well have been "written in invisible ink."[230] But, in his opinion for the Court, Justice

---

[221]Id. at 935–36.

[222]Id. at 936.

[223]*Lopez,* 514 U.S. at 584.

[224]*Printz,* 521 U.S. at 939. Justices Breyer and Souter also offered separate dissenting opinions.

[225]521 U.S. 898 (1997) at 944.

[226]Id. at 945.

[227]Id. at 954.

[228]Id. at 959.

[229]119 S. Ct. 2240 (1999).

[230]Aaron Epstein, Court Decisions Give More Power to States, Raleigh News and Observer, May 15, 1999, at A5 ("Court Decisions").

Kennedy declared that the Eleventh Amendment gave states immunity from such suits. He further maintained that "any doubt regarding the constitutional role of the States as sovereign entities is removed by the Tenth Amendment,"[231] adding: "Although the Constitution grants broad powers to Congress, our federalism requires that Congress treat the States in a manner consistent with their status as residuary sovereigns and joint participants in the governance of the Nation."[232]

For the dissenters, Justice Souter, joined by the familiar trio of Justices Breyer, Ginsburg, and Stevens, pointed out that, although Kennedy had cited the Tenth Amendment, the Court's reasoning rested both on "an indefeasible, natural law view of sovereign immunity"[233] and a murky conception of the rights of states somehow inhering in the American system of federalism, a claim with no historical foundation. Furthermore, Souter maintained, "[t]he State of Maine is not sovereign with respect to the national objective of the FLSA."[234] He went on to say that "if today's decision occasions regret at its anomalous versions of history and federal theory, it is the more regrettable in being the second time the Court has suddenly changed the course of prior decision."[235] In truth, as he elsewhere noted, it was actually the third turnabout, for, in circumscribing the reach of the FLSA in *National League of Cities,* the Court had reversed *Wirtz,* and *National League of Cities* in turn had, within a decade, lost out to *Garcia.*

On that same June day in 1999, once again by 5–4, in *Florida Prepaid Postsecondary Education Expense Board v. College Savings Bank,*[236] the Court invalidated the Patent Remedy Act as violating state sovereignty by subjecting states to patent infringement suits. The characteristically terse opinion for the Court by Chief Justice Rehnquist drew a blistering dissent from Justice Stevens. "The Constitution vests Congress with plenary authority over patents and copyrights," Stevens began, and "nearly 200 years ago, Congress provided for exclusive jurisdiction of patent infringement litigation in the federal courts."[237] It was "quite unfair" for the Court to strike down an act of Congress on the basis of a stipulation—the need for substantial findings of patent infringements by the states themselves—that the Court had not yet articulated, he continued, especially since Congress had taken pains to address a problem the Court had raised in a 1985 decision.[238] Moreover, Congress had, in fact, heard testimony, not least from the Acting Commissioner of Patents, showing the need for such a statute.

---

[231] 119 S. Ct. at 2247.

[232] Id. at 2263.

[233] Id. at 2277.

[234] Id. at 2288.

[235] Id. at 2291–92.

[236] 119 S. Ct. 2199 (1999).

[237] Id. at 2211 (Stevens dissenting).

[238] Id. at 2214 (citing Atascadero State Hospital v. Scanlon, 473 U.S. 234 (1985)).

"The Court's opinion today threatens to read Congress' power to pass prophylactic legislation out of Section 5 [of the Fourteenth Amendment] altogether,"[239] Stevens charged, although the patent law was "a paradigm of an appropriate . exercise of Congress' § 5 power."[240]

The decision, Stevens concluded, offered further evidence of the mischief the Court had wrought by the "dramatic expansion of the judge-made doctrine of sovereign immunity" in *Seminole Tribe*. In maintaining that the future reach of that ruling was "defined only by the present majority's perception of constitutional penumbras rather than constitutional text,"[241] he chose a word that was intended to sting, for "penumbras" brought to mind Justice Douglas's execrated opinion in *Griswold v. Connecticut,*[242] a decision that paved the way for *Roe v. Wade*.[243] In sum, the Rehnquist majority, Stevens was saying, was guilty of the same reckless judicial activism it had condemned in the Warren Court.

The assault continued in the Court's October 1999 term, albeit with curiously mixed results. Early in 2000, in *Kimel v. Florida Board of Regents,*[244] the Court continued the parade of federalism rulings by invalidating the provision of the Age Discrimination in Employment Act abrogating the states' immunity from suits by its employees. Since *Seminole Tribe* had barred use of the commerce power to abrogate state immunity, the plaintiffs in *Kimel* had sought redress in Section 5 of the Fourteenth Amendment. But the Court rejected that route, too, as not "appropriate."[245] In her opinion for the Court, Justice O'Connor did not hesitate to pass judgment on the wisdom of the legislation, asserting that "Congress' 1974 extension of the Act to the States was an unwarranted response to a perhaps inconsequential problem."[246] Several paragraphs later, she was even more confident of this point. "Congress," she declared, "had virtually no reason to believe that state and local governments were unconstitutionally discriminating against their employees on the basis of age."[247] The 5–4 division "was the same as in other rebuffs that justices have dealt Congress in the last five years," observed Linda Greenhouse. "The difference this time was a notable hardening of tone."[248]

---

[239]Id. at 2217.

[240]Id. at 2219.

[241]Id.

[242]381 U.S. 479, 484 (1965).

[243]410 U.S. 113 (1973).

[244]120 S. Ct. 631 (2000).

[245]Id. at 645. The Court had only recently established the standard that legislation enacted under Section Five of the Fourteenth Amendment must be "appropriate" in City of Boerne v. Flores, 521 U.S. 507 (1997).

[246]*Kimel,* 120 S. Ct. at 648–49.

[247]Id. at 649.

[248]N.Y. Times, January 12, 2000.

Justice Stevens began his dissent by saying forcefully, "Congress' power to regulate the American economy includes the power to regulate both the public and private sectors of the labor market."[249] Sounding much like Justice Harlan Fiske Stone in 1936, he maintained that "the Framers did not . . . select the Judicial Branch as the constitutional guardian of . . . state interests."[250] He further insisted that "[t]here is not a word in the text of the Constitution supporting the Court's conclusion that the judge-made doctrine of sovereign immunity limits Congress' power to authorize private parties . . . to enforce federal law against the States."[251] Furthermore, he contended, the Court, in its "profoundly misguided" ratiocination,[252] was misconstruing the Eleventh Amendment, which applied only to diversity jurisdiction, just as it had misfired in *Seminole Tribe.* He valued the principle of *stare decisis,* but so "profoundly mistaken" was the reasoning in that recent ruling that it had "forsaken any claim to the usual deference or respect owed to decisions of the Court."[253] O'Connor responded sniffily. The dissenters' refusal to accept precedents the majority thought salient, she said, "makes it difficult to engage in additional meaningful debate on the place of state sovereignty immunity in the Constitution."[254]

Just one day after *Kimel,* the Court handed down a decision on another federalism case that commentators anticipated would further invigorate the Tenth Amendment. *Reno v. Condon* [255] grew out of a suit filed by the attorney general of South Carolina, Charlie Condon, against the United States government (in the person of Attorney General Janet Reno) challenging the Driver's Privacy Protection Act of 1994. Congress had been motivated to enact the DPPA, restricting the right of state governments to make available personal information in the files of motor vehicle agencies, by the murder of actress Rebecca Schaeffer, costar of the television program *My Sister Sam,* by a stalker who had gotten her unpublished address from the records of a state driver's license bureau. Moreover, citizens were irked by unwanted solicitations from firms who had obtained their addresses, as well as their photographs, from state agencies that did a lucrative trade in selling this information to commercial database services.

It seemed improbable that the statute would survive its rough ride through the federal courts. In 1998, the United States Court of Appeals for the Fourth Circuit, the graveyard for federal legislation, sustained a district court ruling

---

[249]*Kimel,* 119 S. Ct. at 650 (Stevens dissenting).

[250]Id. at 651.

[251]Id. at 652.

[252]Id. at 653.

[253]Id.

[254]Id. at 643. The Rehnquist Court has also narrowed the authority of the federal government over state suffrage requirements under the Voting Rights Act. See Abrams v. Johnson, 521 U.S. 74 (1997).

[255]120 S. Ct. 666 (2000).

invalidating the act on the grounds that the commerce power of Congress is circumscribed by the Tenth Amendment.[256] In dissent, Senior Circuit Judge Phillips pointed out that the provisions of the law "only apply once a State makes the voluntary choice to enter the interstate market created by the release of personal information in its files,"[257] but questioning during oral argument in the U.S. Supreme Court Chamber in the fall of 1999 gave the solicitor general, who defended the statute, reason for foreboding. Justice Scalia commented, "[w]hat a state does with its own records is its own business," and Justice Kennedy said that one had to assume that the states did not have a privacy shield "because their voters don't want it. . . . Here, the federal interest is unnecessary and intrusive."[258]

But on January 12, 2000 the Supreme Court pulled a surprise by reversing the Fourth Circuit and sustaining the law.[259] In a unanimous opinion, Chief Justice Rehnquist declared "that in enacting this statute Congress did not run afoul of the federalism principles enunciated in" *New York* and *Printz.*[260] Likening the DPPA to the act contested in *South Carolina v. Baker,* he pointed out that it did not "require the States in their sovereign capacity to regulate their own citizens" or commandeer state officials to enforce federal legislation regulating private parties.[261] *Reno v. Condon,* wrote Linda Greenhouse in the *New York Times,* was "a rare federal victory in the ongoing battle at the court over federal versus state authority."[262]

Four months later, this newfound unanimity was severely tested by an especially nasty case. In litigation that became known as *United States v. Morrison,* Christy Brzonkala alleged that shortly after enrolling as a freshman at Virginia Polytechnic Institute in September 1994 she was brutally gang-raped by two members of the football team, one of them Antonio J. Morrison. As the Supreme

---

[256]Condon v. Reno, 155 F.3d 453 (4th Cir. 1998).

[257]Id. at 468 (Phillips dissenting).

[258]David G. Savage, Supreme Court Hears Arguments in Motor Vehicle Records Privacy Case, Raleigh News and Observer, Nov. 11, 1999, at A9.

[259]Reno v. Condon, 120 S. Ct. 666 (2000).

[260]Id. at 671 (citing New York v. United States, 505 U.S. 144 (1992) and Printz v. United States, 521 U.S. 898 (1997)).

[261]Id. at 672 (quoting South Carolina v. Baker, 485 U.S. 505, 514–15 (1988)). Even if the Court had upheld the Court of Appeals, the decision would have had little consequence because Congress had enacted new legislation imposing the same restrictions on the states, which was to take effect 90 days after the Court disposed of this South Carolina case. That measure required compliance as a condition to receipt by the states of federal transportation funds. Since it rested on the broad spending power, the Court was not expected to strike it down. Officials Ask High Court to Stay Out of Case, L.A. Times, Oct. 22, 1999, at A35.

[262]Linda Greenhouse, Justices Uphold Ban on States' Sales of Drivers' License Information, N.Y. Times, Jan. 12, 2000, at A29.

Court later acknowledged, "Morrison admitted having sexual contact with her despite the fact that she had twice told him 'no.'"[263] She further asserted that Morrison told her after raping her a second time, "[y]ou better not have any fucking diseases," and that he later said loudly in the college dining room, "I like to get girls drunk and fuck the shit out of them."[264] So traumatizing was the episode, she related, that she dropped out of school and attempted suicide. After the university behaved with appalling callousness to these very serious charges (Morrison was permitted to complete his senior year on a full football scholarship), Brzonkala filed suit under the provision of the Violence Against Women Act of 1994 "creat[ing] a private cause of action against any 'person . . . who commits a crime of violence motivated by gender.'"[265]

Early in the summer of 1999, the United States Court of Appeals for the Fourth Circuit, splitting 7–4, found the section of the act opening federal courts to female victims invalid because the law did not establish a convincing relationship to interstate commerce or to government violation of civil rights. The majority relied substantially on *Lopez.* Judge J. Michael Luttig, who began his 214-page opinion, "[w]e the people, distrustful of power, and believing that government limited and dispersed protects freedom best,"[266] said of VAWA: "Such a statute, we are constrained to conclude, simply cannot be reconciled with the principles of limited federal government upon which this nation is founded."[267]

Christy Brzonkala, now 23, sat in the Supreme Court Chamber during argument on her appeal from the Fourth Circuit ruling, and she could not have been happy with what she heard. "In an hour of rapid-fire questions and sometimes testy exchanges," reported the *Washington Post,* conservative justices peppered her attorney (from the National Organization for Women Legal Defense Fund) and Solicitor General Waxman (expressing the Clinton administration's backing for the law) with skeptical queries.[268] "Your approach," Sandra Day O'Connor told Waxman, "would justify a federal remedy for alimony or

---

[263]United States v. Morrison, 120 S. Ct. 1740, 1746 (2000).

[264]Brzonkala v. Virginia Polytechnic Inst., 169 F.3d 820, 827 (4th Cir. 1999) (en banc). In an effort to spare our sensibilities, the Court of Appeals refused to spell out some of the more graphic parts of Morrison's statements (for example, "***ing diseases"). That was slightly more inclusive than the approach the chief justice would take, as he simply omitted the words entirely from his version of the facts ("any . . . diseases"). Morrison, 120 S. Ct. at 1746. The case itself resulted from one of two lawsuits that Ms. Brzonkala filed.

[265]*Brzonkala,* 169 F.3d at 827 (quoting 42 U.S.C. § 13981 (c) (1994)).

[266]Id. at 825–26.

[267]Id. at 826.

[268]Joan Biskupic, Sex-Assault Law Under Scrutiny; Justices Skeptical About Congress's Role in Victims' Remedies, Wash. Post. Jan. 12, 2000, at A11.

child support."[269] Justices Ginsburg, Stevens, and Breyer indicated that they were favorably disposed toward the statute, but, noted a correspondent for the Baltimore *Sun,* "they appeared to be outnumbered."[270]

They were. On May 15, 2000, with the same 5–4 division that characterized *Lopez,* the Court struck down the civil remedy provision of the Violence Against Women Act. In reaching this decision, Rehnquist explained, the majority relied on three precedents: *Lopez* and the two notorious Reconstruction era rulings that effectively shut off virtually all efforts to secure equality for African Americans for the next three quarters of a century.[271] "Gender-motivated crimes of violence are not, in any sense of the phrase, economic activity," the chief justice declared.[272] While conceding that, in contrast to the absence of congressional findings in *Lopez,* Congress, in adopting this legislation, had demonstrated "the serious impact that gender-motivated violence has on victims and their families,"[273] that record, he maintained, failed "to sustain the constitutionality of Commerce Clause legislation."[274] If the Court accepted the government's reasoning in this case, it

> would allow Congress to regulate any crime as long as the nationwide, aggregated impact of that crime has substantial effects on employment, production, transit, or consumption. Indeed, if Congress may regulate gender-motivated violence, it would be able to regulate murder or any other type of violence since gender-motivated violence, as a subset of all violent crime, is certain to have lesser economic impacts than the larger class of which it is a part.[275]

Nor, Rehnquist continued, could the legislation be sustained under Section 5 of the Fourteenth Amendment. The 1883 decisions on which that judgment was founded had force, he maintained, not only because of the principle of *stare decisis,* "but also from the insight attributable to the Members of the Court at that time,"[276] an observation that ignored the widespread condemnation of the reasoning of the justices in these cases by more recent commentators. "If the allegations here are true, no civilized system of justice could fail to provide her a remedy for the conduct of respondent Morrison," Rehnquist concluded. "But

---

[269]Id.

[270]Lyle Denniston, Justices Wary of Congress' Reach, Raleigh News and Observer, Jan. 12, 2000, at A4.

[271]*Morrison,* 120 S. Ct. at 1748–54 (citing United States v. Lopez, 514 U.S. 549 (1995)) & 1756–57 (citing United States v. Harris, 106 U.S. 629 (1883); Civil Rights Cases, 109 U.S. 3 (1883)).

[272]Id. at 1751.

[273]Id. at 1752.

[274]Id.

[275]Id. at 1752–53.

[276]Id. at 1756.

under our federal system that remedy must be provided by the Commonwealth of Virginia, and not by the United States."[277] Even this rejection of the claim of Christy Brzonkala, who had already been turned down by the legal system of the Commonwealth of Virginia, did not go far enough for Justice Thomas. In a concurrence, Thomas objected to the Court's giving any credibility to the "substantial effects" doctrine which he said was "inconsistent with the original understanding" and only encouraged Congress to "appropriat[e] state police powers under the guise of regulating commerce."[278]

In a fierce dissent, joined by Justices Breyer, Ginsburg, and Stevens, Justice Souter insisted, "[v]iolence against women may be found to affect interstate commerce and affect it substantially."[279] Congress, he noted, had heard evidence that violence was "'the leading cause of injuries to women ages 15 to 44'" and that battering was "the single largest cause of injury to women in the United States."[280] Hence, a House conference report had with good reason concluded, "[c]rimes of violence motivated by gender have a substantial adverse effect on interstate commerce, by deterring potential victims from traveling interstate, from engaging in employment in interstate business, and from transacting . . . business . . . in interstate commerce."[281]

Souter scoffed at the majority's claim that its ruling rested on precedent. VAWA, he said, "would have passed muster at any time between *Wickard* in 1942 and *Lopez* in 1995."[282] The Court's rejection of "an aggregate effects test,"[283] and of John Marshall's view that the commerce power was plenary in favor of a categorical approach distinguishing between commercial and noncommercial, "comes with the pedigree of near-tragedy," he asserted.[284] "Since adherence to these formalistically contrived confines of commerce power in large measure provoked the judicial crisis of 1937, one might reasonably have doubted that Members of this Court would ever again return to the days before *NLRB v. Jones & Laughlin* . . . brought the earlier and nearly disastrous experiment to an end," he wrote.[285] "And yet today's decision can only be seen as a step toward recapturing the prior mistakes."[286] He accused the majority of restoring to the aura of the Tenth Amendment,[287] of "recycling" a theory of state sov-

---

[277]Id. at 1759.
[278]Id. (Thomas concurring).
[279]Id. at 1764 (Souter dissenting).
[280]Id. at 1761 (quoting S. Rep. 103–138, at 38 & 37 (1993)).
[281]Id. at 1763 (quoting H.R. Conf. Rep. 103–711, at 385 (1994)).
[282]Id. at 1764.
[283]Id. at 1766.
[284]Id. at 1767.
[285]Id. at 1767.
[286]Id.
[287]Id. at 1770 n.18.

ereignty repudiated in *Darby*,[288] and of bestowing on Antonio Morrison the same kind of dubious victory that James Carter had won in *Carter* in 1936.[289] "Why is the majority tempted to reject the lesson so painfully learned in 1937?" he asked.[290] "The federalism of some earlier time" was "no more adequate" to deal with today's problems "than the theory of laissez-faire was able to govern the national economy 70 years ago."[291]

Predictably, conservatives greeted *Morrison* with loud huzzahs. Some publicists had early signaled their belief that any such ruling would be commonsensical. James Kilpatrick, who stated flatly that Christy Brzonkala had been raped, ended a column with two gruff sentences: "Congress has power to regulate commerce. It has no power to regulate rape."[292] After the decision was handed down, he cheered "Five Brave Votes for Checking Congress,"[293] while a delighted George Will wrote that *Morrison* "should inhibit Congress from passing 'hate crimes' legislation," which he dismissed as "moral pork."[294] To one of Morrison's attorneys, the ruling was "a welcome reminder that 'democratic majorities are limited by the text of the Constitution.'"[295] Charles Fried, though lamenting that the continuing 5–4 divide on the Court made for "dismal reading" and had "a baleful effect on the development of the law," chewed out the dissenters for behaving "as if they were the students of Felix Frankfurter defending the New Deal against the devastation of the pre-1937 court and its 'nine old men.'"[296]

The dissenters, though, turned out to have a considerably more numerous and more vocal following. The former chairman of the Senate Judiciary Committee, Joseph Biden of Delaware, accused the *Morrison* majority of "judicial

---

[288]Id. at 1768.

[289]Id. at 1773.

[290]Id. at 1767.

[291]Id. at 1774. Justice Breyer issued a separate dissent, amplifying Souter's reasoning on the commerce power, id. at 1774–78 (Breyer dissenting), a statement that won the support of Ginsburg and Souter, and also asserting the relevance of Section Five of the Fourteenth Amendment, a contention that gained the approval only of Justice Stevens. Id. at 1778–80 (Breyer dissenting).

[292]James Kilpatrick, Rape Is a Problem, But Not Congress' Problem, Raleigh News and Observer, Aug. 30, 1999, at A13.

[293]James Kilpatrick, Five Brave Votes for Checking Congress, Raleigh News and Observer, May 22, 2000, at A11.

[294]George Will, A Revival of Federalism?, Newsweek, May 29, 2000, at 78 ("Revival").

[295]Michael Rosman, quoted in Linda Greenhouse, The Court on Federalism: Women Lose Right to Sue Attackers in Federal Court, N.Y. Times, May 16, 2000, at A14 ("Women Lose Right").

[296]Charles Fried, Opponents of Federalism Are Mired in a Time Warp, Wall St. J., May 16, 2000, at A29.

activism," ironically the same charge that conservatives had leveled at the Warren Court.[297] "The court has imposed by fiat limitations on the exercise of federal power," he said. "What is at issue here is a question of power, whether power will be exercised by an insulated judiciary or by the elected representatives of the people."[298] Biden added, "[t]he damage done to the act is not as bad as the damage done to American jurisprudence."[299] In like manner, Senator Charles E. Schumer of New York protested, "[j]ust at a time when the economic and social conditions of the world demand that we be treated as one country and not as 50 states, the Supreme Court seems poised to undo decades and decades of a consensus that the federal government has an active role to play."[300]

Biden and Schumer had both been sponsors of VAWA, but the loud outcry against *Morrison* was not limited to those who had a special stake in the outcome. The *New York Times* spoke of "Violence Against the Constitution,"[301] and Anthony Lewis criticized "a headstrong majority pressing a dubious historic vision to a serious clash with Congress, and with reality."[302] In an editorial entitled "Door Closed to Women," one of the leading newspapers in the South, saddened that Christy Brzonkala's "brave fight" had been "in vain," charged that the justices were "narrowly focused." The United States Surgeon General, it pointed out, had reported that "half of all rape victims lose their jobs or are forced to quit, 100,000 a year."[303]

In an op ed piece in the *New York Times,* a Yale Law School professor targeted Rehnquist's employment of questionable nineteenth-century precedents. "Without a hint of embarrassment," wrote Jack M. Balkin, "Justice Rehnquist argued that the decision in the Civil Rights Cases was hallowed by time and could not be disturbed." Rehnquist's reasoning, he maintained, "means states can now violate many civil rights with impunity." He added:

> The Supreme Court has taken a wrong turn in these cases. It's striking down the work of a democratically elected legislature. But it's not too late to end this constitutional Catch-22.

> We should get rid of the racist precedents of the 1880's. We should recognize what the framers of the 14th Amendment intended: Congress has an independ-

---

[297]David Stout, Court Limits Rape Cases, Raleigh News and Observer, May 16, 2000, at A1.

[298]E. J. Dionne, The New Conservative Judicial Activism, Boston Globe, July 16, 2000 ("New Conservative").

[299]Women Lose Right, at A16 (cited in note 295).

[300]Id.

[301]Editorial, Violence Against Women, May 16, 2000, at A30.

[302]Anthony Lewis, Abroad at Home: Court and Congress, N.Y. Times, May 20, 2000, at A31.

[303]Door Closed to Women, Raleigh News and Observer, May 26, 2000, at A24.

ent power and obligation to promote and protect equal citizenship and equal rights.[304]

Much of the alarm aroused by Rehnquist's opinion derived from the perception that *Morrison* seemed a curious case to elicit a defense of federalism and that there was more to the decision than met the eye. The Violence Against Women Act, wrote Linda Greenhouse, "appeared an unlikely battleground for the Supreme Court's continuing federalism wars," since the statute "neither told the states to do anything nor prohibited them from taking any action." Moreover, it "did not expose the states themselves to any legal liability." In short, "this was no titanic struggle among co-equal sovereigns." The significance of *Morrison,* she said, lay less in anything Rehnquist said specifically than "in the background music of a decision that rejected a large volume of evidence that the law's sponsors had compiled to show why a national approach to violence against women was needed." Laurence Tribe, she added, believed that the majority had operated on the premise of "its own metatest": "We don't care what the findings are, if accepting them endangers our vision of state sovereignty, our view of the architecture of our system."[305]

The ruling raised doubts that the agenda of the Court was as straightforward as it purported to be. The justices in the majority presented themselves as stalwart defenders of the rights of the states against the predatory leviathan in Washington, but that claim rang hollow since 36 states had signed an *amicus* brief on behalf of federal authority in the Violence Against Women Act, a reality that prompted Justice Souter to note caustically that "[i]t is, then, not the least irony of these cases that the States will be forced to enjoy the new federalism whether they want it or not."[306] David Strauss of the University of Chicago Law School said of the justices in the *Morrison* majority, "I don't think they care about the states; they want to get rid of regulation."[307] That insight brought to mind a point raised some years earlier in the aftermath of *Lopez* by Mark Tushnet: "The present constitutional moment, if it is one, may involve the evaporation rather than devolution of public power. That is, power may not be flowing from Congress to state and local governments, but rather going into thin air—or, more precisely, to private institutions."[308]

Invalidating the Violence Against Women Act on Tenth Amendment grounds intensified the alarm Scalia had triggered in *Printz* on the very last day

---

[304]Jack M. Balkin, The Court Defers to a Racist Era, N.Y. Times, May 17, 2000, at A27.

[305]Linda Greenhouse, Battle on Federalism: In an Era of States' Rights Debates, High Court's Ruling Limits Congress, N.Y. Times, May 17, 2000, at A16.

[306]*Morrison,* 120 S. Ct. at 1773 (Souter dissenting).

[307]New Conservative (cited in note 300).

[308]Living, at 869 (cited in note 1).

of an earlier Term. By using "dramatic" rhetoric about "a relatively minor and technical instance of federal overreaching," Scalia's eleventh-hour opinion, one commentary observed:

> reads as if he wants to generate enough momentum to turn back the clock to older theories of not just "dual sovereignty" but to even more controversial and long-refuted theories of "dual federalism." . . . For several years, the Rehnquist core majority had been building up to this very decision. Now that it has stunningly pronounced it on such a slim case, its commitment to what it's calling the system of "dual sovereignty" will likely prove to be the future flashpoint for issues of judicial federalism. . . .[309]

Furthermore, the contemptuous language of the Court's opinions conveys the sense that the members of the majority conceive of themselves as the triumphant perpetrators of a conservative coup, and are impatient to expand their domain. In his characteristically acerbic manner, Justice Scalia said of one dissent, "Justice Breyer reiterates (but only in outline form, thankfully) the now fashionable revisionist accounts of the Eleventh Amendment set forth in other opinions in a degree of repetitive detail that has despoiled our Northern woods."[310] The attitude of the Court's admirers has also perceptibly hardened. In February 2000, George Will, a columnist once esteemed for his judiciousness, called Clarence Thomas one of President George Bush's "best legacies" and David Souter one of his "worst."[311]

Federal judges may be expected to view *Morrison* as a green light not just to follow the Supreme Court in the *Lopez* direction but to move in advance of it in dismantling the Constitutional Revolution of 1937. *Lopez* emboldened federal courts to breathe new life into clauses such as "privileges or immunities" and doctrines such as improper delegation that had been moribund since the age of Roosevelt. Even more controversial was the language of the United States Court of Appeals for the Fourth Circuit in announcing, "the question before this Court is not whether the DPPA regulates commerce, but whether it is consistent with the system of dual sovereignty established by the Constitution."[312] The repercussions of such thinking may be very far-reaching. "Well, now," wrote George Will, "if the Commerce Clause can justify congressional regulation only of a

---

[309]Sanford F. Schram & Carol S. Weissert, The State of American Federalism, 1996–1997, 27 Publius: The Journal of Federalism 28 (Spring 1997).

[310]College Savings Bank v. Florida Prepaid Postsecondary Education Expense Bd., 527 U.S. 666, 687 (1999). William F. Buckley, Jr., The Court Reenfranchises the States, Nat'l Rev., Aug. 9, 1999, at 58. Buckley commented, "[i]t's wonderful to be alive when such sentences are written." Id.

[311]George Will, Money in Politics: Aiding Speech, Raleigh News and Observer, Feb. 6, 2000, at A27.

[312]Condon v. Reno, 155 F.3d 453, 458 (4th Cir. 1998).

clearly economic activity, what then of some environmental laws, such as the Endangered Species Act?" He noted that David Savage of the *Los Angeles Times* had pointed out, "[s]ome critics have suggested congress has no power to protect a threatened animal or plant that lives in only one state and has no effect on interstate commerce."[313]

Numbers of observers have seen the line of cases starting with *Lopez* as a momentous chapter in our constitutional history. "The Supreme Court," declared Paul Gewirtz of Yale Law School, "is redesigning the basic institutional architecture of our public lives," a development "with enormous consequences,"[314] and a writer for the Knight Ridder chain observed:

> In the unceasing constitutional conflict between the U.S. government and the 50 states, the news from the nation's courthouses is that the states are on the offensive and gaining ground.
>
> The trend seems clear enough already to characterize the 1990s at the Supreme Court as the decade of a resurgence of state authority and a consequent corralling of national power.
>
> In a series of decisions . . . five conservative justices—all appointees of Republican presidents—have signaled a sharp retreat from the high court's longtime willingness to endorse the expansive power of Congress to regulate a vast array of activities.

That retreat appears far from over.[315]

Commentators differed sharply, though, on how to evaluate this trend. In 1999, James Kilpatrick expressed pleasure that "the 10th Amendment, crisply defining the whole concept of federalism, is enjoying new respect."[316] But that same year Anthony Lewis wrote:

> The Supreme Court term just ended showed us a phenomenon that this country has not seen for more than 60 years: a band of radical judicial activists determined to impose on the Constitution their notion of a proper system of government. . . . The five Justices in the majority changed the structure of Ameri-

---

[313]Revival, at 78 (cited in note 294).

[314]Linda Greenhouse, Benchmarks of Justice, N.Y. Times, July 1, 1997, at A1.

[315]Court Decisions (cited in note 230).

[316]James Kilpatrick, Hamilton, Madison Spar Again in Student's Case, Raleigh News and Observer, December 6, 1999, at A15.

can government. And they did so without a word of support in the text of the Constitution.[317]

After *Morrison* was decided in 2000, E. J. Dionne noted, "[t]he liberal fear is that the Supreme Court is marching back to its pre-New Deal days."[318]

Both camps did agree that these rulings represented a triumph for William Rehnquist, who not many years before had been a member of a forlorn minority. David Garrow has written of "how successfully Rehnquist has extended his own staunchly conservative, lifelong beliefs into a judicial agenda that has significantly remade major portions of American law,"[319] and Douglas Kmiec concluded that "the revival of federalism has become the clearest legacy of the Rehnquist Court."[320] Taking full advantage of his position as chief justice of the United States, Rehnquist, in his year-end report on the judiciary in 1998, struck a blow for federalism by chiding Congress for transforming local offenses into federal crimes, thereby overburdening the courts. But it was his activity in massing his slim majority in case after case that made the biggest impact. In the fall of 1999, David O'Brien, scrutinizing the rash of 5–4 decisions, wrote, "[n]ot since before the 1937 constitutional crisis over the court's invalidation of progressive New Deal legislation has a bare majority been so bent on reining in Congress."[321]

There were, however, reasons to ask whether both the jubilation and the resentment were not excessive, or at least premature. Each of the decisions prior to *Morrison* dealt not with society as a whole, but only with the "states as states"— as officials, litigants, or employers. Hence, they were progeny not of *Lopez* but of *National League of Cities* and its descendants. Not one of these cases is remotely of the significance of the 1930s rulings to which they are so freely likened, for they dealt with legislation that bore no resemblance to the enactments of the New Deal, which encompassed vast areas of industry and agriculture. Even Justice Stevens, dissenting in *Seminole Tribe,* characterized the Indian Gaming Regulatory Act as a "rather curious statutory scheme."[322] *Morrison* was clearly of greater significance than the earlier rulings, but not every commentator thought it palpably egregious or momentous. Anthony Lewis acknowledged that *Morrison* "was a close case . . . indeed at the edge of congressional power," and Gerald Gunther of Stanford Law School concluded that, though the justices

---

[317]Anthony Lewis, Abroad at Home: The Supreme Power, N.Y. Times, June 29, 1999, at A19.

[318]New Conservative (cited in note 298).

[319]David I. Garrow, The Rehnquist Reins, N.Y. Times Mag., Oct. 6, 1996, at 65.

[320]Rediscovers, at 60 (cited in note 206).

[321]David M. O'Brien, Supreme Court Can No Longer Duck the Big Issues, L.A. Times, Oct. 3, 1999, at M1.

[322]Seminole Tribe of Florida v. Florida, 517 U.S. 44, 77 (1996) (Stevens dissenting).

should have paid more heed to the legislative record, the decision "was not a catastrophe."[323]

At times, too, the ideological gulf on the Court could be bridged. That feat had been accomplished in *Reno v. Condon* when the Rehnquist bloc had validated an act of Congress restricting state governments. Only one week after *Morrison,* unanimity was achieved again when all nine justices rejected an expansive reading of the commerce power. In *Jones v. United States,*[324] they set aside the long jail sentence of one Dewey Jones, convicted of violating a provision of the Organized Crime Control Act of 1970 for throwing a Molotov cocktail into his cousin's home and setting it afire. The law stipulated that perpetrators could be punished only if their criminal conduct was directed at "real or personal property used in interstate or foreign commerce."[325] It was "surely not the common perception," Justice Ruth Bader Ginsburg said, "that a private, owner-occupied residence is 'used' in the various activities the government alleged connected it with commerce."[326] To regard an assault on a home employed only for "everyday living" as affecting interstate commerce, she observed, would "make virtually every arson in the country a federal offense," though "arson is a paradigmatic common-law state crime."[327] The case required only a simple exercise in statutory construction and the Tenth Amendment was not at issue, but the ruling revealed that the liberal quartet, too, thought there were limits to the commerce power. Ginsburg even cited *Lopez* as a precedent.[328]

Nonetheless, critics of the Court have good cause to be perturbed by the direction it has taken much of the time since *Lopez*. Though the Rehnquist Court is still far from matching the performance of the Four Horsemen and Owen Roberts, it has been behaving in some ways reminiscent of that era. There are echoes of McReynolds and his brethren in the ready willingness of the Court to jettison acts of Congress or restrict their reach on the basis of doctrines imported by the justices and untethered to any constitutional text. Rehnquist continues to treat with respect precedents such as *Heart of Atlanta Motel,* but he does so in the context of enfeebling them. Moreover, in *Morrison* he went out of his way to

---

[323] Anthony Lewis, The Justices Second-Guess Democracy, Raleigh News and Observer, May 27, 2000, at A24.

[324] 120 S. Ct. 1904 (2000).

[325] Id. at 1909 (quoting 18 U.S.C. § 844(1) (1994)).

[326] Id. at 1910.

[327] Id. at 1912.

[328] Id. at 1911–12. Justice Thomas, in a one-sentence concurrence joined by Justice Scalia, made clear that he was keeping open the question of whether the statute was valid when applied to buildings used for commercial activities. Id. at 1913 (Thomas concurring). Stevens, joined by Thomas, filed a separate concurrence stressing the need to read statutes narrowly where they posed the risk of "effectively displac[ing] a policy choice made by the State." Id. at 1912 (Stevens concurring).

cite with approval a concurrence in *Schechter*.[329] As Mark R. Killenbeck has written, "[t]here is . . . every reason to believe that in their single-minded quest to protect the 'residuary and inviolable sovereignty' of the states, these Justices contemplate substantial revision, perhaps even wholesale reversal, of many of the assumptions that have guided American constitutional doctrine and public policy this century."[330]

In the new millennium, the Court lost no time in arousing further controversy. Eleven days before George W. Bush was inaugurated, it curbed federal power once again. Weeks earlier, the conservative bloc had drawn vitriolic abuse for setting aside a decision by the Florida Supreme Court and halting a manual recount of ballots in the disputed presidential election.[331] That intervention had ended all possibility that the Democrat Al Gore, who had received several hundred thousand more popular votes nationally than his Republican opponent, Governor Bush, would gain the required margin in the Electoral College. Since it was hard to square the Court's action with the solicitude for the state judiciary that the Rehnquist bloc professed, boisterous critics accused its members of a blatantly political deed to ensure the victory of the candidate of their party and the champion of their ideology. So raucous were the objections that some commentators thought that the bloc of five would be more circumspect in the future. But on January 9, 2001, the Court, in *Solid Waste Agency of Northern Cook County v. United States Army Corps of Engineers*,[332] resumed the march that had begun with *Lopez*.

The case had originated in the effort of a consortium of Chicago suburbs to dump waste in an abandoned sand and gravel pit that contained ponds frequented by 121 species of birds, notably great blue herons. The Army Corps of Engineers, asserting its authority under the Clean Water Act of 1972 and the Migratory Bird Rule,[333] denied a permit. When the consortium brought suit, it won a summary judgment from a United States district court, but the Court of Appeals for the Seventh Circuit ruled both that the Clean Water Act could be validated under the commerce power and that the Corps was justified by the cumulative impact doctrine in applying the law to this site.[334] In yet another 5–4

---

[329]*Morrison*, 120 S. Ct. at 1753 n.6 (quoting A. L. A. Schechter Poultry Corp. v. United States, 295 U.S. 495, 554 (1935) (Cardozo concurring).

[330]Mark R. Killenbeck, Pursuing the Great Experiment: Reserved Powers in a Post-Ratification, Compound Republic, 1999 Sup. Ct. Rev. 81, 82.

[331]See Bush v. Gore, 121 S. Ct. 525 (2000).

[332]121 S. Ct. 675 (2001).

[333]Federal Water Pollution Control Act Amendments of 1972, Pub. L. 92–500, 86 Stat. 816 (1972). The Migratory Bird Rule was issued by the Corps in 1986. See 51 Fed. Reg. 41,217 (1986).

[334] Solid Waste Agency of Northern Cook County v. United States Army Corps of Engineers, 191 F. 3d. 845, 850 (7th Cir. 1999). The district court opinion may be found at 998 F. Supp. 946 (N.D. Ill. 1998).

decision, with Chief Justice Rehnquist speaking for the majority, the Supreme Court reversed. Without reaching the constitutional question, it found that the Migratory Bird Rule resulted in "federal encroachment upon a traditional state power."[335]

Though the majority chose to view the case as a simple matter of statutory construction, it skated unnervingly close to a constitutional judgment. Rehnquist's opinion spoke of "the outer limits of Congress' power," adding: "Twice in the past six years we have reaffirmed the proposition that the grant of authority to Congress under the Commerce Clause, though broad, is not unlimited."[336] In support of that assertion, he cited not only *Lopez*, but also *Morrison*, 5–4 rulings that commanded considerably less than universal regard.

Justice Stevens began his dissent with the dramatic sentence: "In 1969, the Cuyahoga River in Cleveland, Ohio, coated with a slick of industrial waste, caught fire."[337] In spotlighting what had motivated Congress to enact clean waters legislation three years later, Stevens, in an opinion joined by Justices Breyer, Ginsburg, and Souter, declared: "Our Nation's waters no longer burn. Today, however, the Court takes an unfortunate step that needlessly weakens our principal safeguard against toxic water."[338] Rehnquist and his brethren in the majority, Stevens maintained, had willfully misconstrued the law by concentrating on whether the ponds were navigable and hence within the scope of the commerce power. "During the middle of the 20th century," he pointed out, "the goals of federal water regulation began to shift away from an exclusive focus on protecting navigability and toward a concern for preventing environmental degradation."[339] But, he observed, "the goals of the 1972 statute have nothing to do with *navigation* at all."[340] With the Rehnquist bloc in his sights, Stevens fired away. By drawing an "odd jurisdictional line" in a "miserly construction of the statute" that was "unfaithful" to two recent precedents, the majority, Stevens charged, had done "violence to the scheme Congress chose to put in place."[341]

The Rehnquist Court, and more particularly Justices Scalia and Thomas, may well be impelled farther along the path that began with *Lopez* with the Republicans having regained the White House in 2001. The retirements of William Brennan in 1990 and Thurgood Marshall in 1991 shifted the balance on the Court with regard to federalism, and a couple more Clarence Thomases or Antonin Scalias could have a disproportionate influence in the new century. August 2000, six years after Stephen Breyer took the oath of office, marked the longest

---

[335] *Solid Waste Agency*, 121 S. Ct. at 683.
[336] Id.
[337] Id. at 684 (Stevens dissenting).
[338] Id.
[339] Id. at 686.
[340] Id. at 688.
[341] Id. at 688 & 693.

period without an appointment to the High Court since 1870, and, given the age and ailments of the present bench, there is expectation of more than one vacancy in the next four years.[342] "Any president who serves two terms could appoint approximately half the federal judiciary," George Will has remarked. "So the next president probably will have the power to accelerate, or halt, what the court has begun—a jurisprudential counterrevolution in defense of federalism."[343]

During the 2000 campaign, both liberals and conservatives highlighted speculation about the future composition of the Supreme Court. People for the American Way, which issued a report, *Courting Disaster: How a Scalia-Thomas Supreme Court Would Endanger Our Rights and Freedoms,* summoned voters to the polls with the dire warning: "The United States Supreme Court is just one or two new justices away from curtailing or abolishing fundamental rights that millions of Americans take for granted."[344] Though George W. Bush is said to have shown moderation in his judicial appointments as governor of Texas, he created alarm in liberal and centrist circles by saying that his favorite justices were Scalia and Thomas.[345] "What bothers me about the prospect of a President George W. Bush," wrote the columnist William Raspberry, "is the legacy of his father, also a decent and compassionate conservative, whose enduring bequest to America is: Clarence Thomas."[346] The Republican right, on the other hand, announced its determination to avoid the errors of GOP chief executives in the past who had carelessly named men who had not proven to be doctrinally sound. When the chairman of the Senate Judiciary Committee, Orrin Hatch, campaigned for the Republican presidential nomination, he announced: "No David Souters, I could guarantee that."[347]

Even if new appointments do bolster Scalia and Thomas, however, the tribunes of the Tenth Amendment will continue to bear the burden of two centuries of repellent associations, an unsavory legacy to which, its detractors say, the Rehnquist Court has contributed. Some of the Court's critics linked *Lopez* to the Oklahoma City bombing one week earlier, on the premise that "right-wing zealots (Timothy McVeigh, Chief Justice William Rehnquist) struck a mad blow at a federal government they perceive to be bloated, despotic and out of control."[348]

---

[342]Edward Walsh, In Campaign, High Court Is High on the Agenda; Aging Justices and Close Rulings Energize Partisans on Both Sides, Wash. Post, July 9, 2000, at A8 ("High Court").

[343]Revival (cited in note 296).

[344]High Court (cited in note 342).

[345]Jonathan Alter, The Real Stakes in November, Newsweek, July 10, 2000, at 26.

[346]William Raspberry, The Supreme Question for Bush, Boston Globe, July 16, 2000. President Bush, it should be noted, also appointed Justice Souter.

[347]High Court (cited in note 342).

[348]Fed Up, at 13 (cited in note 186). Rosen was paraphrasing a contention with which he strongly disagreed.

After the Brady Act was invalidated, Senator Dan Coats of Indiana asserted, "[t]he Supreme Court is actively disarming the Congress in the most important conflicts of our time."[349] The ruling in *Kimel,* observed the AARP, was disturbing to older persons because it "sends a message to the nation that ageism is not as reprehensible as other forms of discrimination," while the head of the American Federation of State, County and Municipal Employees commented, "[t]he court . . . has said to these Americans, you have no protections, no recourse under federal law."[350]

Only the most unreasonable faultfinder can believe that in handing down federalism rulings the justices were expressing support for hoodlums, arsonists, and sexual predators, but, once again, the Tenth Amendment (and its sometime auxiliary, the Eleventh Amendment) have surfaced on the unpopular side of moral questions. In the five years since *Lopez,* the federal judiciary has gutted the Brady Law, named after the White House press secretary wounded in the attempt to assassinate President Reagan; has rejected the pleas of librarians and professors against age discrimination; has sanctioned the refusal of a state to pay standard rates of overtime to its employees; and has spurned the pleas of groups such as the National Network to End Domestic Violence on behalf of battered women. When the Fourth Circuit Court of Appeals ruled against Christy Brzonkala, she responded, "I felt like I had been raped again."[351]

## Conclusion

However the future prospects and past record of the Court are assessed, one thing is clear: The Tenth Amendment is no longer a truism. If the Rehnquist bloc has achieved nothing else, it has accomplished that. Scholars, who for decades had ignored the amendment, are now carefully analyzing its origins and are treating it with renewed seriousness. Akhil Reed Amar, for one, has written that "the Tenth Amendment beautifully sums up many of the themes of prior amendments—and it is wholly unsurprising that, alone among the successful amendments, the Tenth was the only one proposed by every one of the state ratifying conventions that proposed amendments."[352] What good news it would be if scholars, and, even more, judges, examined just as closely the subsequent his-

---

[349]Ted Gest, Taking Congress Down Three Pegs: Death, Schools, Clinton in Court, U.S. News & World Report, July 7, 1997, at 33.

[350]Trish Nicholson, Ruling Stirs Criticism: State Employees Lose Ground in Age Bias Cases, 41 AARP Bulletin, Mar. 2000, at 16.

[351]David G. Savage, New Conservative Activism Sweeps the Federal Courts, L.A. Times, June 22, 1999, at A1.

[352]Akhil Reed Amar, The Bill of Rights: Creation and Reconstruction 123 (Yale University Press, 1998).

tory of the Tenth Amendment. In particular, the experience of the Court in the age of Roosevelt continues to be instructive.

I find myself, then, at the cusp of the millennium, so divided in my own mind about where we are that I am reduced to hearing voices. One voice inquires whether, if we could free ourselves from the memories of the 1930s, we might discuss dispassionately, and without anxiety, whether the Court has not, much of the time over the last half century and more, paid too little regard to its role as preserver of our system of federalism. That is the voice of Holgrave in Hawthorne's *The House of Seven Gables,* who asks: "Shall we never, never get rid of this Past? It lies upon the Present like a giant's dead body! In fact, the case is just as if a young giant were compelled to waste all his strength in carrying about the corpse of the old giant. . . . A dead man sits on all our judgment-seats."[353] But there is another voice recalling me to my school days when the Court handed down *Schechter* and *Butler* and *Carter,* and ruled that an exploited woman in a sweatshop was beyond the reach of aid from any government. That voice warns, "Watch out! It's about to happen again."

---

[353]Nathaniel Hawthorne, The Best Known Works of Nathaniel Hawthorne 228 (Blue Ribbon, 1941).

CHAPTER THREE

# American Federalism:
## Was There an Original Understanding?

**Jack N. Rakove**

The evidence continues to mount that the Tenth Amendment is undergoing a rebirth as a lodestar of American constitutionalism. Not so many years ago, the unenumerated rights of the Ninth Amendment seemed more likely to provide a renewable resource of constitutional energy than the reserved powers of the Tenth. And even if earlier reports of the death of federalism—like those of God and the Republican Party after Goldwater—proved greatly exaggerated, the idea that the close of the millennium would bring a radical devolution of power from the Beltway on the Potomac to the byways of state capitols would have seemed equally implausible. Yet since the mid-1990s, a host of signs have indicated that the Tenth Amendment is alive and well and poised to become a serious principle of our governance.

When the state governors arrived in Washington for their annual conference shortly after the Republicans took control of Congress in January 1995, following their long hegira, they carried the Tenth Amendment aloft as their banner. George Will was inspired to use the pulpit of his bullying columns to trumpet its cause, echoing Pete du Pont in asking "[w]hat happened to cause that amendment to become to the Constitution what the Chicago Cubs are to the World Series—of only occasional appearance and little consequence?"[1] In his notewor-

---

[1] George Will, Events and Arguments, Newsweek, Oct. 16, 1995, at 88.

thy dissenting opinion in *United States Term Limits, Inc. v. Thornton*,[2] Justice Clarence Thomas rallied three other members of the Court to his side while relying on the Tenth Amendment to defend the right of the states to impose term limits on their representatives in Congress. And implicitly or otherwise, the core concept of the Tenth Amendment—that the states are the holders of some essential residuary, irreducible elements of sovereignty—seems to underlie many of the Court's recent decisions, strongly indicating that its current conservative majority are willing, even eager, to look for ways to recognize the essential enduring place of the states in American federalism. Even in the Court's recent decisions enhancing the states' sovereign immunity, the aura of the Tenth Amendment looms at least as large as the black letter provisions of the Eleventh—as, for example, when Justice Anthony Kennedy, in his opinion in *Alden v. Maine*, declared that the Constitution "reserves to [the States] a substantial portion of the Nation's primary sovereignty, together with the dignity and essential attributes inhering in that status."[3]

None of these pieces of evidence demonstrates that the Tenth Amendment has lost the essentially truistic character that nationalistic skeptics have ascribed to it. But they do illustrate a crucial if often overlooked feature of the American Constitution. Few if any of its provisions—no matter how obscure or neglected or obsolete—can ever be completely discounted or dismissed as anachronistic. Like sparks of sacred light entombed in the husks of history and usage, they retain a residual capacity for reanimation. If the country learned nothing else from the late unpleasantness in Washington surrounding the impeachment of President Clinton, it is that any clause of the Constitution can be dramatically resurrected under the right (or wrong) circumstances. And that seems to be the case with the last member of the Bill of Rights, a provision adopted to assuage Anti-Federalist anxiety that the new Constitution would soon lead to a consolidated leviathan of a nation-state, rather than a confederated league of semisovereign states.

To make sense of the revival of the Tenth Amendment, it will be useful to consider it from at least two vantage points. The first parades under the familiar banner of "original meaning" or "original intention" or "original understanding."[4] As with other forgotten clauses that come back to life, we need to recon-

---

[2] 514 U.S. 779 (1995).

[3] 527 U.S. 706, 714 (1999). In the previous paragraph, Kennedy had already observed that "[a]ny doubt regarding the constitutional role of the States as sovereign entities is removed by the Tenth Amendment, which, like the other provisions of the Bill of Rights, was enacted to allay lingering concerns about the extent of the national power." Id. at 713–14.

[4] I prefer to use these terms in the specific sense in which they are defined in Jack N. Rakove, Original Meanings: Politics and Ideas in the Making of the Constitution 7–11 (Knopf, 1996) ("Original Meanings").

struct why this particular provision was incorporated in the text of the Constitution, and that of course entails reviewing the debates that led to its adoption, and not simply reciting the text as a mantra. Second, it might also be profitable to reflect on the circumstances that have made the surprising revival of the Tenth Amendment—so long tarred by its association with segregation—possible. It would be easy to account for this revival in terms emphasizing such striking political and intellectual developments as the Reagan revolution of the 1980s, the growing influence and respectability of conservative scholarship, the results of the 1994 election, and the coalescence of a precarious but sometimes effective conservative majority on the Supreme Court. But a deeper explanation of these developments can be found in the underlying centrifugal structure of American constitutionalism, a structure that still fulfills the ambiguous legacy of 1787.[5]

Whether we regard our federalism as a layer cake, a marble cake, or simply as a dish as American as apple pie, one interpretation of its origins has always proven a recipe for intellectual confusion and political disaster. Little if anything is to be gained by asking that hoary question that theorists of state sovereignty and national supremacy have both agitated: Which came first, the union or the states? True, recourse to this question of origins has offered an enticing avenue of escape whenever the task of disentangling the nuances of federalism becomes too tedious or threatening to pursue, but (from the vantage point of the historian) it suffers from two closely linked disabilities.

First, it is in some sense anachronistic in that it ascribes to the Founders of the American states and their confederation a clarity of purpose and understanding that they probably did not have; it attempts to impose a false precision that

---

[5]In this essay, I draw primarily on my two books: Original Meanings (cited in note 4), and The Beginnings of National Politics: An Interpretive History of the Continental Congress (Knopf, 1979) ("Beginnings"). I have offered some further speculations about the difficulty of applying any serious doctrine of sovereignty to the American case in a two-part essay, Making a Hash of Sovereignty, Parts I & II, 2 The Green Bag 35 (1998) and 3 The Green Bag 51 (1999). My thinking about the historical origins of American federalism has also been shaped by Peter S. Onuf, The Origins of the Federal Republic: Jurisdictional Controversies in the United States, 1775–1787 (University of Pennsylvania Press, 1983) ("Onuf, Origins"), and Samuel H. Beer, To Make a Nation: The Rediscovery of American Federalism (Belknap Press, 1993) ("To Make a Nation"). An important interpretive essay is Harry N. Scheiber, Federalism and the Constitution: The Original Understanding, in Harry N. Scheiber and Lawrence M. Friedman, eds., American Law and the Constitutional Order: Historical Perspectives (Harvard University Press, 1978). The best short account of the drafting of the Tenth Amendment is by the pioneering originalist Charles A. Lofgren, The Origins of the Tenth Amendment: History, Sovereignty, and the Problem of Constitutional Intention, in Charles A. Lofgren, "Government by Reflection and Choice": Constitutional Essays on Foreign Relations and Federalism 70–115 (Oxford University Press, 1986) ("Lofgren, Origins").

has far more to do with our concerns than with theirs. American federalism has its constitutional origins in a revolutionary situation in which neither state nor national leaders (and of course these two categories are themselves indistinct) had any strong reason or incentive to worry about the exact relation between the union and the states. Like many exercises in originalism, this one risks asking historical actors to take positions on issues that they either did not perceive or perceived rather differently from us.

Second, insofar as we can reconstruct the origins of American federalism, the most persuasive story we can tell is one that emphasizes the simultaneity with which concepts of both statehood and union emerged in the revolutionary crucible of the mid-1770s. No single vector charts how political authority and constitutional legitimacy flowed at the moment in historical time when the American colonies and their federal union acquired their new identities as both independent and united states. If the states were truly sovereign and independent when British rule collapsed, they should not have had to ask the Continental Congress for permission to write new constitutions of government to emerge from that version of the state of nature—or at least a dissolution of government—into which Americans felt they had been plunged after civil war erupted in 1775. By the same token, a Congress that had possessed an effective monopoly over the control of foreign relations from its inception in 1774 nevertheless felt it could not act to declare independence until it had fairly substantial evidence that the extralegal authorities in each of the colonies-becoming-states had signaled their approval. In a revolutionary situation, the acquisition of legitimacy for these new institutions was a reciprocal process in which power and authority flowed from one level of the emerging polity to another.

One has to make this point because the image of priority and its accompanying binary choice between either the union or the states as the primordial repositories of sovereignty still seems to resonate in our constitutional discourse. But historians have no obligation to render decisive, conclusive answers; we are perfectly happy (indeed sometimes happiest) when we can muddy the waters with ambiguities, and that is what the remainder of this essay shall do.

At the minimum, any attempt to fix an original meaning or range of meanings for the Tenth Amendment within a larger narrative about the origins of American federalism should cover at least four points. First, it should begin with an account of the pragmatic division of sovereignty between the Union and states that was embodied in the Articles of Confederation. Second, it should describe the range of expectations about the purposes of union that informed the debates at the Federal Convention of 1787. Third, it should attempt to understand what Anti-Federalists meant by the term consolidation, for it was their charge that the Constitution would produce a consolidated Union in which the states would wither away that shaped the underlying debate about federalism in 1787–1788. Fourth, and perhaps most important, this narrative should provide some explanation of the concerns that led James Madison and his colleagues in the First Federal Congress to add the "truism" of the Tenth Amendment to the articles we know as the Bill of Rights.

## The Articles of Confederation

A division of sovereignty has been evident in American federalism from its inception. This claim may seem surprising. It flies in the face of a common view that the first American union was a confederation of sovereign states in which the national government had little independent authority and fewer resources to execute its own decisions. And it seems to defy Article II of the Confederation, which affirms that "[e]ach state retains its sovereignty, freedom, and independence, and every power, jurisdiction, and right, which is not by this confederation expressly delegated to the United States, in Congress assembled."[6] Moreover, it may seem further surprising when we consider the immediate context in which the articles were formed, for after spending a decade disputing the authority of Parliament to legislate for the colonies "in all cases whatsoever," the revolutionaries could hardly have been expected to yield their rights of provincial self-government to a new leviathan, even one of their own choosing.

Nevertheless, when we track the adoption of the Articles of Confederation from drafting through ratification and brief implementation, a more complicated and indeed surprising picture emerges. Rather than agonize over the location of sovereignty in a federal system, the drafters of the articles moved instead to adopt a fairly pragmatic and largely noncontroversial division of powers between Congress and the states. There was broad agreement that Congress would exercise exclusive control over the great affairs of state, war, and foreign relations, while the states would retain exclusive control over the entire realm of "internal police"—the matters of governance that involved all the ordinary aspects of domestic or municipal legislation. In the one area of governance where these spheres directly overlapped—the control and disposition of western lands—successive drafts of the Confederation narrowed the authority the union could exercise, even at the expense of weakening its capacity to manage relations with Indian nations in the interior. Yet even here, through an extraconstitutional process of negotiation, Congress managed to acquire the authority to govern a substantial national domain north of the Ohio River.[7]

In allocating powers between these two levels of government, the framers of the Confederation did not assume that the states would serve as independent, sovereign arbiters of the wisdom and propriety of the recommendations, resolu-

---

[6]Act of Confederation of the United States of America (15 Nov. 1777), Art. II, in Merrill Jensen, ed., 1 The Documentary History of the Ratification of the Constitution, at 86, 86 (State Historical Society of Wisconsin, 1976) ("Documentary History").

[7]The best account of this process is Onuf, Origins (cited in note 5).

tions, and requisitions of Congress. The original American theory of federalism was that the states would freely and voluntarily comply with all the measures Congress legitimately asked them to implement, shaping its recommendations to the particular circumstances of their own communities. The states were, in this sense, the administrative auxiliaries of Congress. Naive and problematic as this conception of federalism soon proved, it reflected the revolutionary origins of the American union. That is, it was an entirely plausible manifestation of the enthusiasm that carried the colonists from resistance to revolution in the mid-1770s. James Madison grasped this point when he dissected the "vices" of the Confederation on the eve of the Federal Convention. The failure of the articles to give Congress any power of "coercion" over the states arose naturally, he observed, "from a mistaken confidence that the justice, the good faith, the honor, the sound policy, of the several legislative assemblies would render superfluous any appeal to the ordinary motives by which the laws secure the obedience of individuals, a confidence which does honor to the enthusiastic virtue of the compilers, as much as the inexperience of the crisis apologizes for their errors."[8]

None of this is meant to deny that the states did indeed retain substantial aspects of sovereignty, or even to imply that they were inferior to Congress on this score. The states alone could legislate directly on the American people, and they alone were vested with the power to tax. Yet they were manifestly not sovereign when it came to other equally important aspects of governance that contemporaries would have associated with the powers of a nation-state. Nor did the affirmation of the principle of sovereignty in the second Article of Confederation have any material impact on this pragmatic understanding of the separate spheres of national and state power. True, Thomas Burke, the original author of this article, fits the bill of a genuine apostle of states' rights; and James Wilson, his leading critic on this point, already appears as an advocate of national supremacy, implied powers, and perhaps even popular sovereignty. But most members of Congress probably fell comfortably between them.

## The Federal Convention

The recognition that any system of federal government relying on the voluntary compliance of the states was doomed to "imbecility" (to use a favorite term of the 1780s) was the crucial point of departure for the program of reform that James Madison carried to Philadelphia in 1787. Once this point was accepted, it followed that the anomalous union embodied in the unicameral Continental

---

[8]Vices of the political system of the U. States (April 1787), in Robert Rutland & William M. E. Rachal, eds., 9 The Papers of James Madison, at 351 (University of Chicago Press, 1962–91) ("Madison's Papers"). In this paragraph I summarize the broader argument I made in Beginnings, at 135–91 (cited in note 5).

Congress had to be reconstituted as a government in the normal sense of the term, with a bicameral legislature and independent executive and judiciary endowed with greater powers than their counterparts in the states. To create these new institutions, the Framers had to devote a hefty amount of their time and attention to questions relating to rules of election, appointment, and tenure. By contrast, efforts to determine what the national government would actually do, or to define the respective scopes of national and state power, often seem to have been considered in less detail, or at least debated with less eloquence.[9]

One of the great puzzles about the Federal Convention, in fact, is to determine whether some delegates were willing to create a national government with a plenary authority to legislate. That is certainly the impression that the relevant language of the Virginia Plan conveys. Its sixth article declared that "the National Legislature ought to be empowered to enjoy the Legislative Rights vested in Congress by the Confederation & moreover to legislate in all cases to which the separate States are incompetent, or in which the harmony of the United States may be interrupted by the exercise of individual Legislation."[10]

This open-ended language can be read, however, in two very different ways. Taken at face value, it certainly sounds like a formula for a national government whose legislative power would be limited only by its own discretion, one in which the reserved powers of the states would always be subject to national supersession. This impression is reinforced when we recall that a congressional negative on state legislation was a key element of the Madisonian program. But the open-ended language of Article VI can also be read as a sort of textual placeholder, to be used so long as the great issue of representation remained unresolved, but then to be modified or even replaced by a list of particular powers. Through June and well into July, Madison and his allies repeatedly resisted efforts to specify exactly what legislative powers their proposed new government would have, insisting that no conclusion could be reached on that point until the crucial problem of determining the basis for representation in both houses of Congress was resolved. In the meantime, both sides had a rhetorical incentive to speak as if the new government would indeed possess unlimited legislative power. Because the national government should be so powerful, large state delegates argued, justice demanded that equitable principles of apportionment be applied to both houses of Congress. If it would be so powerful, small state delegates replied, the security of their states required retention of the equal vote in one chamber at least.

Once the misnamed "great compromise" of July 16, 1787 gave the small states their equal vote, support for the idea of a plenary national legislative

---

[9]In this and the following paragraphs, I draw extensively on *Original Meanings*, at 60–62, 79–83, and more generally, 161–202 (cited in note 4).

[10]The Virginia Resolutions (29 May), in 1 *Documentary History*, at 243, 244 (cited in note 6).

power quicky evaporated. Madison's congressional veto over state laws was the first casualty of this decision (initially replaced by the weak version of the supremacy clause first proposed in the New Jersey Plan a month earlier).[11] Although the Convention briefly reaffirmed the language of the Virginia Plan, it seems likely that most delegates were already prepared to accept the significant change that the Committee of Detail soon proposed (in its report of August 6) when it replaced the discretionary language of the Virginia Plan with a list of enumerated legislative powers. None of the Framers protested that this seemingly substantive change had somehow thwarted or subverted their prior intentions—which in turn supports the hypothesis that the original article of the Virginia Plan was indeed a textual placeholder,[12] used only so long as the impasse over representation went unresolved.[13]

Moreover, when the report of the Committee of Detail came under debate after August 6 it is noteworthy that the Framers discussed the scope of congressional activity in modest terms that contrast sharply with the potential leviathan evoked in June and July. To "the Legislative Rights vested in Congress by the Confederation," the Committee proposed to add the power to lay and collect taxes, regulate interstate and foreign commerce, establish a uniform rule of naturalization, subdue rebellion within individual states, raise an army without relying on the states for the recruitment of soldiers, and "to call forth" the militia to enforce national laws and treaties and to "suppress insurrections, and repel invasions."[14] In practical terms, the Committee thus defined the "common interests" to embrace little more than manners of foreign relations and general commerce. Far from being surprised by the report, most Framers agreed that the scope of national lawmaking would remain modest. As ardent a nationalist as Gouverneur Morris even wondered if Congress would need to meet annually, as the Committee proposed. This was "improper," he asserted on August 7.[15] "The public business might not require it," Rufus King agreed. Earlier he had confessed that while he "doubted much the practicability of annihilating the states," he "thought that much of their power ought to be taken from them."[16] Now King observed that "[t]he most numerous objects of legislation belong to the states. Those of the Natl. Legislature were but few. The chief of them were commerce & revenue. When these should be once settled, alterations would be

---

[11]2 Max Farrand, ed., The Records of the Federal Convention of 1787, at 27–28 (rev. ed., Yale University Press, 1966) ("Farrand").

[12]Id.

[13]For a different view, see Joseph Lynch, Negotiating the Constitution: The Earliest Debates over Original Intent 8–30 (Cornell University Press, 1999).

[14]See generally 2 Farrand, at 182 (cited in note 11).

[15]Id. at 198.

[16]Id. & 1 id. at 324.

rarely necessary & easily made."[17]   Other delegates, such as George Mason and Roger Sherman thought this assessment too sanguine.   "The extent of the Country will supply business," Mason argued, and even if it did not, annual meetings were "an essential safeguard of liberty" still required because Congress would also possess "inquisitorial powers, which can not safely be kept in suspension."[18] But the common expectation was voiced by James Wilson, another ardent nationalist, when he noted that "War, Commerce, & Revenue were the great objects of the Genl. Government."[19]   Though additional powers were added to Article I in the closing weeks of deliberation, they did not alter the underlying conception of governance on which the Framers acted after mid-July.   By default, every other aspect of governance, including most of the matters that would affect Americans in the daily conduct of their affairs, would remain with the states.

The comments of nationalist-minded delegates like Wilson and King reflect a common-sense view rooted in the realities of eighteenth-century American life, when most of the business of government devolved less upon the state governments than upon county courts and town meetings.   The Framers were products of that world; much as they hoped that the reconstitution of the union would give a new stability to the American Republic, they could not escape the essentially parochial character of governance in this highly decentralized polity.   Nor could they easily think of the states as malleable jurisdictions subject to a radical erosion of their standing functions.   Too much history, in the form of distinct traditions of statutory law and common law alike, had already passed for the Framers to imagine 1787 as a moment of pure creation.   How could they do otherwise, when the internal police of the 13 states already included such disparate laws as those that protected the peculiar institution of slavery and the variety of religious establishments and disestablishments of this intensely Protestant society?

## The Federalist Persuasion

On balance, this interpretation supports a view of federalism emphasizing both the limited objects to which the national legislative power would be directed and the self-sufficiency that Congress would enjoy by virtue of its broad powers of taxation and the two additional clauses that Anti-Federalists soon identified as the principal engines of the "consolidation" they predicted: The Necessary and Proper and Supremacy Clauses.   Though some Framers occasionally implied that the national government might continue to act through the states in much

---

[17] 1 id. at 198.
[18] Id. at 199.
[19] Id. at 275.

the same fashion as had the Continental Congress, the dominant expectation was that national laws would operate directly on the American people without the intervention of the state legislatures.  But when one took a sober look at the respective responsibilities of national and state government, it was hard to escape the conclusion that national legislation would be no more than a thin template floating lightly above a broad base of state activity.

The Philadelphia merchant Tench Coxe accurately forecast this situation while explaining why the Constitution would not lead to the "annihilation" of the state governments.  Most objects of legislation would remain the exclusive or preponderant preserve of the states, Coxe observed: The regulation of religion; the law of descents and entail; altering and amending constitutions; chartering "corporations for literary, religious, commercial, or other purposes"; enforcing criminal law; and "all the innumerable disputes about property Lying within their respective territories between their own citizens, such as titles and boundaries of lands, debts by assumption, note, bond, or account, mercantile contracts." Nor was even this catalogue exhaustive:

> 14thly. The several states can create corporations civil and religious; prohibit or impose duties on the importation of slaves into their own ports; establish seminaries of learning; erect boroughs, cities and counties; promote and establish manufactures; open roads; clear rivers; cut canals; regulate descents and marriages; license taverns; alter the criminal law; constitute new courts and offices; establish ferries; erect public buildings; sell, lease, and appropriate the proceeds and rents of *their lands,* and of every other species of *state property;* establish poor houses, hospitals, and houses of employment; regulate the police; and many other things of the utmost importance to the happiness of their respective citizens.[20]

Coxe went on to note that the "lordship of the soil" which "remains *in full perfection* with every state" constituted "one of the most valuable and powerful appendages of sovereignty," and he further enumerated the various sources of revenue that the states would retain as "indisputable proofs of sovereignty."[21]

Yet to reduce the expectations of the Framers of the Constitution to a mere catalogue of powers that were either delegated to the union or reserved to the states obscures as much as it explains. Those Framers who were most concerned with the equilibrium of federalism were clearly thinking in political as well as constitutional terms.  That is, they understood that the future balance of power within the federal system would rest on something more than the formal allocation of authority between the two levels of governance.  It would also depend, over time, on their respective capacity to mobilize the political loyalty of their constituents.  Whether the establishment of an effective national government

---

[20]14 Documentary History, at 454–58 (cited in note 6).
[21]Id. at 508–11; 16 id. at 50–51.

would wean Americans from their provincial attachments was the great question that the legal ratification of the Constitution left unanswered and problematic.

The two Framers whom we regard as the principal architects of national government illustrate how difficult it was to imagine how national loyalties would be cultivated. Both James Madison and Alexander Hamilton left Philadelphia convinced that the proposed Constitution would not do nearly enough to check the centrifugal tendencies of American federalism. Both men assumed that the real political advantages would continue to lie with the states, and that the national government would be sorely pressed to defend itself against the continued rivalship and potential interference of the states. That (more than the celebration of the British constitution) was the great theme of Hamilton's famous speech at the Convention of June 18. So long as the states continued to exist as such, Hamilton warned, they would command all the resources needed to secure

> an habitual attachment of the people. The whole force of this tie is on the side of the State Govt. Its sovereignty is immediately before the eyes of the people: its protection is immediately enjoyed by them. From its hand distributive justice, and all those acts which familiarize & endear Govt. to a people, are dispensed to them.[22]

Only if the states were reduced to something like English shires would this advantage be broken. Hamilton continued to revolve this concern after the Convention adjourned. In a private memorandum written a few later, he observed that, at the minimum, a "good administration" under the likely presidency of Washington would be required to "conciliate the confidence and affection of the people and perhaps enable the government to acquire more consistency than the proposed constitution seems to promise for so extended a country. It may then triumph altogether over the state governments and reduce them to an entire subordination, dividing the large states into smaller districts." But should this not occur, Hamilton ventured, "it is probable that the contests about the boundaries of power between the particular governments and the general government and the momentum of the larger states in such contests will produce a dissolution of the union."[23]

For Hamilton, the solution to the debilities of federalism was a matter of policy and politics more than of formal adherence to constitutional design. As first secretary of the treasury, he pursued a set of policies designed to attach key interest groups to the national government, in the realistic expectation that this was the best way to counter the innate advantages of the states. It was the disagreement over these policies that first opened up the fissures between Hamilton

---

[22] 1 Farrand, at 284 (cited in note 11).
[23] 13 Documentary History, at 278 (cited in note 6).

and Madison that led to the creation of the first political party system of the 1790s. But in 1787, Madison believed, with Hamilton, that the national government would likely operate from a position of political and constitutional weakness. As Madison explained in his remarkable letter to Jefferson of October 24, 1787, a national government deprived of a negative over state laws and forced to rely on the flimsy authority of the judiciary would be ill poised either to defend its powers against the encroachments of the states or to prevent the states from enacting laws infringing the rights of minorities within their own boundaries.[24]

In *The Federalist,* however, Madison turned this private pessimism into a public rationale to demonstrate that the Anti-Federalist charge of consolidation was implausible on its face. Madison was willing to concede that "manifest and irresistible proofs of a better administration" might ultimately transfer popular loyalties and affection from the states to the union.[25] But on balance it seemed likely that "The State governments will have the advantage of the Federal government" in every political respect, regardless of the legal force of the supremacy clause or the reach of the necessary and proper clause. Not only would the people at large feel more deeply interested in the activities of the state governments—which would remain more intimately involved in the regulation of their ordinary affairs—but the rewards and benefits that they could bestow would exceed those emanating from a distant union. Nor was it even likely that congressmen would possess great "prepossessions" in favor of enhancing national authority at the expense of the states.[26] Madison found it difficult to imagine, moreover, that the plausible objects of national governance would extend very far. In comparison to his co-author of *The Federalist,* it seems evident that Madison was much less convinced of the imperatives of state-building than Hamilton; much less fearful that world events would seriously endanger the national security once the newly empowered national government negotiated a framework of commercial treaties with other Atlantic nations; and much more willing to concede that there were practical reasons for thinking that most domestic affairs would long remain subject to state regulation. "The operations of the Federal Government will be most extensive and important in times of war and danger," he wrote in Federalist 45; "those of the State Governments in times of peace and security. As the former periods will probably bear a small proportion to the latter, the State Governments will here enjoy another advantage over the Federal Government."[27] Over the short run of the next quarter century, the French Revolution and its aftermath made Hamilton the superior prophet; but it

---

[24]Letter from Madison to Jefferson (Oct. 24, 1787), in 10 Madison's Papers, at 209–14 (cited in note 8).

[25]Federalist 46 (Madison), in 15 Documentary History, at 488–89 (cited in note 6).

[26]Federalist 45 (Madison) and 46 (Madison), in 15 id. at 478 & 490–91.

[27]Id. at 479–80.

was Madison who better captured the reality of American governance for the better part of the next century.

In their different ways—each representing a different form of constitutional realism—both men were responding to the recognition that no constitution, however nationalist, could unilaterally reverse the inertial forces that favored the residual authority of the states. Yet the one Framer who perhaps best grasped the deeper possibilities of federalism was neither Hamilton nor Madison but rather James Wilson, the Scottish lawyer-immigrant whom Jennifer Nedelsky and Samuel Beer have described as the most democratic of the major architects of the Constitution.[28] True, Wilson's commitment to democracy as a constitutional principle does not sit well with the somewhat elitist tenor of his politics in the factious commonwealth of Pennsylvania. Yet Wilson understood that the idea of popular sovereignty was something more than a theoretical sleight-of-hand to get around the conventional wisdom that held that sovereignty could never be divided between two levels of government (because "*imperium in imperio* is a solecism in politics").

The fact that in 1787 the American states enjoyed the advantage in commanding the political loyalties of their citizenry was no guarantee that this would always be the case. After all, given the underlying structural weakness of the Confederation, what other choice or possibility had there been? But once an effective national government was created, Wilson understood, an entirely different set of attachments might form. Once it was realized that state and national governments were equally the vehicles of democratic politics, the extent of their respective spheres of authority and influence could be recognized as a mutable function of popular preferences. "A private citizen of a State is indifferent whether power be exercised by the Genl. or State Legislatures, provided it be exercised most for his happiness," Wilson told the Framers on June 20 and again the next day.[29] Wilson's immediate point was that the interests of state legislators in preserving their own authority could not be uncritically equated with those of their electors. But implicitly he was arguing a more powerful point: Through the mechanisms both of constitutionalism *and* of representation, a sovereign people would henceforth be free to shift its support to whichever level of government proved most capable of asserting its interests.

How Wilson came to this perception is not entirely clear: His extant papers cannot support the same biographical detail we expect of Hamilton, Madison, or Jefferson. Perhaps as an immigrant he lacked the intuitive provincial loyalties of the Virginians; perhaps his roots in the moral philosophy of the eighteenth-century Scottish Enlightenment made him more receptive to the con-

---

[28] Jennifer Nedelsky, Private Property and the Limits of American Constitutionalism: The Madisonian Framework and Its Legacy 96–140 (University of Chicago Press, 1990); To Make a Nation, at 341–77 (cited in note 5).

[29] 1 Farrand, at 344 & 359 (cited in note 11).

structed bonds of human sociability. In any case, in his speeches on representation and popular sovereignty, Wilson came closest to perceiving that the initial advantages the states would enjoy in their competition with the union need not last forever. If new attachments replaced old ones, a people who always retained "the fee simple" of government would be free to give a decisive advantage to the union, once it demonstrated its competence to pursue their happiness.

## The Anti-Federalist Brief

In one crucial respect, Wilson's efforts to present his views in simplified form also laid a foundation for much of the Anti-Federalist critique of the Constitution. Wilson began his widely reprinted public speech of October 6, 1787— delivered before a crowd assembled outside the Pennsylvania statehouse—by rebutting the claim that the Federal Convention had grievously erred by omitting a Bill of Rights from the Constitution. There was a fundamental difference, Wilson observed, between the state constitutions and the proposed national one:

> When the people established the powers of legislation under their separate governments, they invested their representatives with every right and authority which they did not in explicit terms reserve; and therefore upon every question, respecting the jurisdiction of the house of assembly, if the frame of government is silent, the jurisdiction is efficient and complete. But in delegating federal powers, another criterion was necessarily introduced, and the congressional authority is to be collected, not from tacit implication, but from the positive grant expressed in the instrument of union.[30]

In the states, Wilson concluded, "everything which is not reserved is given"; but in the national Constitution, "everything which is not given, is reserved." Wilson deployed this argument to explain why a Bill of Rights would be not only superfluous but dangerous. To reserve rights where powers had not in fact been granted would have the perverse effect of making the national government appear stronger than it was intended to be. If the new government had been given no power to regulate freedom of speech or rights of conscience, the incorporation of a declaration protecting these rights might be read to imply that some substantive power had actually been delegated.[31] But his position had a deeper implication still. For it stated in the clearest form possible the theory that the powers granted in the Constitution were finite and limited.

Wilson's speech was critical to the ensuing ratification debate for two reasons: First, because it stated the theory of delegated power and reserved rights in

---

[30]2 Documentary History, at 167–68 (cited in note 6).
[31]Id.

so succinct but also vulnerable a fashion; second, because Wilson was the only Framer to defy rhetorical convention and make a public speech presumably providing an authoritative interpretation of the Constitution. Characterized as a "recourse to the most flimsey sophistry,"[32] Wilson's remarks did nothing to allay the Anti-Federalist conviction that the Constitution was a formula for a consolidated national government. As they used this loaded term, consolidation had two distinct meanings. It could mean either that consolidation would occur immediately, simply because the union would possess an "absolute and uncontroulable power" over those "objects" placed under its control; or that consolidation would unfold gradually but ineluctably as the new government deployed its powers and monopolized the most productive sources of revenue to render the states impotent for all effective purposes of government. Used in the first sense, the Constitution amounted to consolidation merely because it ceased to be a pure confederation in which "the state governments stand between the union and individuals" and "the laws of the union operate only on states, as such, and federally."[33] Used in the second sense, consolidation marked the ultimate destination toward which the Constitution must verge. While conceding that "a partial consolidation" might be possible in theory, or even that the Constitution "appears to be partly federal," leading Anti-Federalists insisted that the Constitution was "calculated ultimately to make the states one consolidated government," and dismissed Federalist rebuttals on this head as disingenuous.[34] Seizing on another point of Wilson's speech, they argued that the various electoral functions of the states hardly dispelled the fear that the Constitution was "designedly framed, to reduce the state governments to mere corporations, and eventually to annihilate them." Far from giving the states a vital role in the federal system, these tasks would survive only as vestigial symbols of a hollow sovereignty. "Who is so dull as not to comprehend," wailed Centinel (with implicit homage to Machiavelli), "that the semblance and forms of an ancient establishment, may remain, after the reality is gone[?]"[35] What confidence or even interest would the people bestow on the state legislatures, Melancton Smith asked, should they be reduced to "meet once in a year to make laws for regulating the height of your fences and the repairing of your roads?"[36]

In one way or another, nearly all of the Anti-Federalist criticisms of the Constitution were designed to demonstrate that its adoption could only lead to

---

[32]Centinel, Philadelphia Freeman's Journal (Oct. 24, 1787), in 13 id. at 459.

[33]Federal Farmer, XVII (Jan. 23, 1788), in Herbert Storing, ed., 2 The Complete Anti-Federalist, 331–32 (University of Chicago Press, 1981) ("Storing").

[34]Federal Farmer I and II, in id. at 228–34.

[35]Centinel II, id. at 146. On the connection to Machiavelli, see Paul Rahe, Republics Ancient and Modern: Classical Republicanism and the American Revolution 527 & epigraph 521 (University of North Carolina Press, 1992).

[36]Speech of June 25, 1788, in 6 Storing, at 166 (cited in note 33).

the "annihilation" of the state governments and the consolidation of all real power in the aristocratic national government the Constitution would create. Without a Bill of Rights, the people would literally never know when the national government had overstepped its bounds in arrogating powers it did not rightly possess. Without a limitation on its power of taxation, the national government would monopolize all the productive sources of revenue, leaving the states to wither away from lack of financial resources. Without some restriction on the appellate jurisdiction of the federal courts, the new third branch of government would license Congress to stretch a "necessary and proper" clause as far as it wished, in effect teaching and even inviting the aristocratic legislators in both houses to perceive that their authority to legislate was uncircumscribed. Armed with the Supremacy Clause, the Necessary and Proper Clause, and the authority to raise a standing army sustained by unlimited sources of revenue, the new government could run roughshod over the residual powers of the state government whenever it wished. Even if the Constitution did not "go to a perfect and entire consolidation," the Anti-Federalist Brutus warned, "yet it approaches so near to it, that it must, if executed, certainly and infallibly terminate in it." For all intents and purposes, the powers of the national government were "absolute and perfect . . . with respect to every object to which it extends," and because those objects would "extend to every case that is of the least importance—there is nothing valuable to human nature, nothing dear to freemen, but what is within its power." Merely by wielding its "great engine of tyranny and oppression"—the power of taxation—"the government of a particular state might be overturned at a single stroke, and thereby be deprived of every means of its support."[37]

If Anti-Federalists could be polled, then, as to whether they thought that the original Constitution of 1787 adequately secured the reserved powers of the states, the logic of their position would have compelled them to answer in the negative. Their original understanding of the Constitution was that it was a formula for consolidation, perhaps immediately, certainly over time. Of course, as losers in the struggle over ratification, their views need not be factored into our own reconstruction of what the Constitution originally meant at the moment when it became the supreme law of the land in 1788, superior in legal force to all the existing state constitutions.[38] Not only had it had been adopted more recently, but it had also been ratified under procedures juridically superior to, or more properly constitutional than those employed when nearly all the state constitutions were promulgated (Massachusetts and New Hampshire being the ex-

---

[37]Brutus, in 13 Documentary History, at 411–21 (cited in note 6).

[38]Though many observers of the current Supreme Court have been tempted to wonder whether some of the justices might be inclined to accord the Anti-Federalist losers in this debate the same authority as the Federalist victors.

ceptions).[39] But, of course, it is equally obvious that the Anti-Federalist misapprehension is germane to the original meaning of the Tenth Amendment, because it was to allay their concerns, however ill-grounded, that James Madison and his colleagues in the First Congress proposed the formula that is now before us: "The powers not delegated to the United States by the Constitution, nor prohibited by it to the States, are reserved to the States respectively, or to the people."

## The Origins of the Tenth Amendment

From the Pennsylvania ratification convention on, proposals to add something very like this eventual text to the amendments that Anti-Federalists desired were heard frequently. Its repetition from convention to convention bears few marks of refinement or improvement, with the noteworthy exception of New York, the only state to suggest that undelegated powers remained in the possession of either the state governments or their people.[40] But if these early efforts to state a

---

[39]For further discussion, see Original Meanings, at 94–130 (cited in note 4).

[40]Here are the relevant variants:

In the amendments proposed by the Anti-Federalist minority to the Pennsylvania convention: "15. That the sovereignty, freedom, and independency of the several states shall be retained, and every power, jurisdiction and right which is not by this Constitution expressly delegated to the United States in Congress assembled." Neil H. Cogan, ed., The Complete Bill of Rights: The Drafts, Debates, Sources, & Origins, at 675 (Oxford University Press, 1997).

In the amendments proposed by the Massachusetts convention: "First. That it be explicitly declared, that all Powers not expressly delegated by the aforesaid Constitution are reserved to the several States, to be by them exercised." Id. at 674.

In the amendments proposed by the Virginia convention: "First. That each State in the Union shall respectively retain every power, jurisdiction, and right, which is not by this Constitution delegated to the Congress of the United States, or to the departments of the Foederal Government." Id. at 675. The same language was also used in the first proposed amendment of the first North Carolina convention, which rejected the Constitution.

The relevant language proposed by the New York constitution offer the most noteworthy (and expansive) variation:

That the powers of Government may be reassumed by the People, whensoever it shall become necessary to their Happiness; that every Power, Jurisdiction, and right, which is not by this said Constitution clearly delegated to the Congress of the United States, or the departments of the Government thereof, remains to the People of the several states, or to their respective State Governments, to whom they may have granted the same; And that those Clauses in the said Constitution, which declare, that Congress shall not have or exercise certain Powers, do not imply that Congress is entitled to any Powers not given by

principle of reserved powers seem formulaic at best, that was because Anti-Federalists were also intent on securing substantive amendments that would erect barriers blocking the various roads to consolidation the Constitution was paving. That is, in addition to funding a way to affirm that the national government was indeed vested with limited powers, Anti-Federalists sought more explicit restrictions on its authority to levy and collect taxes, to raise a "standing army" or control the militia, or to use the federal judiciary to ratify its inroads on the reserved powers of the states.

In taking it upon himself to force the "nauseous project of amendments" down the craw of a reluctant First Congress,[41] it was James Madison's manifest intention to restrict these changes to a general statement of rights, while leaving the structure and powers of the national government untouched. Convinced that only experience could determine which aspects of the Constitution needed improvement, Madison was primarily concerned with assuaging the misguided but plausible fears of those moderate Anti-Federalists who sincerely believed that their liberty would be insecure if a Bill of Rights went unadopted. Privately he still thought that bills of rights were "parchment barriers" that would prove least effective when most needed. But he had also come to recognize that the adoption of a suitable set of amendments might over time serve a valuable purpose ("acquire efficacy") if the inculcation of the principles it embodied worked to brake not the arbitrary impulses of the rulers but the factious passions of the people themselves.[42]

If these were Madison's motives in seeking amendments, what of his colleagues? Contrary to the usual story suggesting that a binding commitment to amendments (at least in the form of a Bill of Rights) was the chief achievement of the Anti-Federalist opponents of the Constitution, there was little pressure on Congress to act when it assembled in the early spring of 1789. Understanding that the real, substantive changes they sought lay beyond their reach, Anti-Federalists (in Congress and perhaps out) had little interest in the innocuous amendments they knew their opponents would now promote. Politics had not stood still since 1788; the failure of Anti-Federalists to do well in the winter's elections for the new government had largely deflated the pressure for amendments.

Under these conditions, it is difficult to avoid seeing the Tenth Amendment as anything more than the truism it is often taken to be—that is, a formula en-

---

the said Constitution; but such Clauses are to be construed either as exceptions to certain specified Powers, or as inserted mainly for greater Caution.

Id. at 674. Madison adapted the two concluding independent clauses of this article in his original version of what became the Ninth Amendment.

[41]The phrase comes from Madison's letter to Richard Peters of Aug. 19, 1789, in 12 Madison's Papers, at 346 (cited in note 8).

[42]Original Meanings, at 330–36 (cited in note 4).

dorsing Wilson's basic position on the nature of the essential grant of power, but one that stopped short of further explication of the actual division of authority. In his original amendments, introduced in his speech to the House of June 8, 1789, Madison appears to have had two specific purposes in mind in drafting the language that evolved into the texts of the Ninth and Tenth amendments. First, he was trying to resolve the genuine theoretical dilemma that James Wilson had opened in his public speech of October 6, 1787, asserting that:

> the exceptions . . . made in favor of particular rights, shall not be so construed as to diminish the just importance of other rights retained by the people, or as to enlarge the powers delegated by the Constitution; but either as actual limitations of such powers, or as inserted merely for greater caution.[43]

Recognizing that the positive enumeration of some rights might be interpreted to relegate others equally fundamental to an inferior status, Madison was explicitly stating that other rights retained their authority even if unincorporated in the revised text. More to the point, he was refuting the Anti-Federalist charge that the explicit recognition of some rights in the original Constitution gave the lie to Wilson's argument that the inclusion of a Bill of Rights might be wrongly construed to imply that powers not intended to be given the national government were in fact vested there. Even without the restrictions imposed in Article I, Section 9, Congress would have had no authority to suspend *habeas corpus* or to enact bills of attainder or *ex post facto* laws. So too, the proposed addition of clauses protecting rights of conscience or the freedom of the press could not be read to imply the existence of a regulatory authority over religion or speech that had never been explicitly delegated. They were simply being proposed for "greater caution."

In framing the forerunner of the Tenth Amendment, Madison took a minimalist approach that stripped the language proposed by the state conventions as far back as he could. Madison's proposed text did not affirm "the sovereignty, freedom, and independency" of the states; or extend their reserved authority to "every power, jurisdiction, and right" not yielded to the national government; or allude to powers "expressly delegated" to the union. It simply said that "[t]he powers not delegated by this Constitution, nor prohibited by it to the States, are reserved to the States respectively."[44] In this primitive form, this language would do nothing more than affirm that powers not delegated to the union remained with the states. Any attempt to ascertain which powers remained to the states would still have to revert to all the other clauses of the Constitution that

---

[43]Madison, Speech of June 8, 1789, in 12 Madison's Papers, at 201–02 (cited in note 8).

[44]Philip Kurland & Ralph Lerner , eds., 5 The Founders Constitution, at 26 (University of Chicago Press, 1987).

mapped the contours of the federal system. It may be mildly noteworthy that Madison proposed placing this clause in a new article, rather than inserting it at a particular point in the original text (as he proposed to do with his other amendments).[45]

Debate on this clause was desultory. When the House took it up on August 18, Thomas Tudor Tucker of South Carolina proposed amending the article in two ways: First, "by prefixing to it [the statement that] 'all powers being derived from the people'"; and second, by adding the adverb "expressly" before "delegated." Madison rebuffed Tudor's second change by alluding to the "full and fair discussion" that had taken place on this point at the Virginia convention: "[I]t was impossible to confine a Government to the exercise of express powers; there must necessarily be admitted powers by implication, unless the Constitution descended to recount every minutia." Roger Sherman, who had repeatedly favored a narrow enumeration of national powers at the Federal Convention, agreed. Tucker still dissented, but the House then rejected his amendment. At this point Daniel Carroll of Maryland (a Framer) proposed adding "or to the people" at the end of the clause, and his change was approved. Three days later, Elbridge Gerry (a nonsigning Framer and Anti-Federalist) again moved to add expressly, but his amendment lost by a roll call vote of 32–17.[46]

In this otherwise desultory story, what significance can we attach to the addition of the term "or to the people" to the Tenth Amendment? As Charles A. Lofgren has explained, the most likely account of the meaning of this change is tied to the fate of Madison's original proposal to prefix to the Constitution a threefold declaration to the effect that all government is derived from the people, instituted for their benefit, and subject to their "indubitable, unalienable, and indefeasible right to reform or change it."[47] But a prefix to a preamble hardly amounted to an amendment of the Constitution; and moreover, once Congress decided it preferred separate amendments to Madison's scheme of interleaved alterations, this idea seemed more redundant still—especially in a Constitution whose opening words, "We the people," were, Sherman observed on August 14, 1789, as "copious and expressive as possible." Once Madison's revision of the preamble was abandoned, the eventual Tenth Amendment became a convenient

---

[45]The first member of this new seventh article would have been a similar clause affirming that the powers delegated to the particular departments of the new government had not been delegated to the other department—another truism.

[46]5 id. at 403–04. For Sherman's notion of a proper division of powers, see 2 Farrand at 17 (cited in note 11). For the resolutions I am convinced he presented to the Convention on July 17, following the so-called "great compromise," see 3 id. at 615–16, although Farrand suggests they were prepared in conjunction with the New Jersey Plan. As late as September 15, Sherman still hoped to incorporate in the Constitution a statement protecting the states in their "internal police." 2 id. at 630.

[47]Lofgren, Origins, at 106–09 (cited in note 5).

refuge for a stripped-down version of the sacred axiom that "all powers [of government are] derived from the people."[48] It was no less a truism than the language to which it was attached.

Or was it?

James H. Hutson has interpreted the Tenth Amendment as "a kind of anti-bill of rights" because "[i]t repeated the stock Federalist charge used during the ratification campaign to deny that a bill of rights was needed: powers not granted to the government were reserved to the people." Properly read, the Tenth Amendment was "a gloss on the Ninth. . . . To the question posed by the Ninth Amendment—What other rights and powers are retained by the people?— the Tenth Amendment answers: all powers not delegated to the United States."[49]

Yet it may be possible to give the Tenth Amendment a broader (or I should say, Wilsonian) reading that may better capture the place it now promises to gain in our constitutionalized politics. When Thomas Tudor Tucker sought to add the reminder "all powers being derived from the people" to this amendment, he was looking for a shorthand way to restate the fundamental premise of popular government. When Daniel Carroll in turn revised this effort by placing "or to the people" at the end of the amendment, however, he opened a new possibility, suggesting that an entity called "the people"—whether gathered separately in the states or collectively as "We the people of the United States" is not clear—were an alternative repository of power to the state governments in which were vested all powers of government delegated elsewhere than the union. In the absence of debate, one should hesitate, even balk, at ascribing intentionality of any kind to this change. Yet there is a sense in which the identification of the people as an entity distinct from both state and national governments illuminates the political underpinnings of federalism.[50]

## Conclusion

I suggested earlier that James Wilson was the one Framer who seemed to glimpse most clearly the possibility that popular loyalty might swing freely between (or even within) the different levels of governance in a compound federal

---

[48]For the debate on Madison's preamble, see Charlene Bangs Bickford et al., eds., 11 Documentary History of the First Federal Congress, at 1235–43 (Johns Hopkins University Press, 1977), and id., at 1242 (Sherman's comment).

[49]James H. Hutson, The Bill of Rights and the American Revolutionary Experience, at 95, in Michael J. Lacey and Knud Haakonssen, eds., A Culture of Rights: The Bill of Rights in Philosophy. Politics, and Law—1791 and 1991 (Cambridge University Press, 1991).

[50]Aviam Soifer hints at this position in his essay, Truisms That Will Never Be True: The Tenth Amendment and the Spending Power, 57 U. Colo. L. Rev. 809 (1986).

republic. He shared the worries of Madison and Hamilton that the states might well get the better of the national government in this competition. But as an immigrant, a nationalist, and a Scot, he may have understood as well that new attachments would flow to whichever level or institutions of government performed most effectively. And that was the image of popular sovereignty that Wilson repeatedly expressed at both the Federal Convention and especially in his public speeches after the Framers dispersed to their states. In the American Republic, Wilson told the Pennsylvania ratifiers on December 4, 1787, sovereignty resided not in the state governments but in the people: "They can delegate it in such proportions, to such bodies, on such terms, and under such limitations, as they think proper." In practice, Wilson continued, the people formed two communities, one national, the other ("on a lesser scale") based in their states. The states had been "made for the People, as well as for them," and "the People, therefore, have a right, whilst enjoying the undeniable powers of society, to form either a general government, or state governments, in what manner they please; or to accommodate them to one another; and by this means preserve them all."[51]

Wilson was speaking, of course, about a constitutional allocation of authority. But given the blurring of boundaries that is inherent in federalism, it is possible to think of this process of "accommodation" and reallocation as an ongoing political process as well. The adoption of the Constitution did little, of itself, to convert the American union into a viable nation-state. After the initial flurry of Hamilton state-building blew over, the United States remained little more than a confederation well into the next century. That it slowly began to resemble a nation by the late nineteenth century owed less to the legacy of 1787—or even 1865—than it did to the gradual coalescing of constituencies and interests eager to bend national power to their own ends. Even then, it took the multiple legacy of depression, global war, cold war, and the Second Reconstruction to allow the term "The United States of America" to become a singular rather than a plural noun. The cumulative response to these developments brought an era of liberal nationalist (Democratic) consensual hegemony that fulfilled the Wilsonian promise, overcoming the centrifugal forces that Madison hoped to tap as he constructed a government that would operate within a vital yet circumscribed orbit.

The sources of the unraveling of that hegemony are now all too evident: Prolonged prosperity, resentment of the perceived excesses of bureaucracy, the extinction of the Soviet bear (or bugbear), and perhaps most important, the backlash of race have given the centrifugal forces of the decentralized American polity a new release of energy. In retrospect, we may have to understand that the history of American federalism cannot be written as a story of the gradual progressive integration of a nation-state. The alternative story may be that integration on any substantial scale required the massive pressures that prevailed in the

---

[51] 2 Documentary History, at 472 (cited in note 6).

era from 1930 to (say) 1975; remove one or more of those pressures, and the fragility of the nationalist consensus lies exposed at its very foundation. But the conclusion of this story remains unwritten, for its outcome can only be a function of the political contestation in which we are now immersed. In this contestation, the Tenth Amendment and the concept of reserved powers are not yet a principle demanding vindication; they are merely symbols of the devolutionist side of this struggle. But wielded in the right way, they may acquire more authority than they have had at any time since the decades preceding the Civil War. For a Madisonian like myself, who happens to think that the national government has indeed played a crucial role in enlarging rather than limiting fundamental rights and liberties, this is not a happy thought.

CHAPTER FOUR

# Federalism and Judicial Review

**John Choon Yoo**

In recent years, the Supreme Court has reasserted its constitutional role in guarding the states from the force of excessive federal regulation. In cases such as *Gregory v. Ashcroft*,[1] *New York v. United States*,[2] *United States v. Lopez*,[3] *Seminole Tribe of Florida v. Florida*,[4] *Alden v. Maine*,[5] and *Kimel v. Florida Board of Regents*,[6] the justices have declared the applicability of judicial review to questions concerning state sovereignty and the proper balance between the powers of the federal and state governments. In these cases, the Court has demonstrated its intention to establish areas of state activity and control that are to remain outside federal jurisdiction, and it has suggested that such areas can be identified by policing Congress's use of its enumerated powers. Although the Court is certain to continue the debate over where the line is to be drawn between state and national power, it seems that the Court believes it has an obligation to draw that line.

---

[1] 501 U.S. 452 (1991).
[2] 505 U.S. 144 (1992).
[3] 514 U.S. 549 (1995).
[4] 517 U.S. 44 (1996).
[5] 527 U.S. 706 (1999).
[6] 120 S. Ct. 631 (2000).

The Supreme Court's reorientation of judicial review stands in direct con-
tradiction to the proposition that the national political branches ought to decide
which matters should be regulated by the federal government and which by the
states. First adopted by the Court in *Garcia v. San Antonio Metropolitan Transit
Authority,*[7] the political safeguards of federalism theory dictated that judicial
review is unnecessary to protect state sovereignty because the states are well
represented in the organs of the national government itself.[8] States select the
senators, have an influential role in the Electoral College, and have authority
over congressional districting and voting rules. The Court in *Garcia* held that
there is no need for federal courts to intervene to protect the states from possibly
unconstitutional federal law. As long as the national political process functions
properly, the states themselves have assented to passage of the legislation. Although the Court has not overruled *Garcia* directly, it clearly has rejected the
political safeguards of federalism approach to judicial review. Indeed, if there is
any clear lesson to be gleaned from its most recent decisions, and in particular,
*United States v. Morrison,*[9] it is that even the most deeply examined congressional judgments are not immune.[10]

This essay examines the history of the ratification of the Constitution to
show why the Court is correct to reinvigorate its institutional role in maintaining
the constitutional balance between the federal and state governments. Evidence
from the framing period indicates that questions of state and national power
were to receive the fullest—if not the primary—attention of the Supreme Court.

---

[7]469 U.S. 528 (1985).

[8]See, for example, Herbert Wechsler, The Political Safeguards of Federalism: The
Role of the States in the Composition and Selection of the National Government, 54
Colum. L. Rev. 543 (1954); Jesse Choper, Judicial Review and the National Political
Process (University of Chicago Press, 1980) ("Judicial Review"); Jesse H. Choper, The
Scope of National Power Vis-à-Vis the States: The Dispensability of Judicial Review, 86
Yale L. J. 1552 (1977); D. Bruce LaPierre, The Political Safeguards of Federalism, Re-
dux: Intergovernmental Immunity and the States as Agents of the Nation, 60 Wash. U. L.
Q. 779 (1982); Larry Kramer, Putting the Politics Back Into the Political Safeguards of
Federalism, 100 Colum. L. Rev. 215 (2000).

[9]120 S. Ct. 1740 (2000). In *Morrison* the Court invalidated the civil suit provision of
the Violence Against Women Act, finding that "Congress' effort . . . to provide a federal
civil remedy can be sustained neither under the Commerce Clause nor § 5 of the Fourteenth Amendment. . . . Under our federal system that remedy must be provided by the
Commonwealth of Virginia, and not by the United States." Id. at 1759.

[10]The Court stressed that "[i]n contrast with the lack of congressional findings that
we faced in *Lopez,* [the civil remedy provision] *is* supported by numerous findings regarding the serious impact that gender-motivated violence has on victims and their families." Id. at 1752. But it rejected the force of those findings, stressing, as it did in *Lopez,*
that this was "'ultimately a judicial rather than a legislative question, and can be settled
finally only by this Court.'" Id. (quoting *Lopez,* 514 U.S. at 557 n.2).

Although there is a great deal of historical support for the idea that the national government itself would protect state interests, there is no evidence that the Framers understood the national political process to be the exclusive safeguard of federalism. Instead, available historical materials strongly indicate that the Framers believed judicial review was necessary because of the chance that members of the national government would subvert the Constitution for their personal ends.

After establishing that the Framers understood judicial review to protect the states, this essay discusses what benefits are produced by judicial protection of the states. Judicial review was necessary because of the role that the states were to play in the national political system. States were to be much more than field offices of the national government,[11] and more than instruments of decentralization for the federal administration.[12] Despite their initial efforts to undermine state sovereignty, the Federalists recognized that the states were a permanent feature of the political landscape, and that they were to play the primary role in regulating and protecting the lives of their citizens. By the end of the ratification debates, the states were understood to be the primary defenders of the rights of the people. States would protect these rights not only by creating and enforcing new rights, but also by checking the power of the federal government. Judicial review, then, would protect rights by directly blocking federal laws that infringed on an individual's right. It would also protect rights by preserving the independence of other political institutions that had an interest in protecting individuals' rights.

History is of the utmost relevance here for several reasons. First, and perhaps most importantly, history underlies the Court's renewed interest in the Constitution's protections for state sovereignty. For example, in concluding in *Gregory v. Ashcroft* that "the principal benefit of the federalist system is a check on abuses of government power," Justice O'Connor relied primarily on *The Federalist Papers*.[13] In *New York v. United States,* Justice O'Connor and the majority again closely reviewed the records of the Constitutional Convention, *The Federalist Papers,* and the ratification debates to conclude that the federal government did not have the power to regulate states *qua* states.[14] *Lopez* and *Seminole Tribe* also were replete with examinations and quotations to the his-

---

[11]Saikrishna Prakash, Field Office Federalism, 79 Va. L. Rev. 1957 (1993) ("Field Office"); but see H. Jefferson Powell, The Oldest Question of Constitutional Law, 79 Va. L. Rev. 633 (1993); Evan H. Caminker, State Sovereignty and Subordinacy: May Congress Commandeer Officers to Implement Federal Law, 95 Colum. L. Rev. 1001 (1995) ("State Sovereignty").

[12]But see Edward L. Rubin & Malcolm Feeley, Federalism: Some Notes on a National Neurosis, 41 UCLA L. Rev. 903 (1994) ("Federalism Notes").

[13]Gregory v. Ashcroft, 501 U.S. 452, 458 (1991).

[14]New York v. United States, 505 U.S. 144, 163–66 (1992).

torical record of the ratification of the Constitution.[15] If the Court is to honestly confront the tension it has created between *Garcia* and its recent federalism jurisprudence, it will almost certainly refer to the original understanding to guide its approach to judicial review and states' rights.

Second, the Supreme Court has come to accept that evidence of the Framers' intent is relevant to any discussion of the meaning of the Constitution. Naturally, there is significant room for disagreement as to the weight to give to the original understanding of the Constitution's text. Some justices of the Supreme Court, such as Justices Scalia and Thomas, would make historical evidence dispositive on questions of constitutional interpretation.[16] Other recent decisions by the Court indicate that a majority at least believe history to be relevant, if not decisive, on questions of constitutional structure and of constitutional rights.[17]

Third, leading academics also believe that evidence of the Framers' intent is relevant to any discussion concerning the structural provisions of the Constitution. Like the differences on the Court, academic debates, for the most part, concern how much deference to provide the Framers, not whether to do so at all. In the area of separation of powers, for example, both sides of a sharp debate over the nature of the executive power place heavy reliance upon the original understanding.[18] Similarly, much of the recent scholarship on the Court's resurrection of federalism has focused on the Framers' intent concerning the Commerce Clause and the Tenth Amendment.[19] To be sure, some scholarship on federalism is decidedly ahistorical, but this scholarship often has less to do with the meaning of constitutional provisions than with the normative goals furthered by federalism.[20] Regardless of where one falls in these debates, however, the history at

---

[15]See, for example, United States v. Lopez, 514 U.S. 549, 584 (1995) (Thomas concurring); Seminole Tribe of Florida v. Florida, 517 U.S. 44 (1996).

[16]See, for example, McIntyre v. Ohio Elections Commission, 514 U.S. 334, 358 (1995) (Thomas concurring); Antonin Scalia, Originalism: The Lesser Evil, 57 U. Cin. L. Rev. 849 (1989).

[17]See, for example, Seminole Tribe of Florida v. Florida, 517 U.S. 44, 100 (1996) (Souter dissenting); United States Term Limits v. Thornton, 514 U.S. 779 (1995).

[18]See, for example, Steven G. Calabresi & Saikrishna B. Prakash, The President's Power to Execute the Laws, 104 Yale L. J. 541 (1994); Lawrence Lessig & Cass R. Sunstein, The President and the Administration, 94 Colum. L. Rev. 1 (1994); Steven G. Calabresi & Kevin H. Rhodes, The Structural Constitution: Unitary Executive, Plural Judiciary, 105 Harv. L. Rev. 1153 (1992).

[19]See, for example., H. Jefferson Powell, Enumerated Means and Unlimited Ends, 94 Mich. L. Rev. 651 (1995) (discussing *Lopez*); Daniel A. Farber, The Constitution's Forgotten Cover Letter: An Essay on the New Federalism and the Original Understanding, 94 Mich. L. Rev. 615 (1995) (same); State Sovereignty (cited in note 11) (discussing *New York*); Field Office (cited in note 11) (same).

[20]See, for example., Federalism Notes (cited in note 12).

least can illuminate the constitutional structure we are examining and can inform our discussion.

A critic of this approach could respond, of course, that historical intent is impossible to determine, or that one can assemble a few quotes of the Framers on one side to counterbalance the quotes on the other side.[21] I admit that this might be the case when the Framers simply did not think about a certain issue, or engaged in a confusing and inconclusive debate about a constitutional provision. This, however, was not the case with issues of federalism. Federalists and Anti-Federalists conducted an extensive, sophisticated debate (of which *The Federalist Papers* were only the most famous example) over the spheres to be occupied by the federal and state governments. Opponents and supporters of the new Constitution were obsessed with the relationship between the federal and state governments, and it might not be too much of an overstatement to say that the most pressing problem that prompted the Constitutional Convention was how to create a nation out of a collection of autonomous states.

We should approach the evidence as a dialogue, in which Federalists advanced various justifications for constitutional provisions in response to specific Anti-Federalists complaints. As the debates began in the press and in the ratifying conventions soon after the end of the Philadelphia Convention's work, different arguments were raised, tested, and discarded. Out of this crucible emerged the justifications and explanations for the Constitution that won the day. It is these arguments that we should accept, not just as indications of "Framers' intent" but also as evidence of what the Framers, both Federalist and Anti-Federalist, believed the Constitution's terms meant. Furthermore, the public explanation of the Constitution's meaning must bear controlling weight, for it was that explanation that informed and reflected the understanding of the people who ratified the Constitution.

On this last methodological point, I am following the distinctions made by several historians of the ratification period.[22] These scholars distinguish between "original intent" and "original understanding." The former refers to the purposes and decisions of the Constitution's authors (reflected primarily by their comments and actions during the Constitutional Convention in Philadelphia), while the latter includes the impressions and interpretations of the Constitution held by its "original readers—the citizens, polemicists, and convention delegates who

---

[21] See, for example, Judicial Review, at 242–43 (cited in note 8); Paul Brest, The Misconceived Quest for the Original Understanding, 60 B.U. L. Rev. 204 (1980).

[22] See, for example, Jack N. Rakove, Original Meanings: Politics and Ideas in the Making of the Constitution 8–9 (Knopf, 1996) ("Original Meanings"); Leonard Levy, Original Intent and the Framers' Constitution (Macmillan, 1988) ("Original Intent"); Charles A. Lofgren, The Original Understanding of Original Intent?, 5 Const. Comm. 77 (1988) ("Original Understanding").

participated in one way or another in ratification."[23] Our choice of what evidence to treat as relevant depends on the normative premises we bring to the job of constitutional interpretation, and therefore whether we believe the original intent or the original understanding is more significant. If we analogize to the task of statutory interpretation, we must decide whether to choose between the individual or group that drafted a statute and the legislators who voted for it.

If one is looking at the history simply to inform a contemporary decision regarding the Constitution, for example, then all sorts of material, including both the debates from the Philadelphia Convention and postratification interpretations of the Constitution, become reasonably authoritative.[24] If we begin, however, from the normative starting point that the Constitution's authority derives from its popular ratification, then a smaller subset of sources becomes relevant to the enterprise of interpretation. If it is the approval of the Constitution in 1787–88 that gives its provisions supremacy today, then the understanding of those who participated in the ratification should guide our interpretation of the text.[25] Therefore, the most relevant evidence will be speeches, articles, and other documents that indicate what the ratifiers—those whose actions gave the Constitution its legal force—believed the text and structure of the Constitution to mean. In other contexts, for example, I have argued that great importance should be placed on the revolutionary state constitutions, because they formed the legal background within which the ratifiers would have understood the Constitution's text.[26]

This approach finds less relevant other sources that are commonly relied on by some to determine original intent. Decisions and events that took place out of the public eye (such as the choices made during the Philadelphia Convention or private letters and conversations) or government actions that occurred after the ratification (such as during the Washington, Adams, or Jefferson administrations) will not prove as central to the determination of the original understanding. To be sure, these sources can help illustrate the general understanding of certain words during the late 18th and early 19th centuries. They cannot, however, provide direct evidence of the understanding of the Constitution held by the delegates to the ratification conventions, and indeed by the American public, from 1787–88.

---

[23] Original Meanings, at 8 (cited in note 22).

[24] Id. at 8–9.

[25] Id. at 9. See also Original Intent (cited in note 22); Original Understanding (cited in note 22).

[26] John Yoo, The Continuation of Politics by Other Means: The Original Understanding of War Powers, 84 Calif. L. Rev. 167, 172–73 (1996) ("Continuation of Politics"); John Yoo, Our Declaratory Ninth Amendment, 42 Emory L. J. 967 (1993) ("Declaratory Ninth").

Finally if one does not agree that the original understanding is relevant—either as the jumping off point for a contemporary discussion or as the definitive interpretation of the Constitution—there is yet one more reason to give the most serious consideration to the Framers. We should pay deference to the views of men such as James Madison and Alexander Hamilton and the other Federalists, and Anti-Federalist writers such as Martin Luther, Brutus, and Cato, because they were some of the greatest political thinkers our nation has known. They anticipated many of the arguments that are raised today in defense of the political safeguards of federalism; indeed, we will see below that the Federalists themselves first developed the theory that Professors Wechsler and Choper would resurrect to such great effect. The Federalists not only anticipated these arguments, but they rejected them with powerful answers that are as compelling today as they were more than 200 years ago. Thus, the views of Madison, Hamilton, and the other Framers are important not just because they reflect the original understanding, but also because they represent penetrating lines of thought whose force has endured to this day. In other words, the Framers' views are important not just as history, but as an argument on the merits.

## Judicial Review and State Sovereignty

### Prelude to the Constitution

In order to understand the Framers' approach to federalism and judicial review, it is useful to examine the political and legal background that would have informed their thinking on the issue. If federalism refers to a political system that allocates authority between different types of sovereign governments that co-exist within the same territory, then the question of federalism was one the British empire and its colonies had struggled with for some time. The Revolution did not truly solve the challenge of distributing power between the national and state governments, and it was the delegates to the Philadelphia Convention who finally attempted to find a solution to the problem. The proposed Constitution that resulted from the Convention, however, is notable not just for its enumeration of new national powers, but also for its rejection of efforts to fundamentally reduce the role of the states in the national political system.

It perhaps would be a conceit to believe that the Framers of the Constitution had invented federalism.[27] The problem of how to distribute authority between local and national governments had confounded Americans well before the

---

[27]For an example of this prevalent assumption, see United States Term Limits, Inc. v. Thornton, 514 U.S. 779, 838 (1995) (Kennedy, J., concurring) ("The Framers split the atom of sovereignty. It was the genius of their idea that our citizens would have two political capacities, one state and one federal, each protected from incursion by the other.")

American Revolution. Indeed, federalism questions were fundamentally the same questions of imperial governance that had challenged the great empires of history. It was a problem that became acute after the Revolution, and it was this central question that led to the calling of the Constitutional Convention.

Perhaps the most important factor in the Framers' political thinking was recent experience, particularly their struggle with the British Crown. In many ways, the American Revolution was fought over the proper allocation of powers between a central government—the Crown—and its peripheries—the colonies. As historian Jack Greene has suggested, the issue of American federalism actually had its roots in the question of imperial organization and governance.[28] In this respect, the British "imperial constitution" approached the question of colonial governance quite differently than did the ancients with whom the revolutionary generation was so familiar. Greek colonies, for example, took the form of autonomous city-states composed of excess population from the mother country, while the Romans used colonies almost as garrisons to control conquered peoples.[29]

Great Britain's American colonies did not hew to either of these models. As expressed in their charters and constitutions, the North American colonies possessed a mixture of both self-governance and political and economic dependency. The revolutionaries sought for themselves what they believed were their rights as Englishmen, as guaranteed by the British constitution, which they construed to include the right to democratic self-government in the area of taxation and spending. As citizens of the British Empire the North American colonists lived under three separate constitutions.[30] First was the British constitution, which governed England and its nearby dependencies, such as Scotland and Wales. Second, there were the constitutions of the individual American colonies, which had their roots in the charters granted to the original settlers of the colonies by the Crown. Third, there was a developing imperial constitution that distributed authority between the mother country and the colonies, with Parliament legislating on general matters, such as war and peace, and the colonial assemblies handling local affairs.[31] The imperial constitution would lay the foundations for the American federal system. As historian Bernard Bailyn puts it, king

---

[28]Jack P. Greene, Peripheries and Center: Constitutional Development in the Extended Polities of the British Empire and the United States, 1607–1788 (University of Georgia Press, 1986) ("Peripheries"); see also Charles Lofgren, The Origins of the Tenth Amendment: History, Sovereignty, and the Problem of Constitutional Intention, in Charles Lofgren, Government From Reflection and Choice 70, 75 (Oxford University Press, 1986) ("The problem of dividing authority between two levels of government was hardly new to the late 1780s").

[29]Peripheries, at 9 (cited in note 28).

[30]Id. at 67.

[31]Id. at 67–68.

and Parliament "touched only the outer fringes of colonial life; they dealt with matters obviously beyond the competence of any lesser authority. . . . All other powers were enjoyed, in fact if not in constitutional theory, by local, colonial organs of government."[32]

Parliament's attempt to change this arrangement during the latter half of the 18th century was a precipitating cause of the American Revolution. In order to pay for the costs of the French-Indian Wars and the continuing military protection of the colonies, Parliament sought to impose direct taxes in the colonies. Parliament's justification for these taxes was based on a theory of Parliamentary supremacy throughout the Empire. The American colonists resisted on the ground that the imperial constitution, which recognized that different sovereign governments could co-exist within the Empire, allocated the power of internal taxation to the local assemblies.[33] To be sure, the revolutionaries also claimed that they were defending the individual rights they had enjoyed as Englishmen. But the defense of these rights was intimately connected to the protection of the limited autonomy and authority of the colonies and their representative assemblies. As Jack Greene describes the controversy: "Throughout the Stamp Act crisis, colonial spokesmen put enormous stress upon the traditional conception of their assemblies as the primary guardians of both the individual liberties of their constituents and the corporate rights of the colonies."[34] The colonial (soon state) assemblies both regulated local matters and protected individual rights by limiting the power of Parliament over their citizens.[35] It was only when Parliament asserted a theory of complete and indivisible sovereignty that the colonists asserted that the colonial assemblies were the equal of Parliament, and that they were part of Great Britain only through their links to the Crown.[36] These themes were to return with a vengeance during the ratification debates.

The Articles of Confederation represented America's first try at creating a workable balance of power between the states and the national government. Taking effect on March 1, 1781, its defects were widely apparent. The Continental Congress had no direct authority over individuals, but instead had to rely on the good faith of the state governments to execute its decisions.[37] The national government had no power to regulate interstate or international commerce, it could not impose taxes or raise armies on its own, and it could not force states to obey treaties or even national legislation. Failure by the states to

---

[32]Bernard Bailyn, The Ideological Origins of the American Revolution 203 (Belknap Press, 1967) ("Ideological Origins").

[33]Id. at 198–229.

[34]Peripheries, at 83 (cited in note 28).

[35]Ideological Origins, at 217–29 (cited in note 32).

[36]Id. at 223–28.

[37]Jack Rakove, The Beginnings of National Politics: An Interpretive History of the Continental Congress (Knopf, 1979).

fulfill Congress's financial requests and to obey the provisions of the peace treaty with Great Britain (known as the Treaty of Paris) suggested that the states would use their sovereign power to frustrate rather than advance the national interest.[38] No Supremacy Clause provided the national government with the authority to supercede conflicting state laws. If one did not realize that the states held the upper hand, the text of the Articles of Confederation served as a reminder by declaring that "each state retains its sovereignty, freedom and independence."[39] By the 1780s, states were passing discriminatory tariff and custom laws against each other, and disputes were breaking out over the peace with Great Britain and the division of the western lands.[40]

Much fault lay with the internal organization of the national government. Under the Articles, each state possessed the power to veto any national legislation, thereby preventing Congress from passing laws that harmed individual states but benefited the nation as a whole. Further, the Articles did not create an executive branch or a judiciary that could enforce federal law throughout the land. The lack of a federal judiciary was especially notable when it came to questions of federalism. While Congress could act as a court for the purpose of deciding interstate disputes, no tribunal existed to hear claims of excessive uses of national power or of state encroachment on national prerogatives.

Frustration with state governments was high among the leaders of the Convention that met in Philadelphia in the summer of 1787 to revise the Articles of Confederation. Earlier that spring, for example, James Madison had written a document, "Vices of the Political System of the United States," which attributed the failures of the Continental Congress not only to the difficulties of collective action by the states, but also to the state governments' internal structural and political defects.[41] He argued that members of the state assemblies often pursued their personal interests rather than the good of their constituents.[42] The people, however, were not free from blame for unjust state laws: "A still more fatal if

---

[38]See John Yoo, Globalism and the Constitution, 99 Colum. L. Rev. 1955 (1999).

[39]Articles of Confederation Art. II (U.S. 1781).

[40]See Harry N. Scheiber, Federalism and the Constitution: The Original Understanding, in Lawrence M. Friedman & Harry N. Scheiber, eds., American Law and the Constitutional Order 85, 86 (Harvard University Press, 1978) ("Constitutional Order").

[41]Robert A. Rutland & William M. E. E. Rachal, eds., 9 The Papers of James Madison, at 345–57, (University of Chicago Press, 1975). Madison was quite explicit in drawing the connection between the failures of government at the national level and the failures of government at the state level. "In developing the evils which viciate the political system of the U.S. it is proper to include those which are found within the States individually, as well as those which affect the States collectively, since the former class have an indirect influence on the general malady and must no by overlooked in forming a compleat remedy."

[42]Id.

not more frequent cause" of injustice "lies among the people themselves."[43] In particular, Madison argued that in a small republic—the only kind that ancient and modern political theorists believed could support democratic self government—"an apparent interest or passion" would move the majority to approve of "unjust violations of the rights and interests of the minority, or of individuals."[44] This insight would become the basis for Madison's argument for an extended republic in *Federalist No. 10,* and it would supply one of the reasons for Madison's efforts to circumscribe state power in the new Constitution

## Federalism and the Philadelphia Convention

The opposition of Madison and others to the power of the states is worth examining, because it highlights their manifest failure to convince the Philadelphia Convention to alter fundamentally the nature of state sovereignty. To be sure, the Constitution vested Congress with numerous powers that it had lacked under the Articles of Confederation. The national government now could impose taxes and duties, borrow money, regulate interstate and international commerce, conduct foreign relations, and operate an independent military.[45] Furthermore, the Constitution prohibited the states from interfering in matters of foreign relations, war, and interstate commerce.[46] The Federalists also succeeded in creating a federal government that could act directly on individuals, without relying upon the intervention of the states. As Alexander Hamilton argued in *Federalist No. 15,* "the great and radical vice" of the Articles lies "in the principle of Legislation for states or governments in their corporate or collective capacities, and as contradistinguished from the individuals of which they consist."[47] With the creation of an independent executive and judicial branch, and the elimination of the state veto on legislation, the national government no longer would be forced to rely on the states to enact, execute, or adjudicate its laws.

The new government, however, would be neither a consolidated nation nor a confederation of sovereign nations. Instead, it would constitute, in Madison's classic phrase, a "compound republic," partly federal and partly national. "The proposed Constitution therefore is in strictness neither a national nor a federal constitution; but a composition of both," Madison wrote.[48] Despite Article I,

---

[43]Id.

[44]Id.

[45]U.S. Const. Art. I, § 8.

[46]U.S. Const. Art. I, §10.

[47]Federalist 15 (Hamilton), in Jacob Cooke, ed., The Federalist (Wesleyan University Press, 1961) ("Federalist").

[48]Federalist 39 (Madison), at 257 ("In its foundation, it is federal, not national; in the sources from which the ordinary powers of the Government are drawn, it is partly federal,

Section 8's enumeration of new national powers vested in Congress, and Article I, Section 10's prohibitions on state action, the Constitution clearly accommodated the independent sovereignty of the states over most affairs in everyday life. In *Federalist No. 39*, Madison declared that the federal government's "jurisdiction extends to certain enumerated objects only," while the states continued to possess "a residuary and inviolable sovereignty over all other objects."[49] Thus, aside from the written exceptions to their powers in the Constitution, the states emerged from the Philadelphia Convention with their sovereignty fundamentally intact, and with the mechanisms of the Senate and of judicial review built into the national government to provide for their continuing protection.

The significance of the inclusion of state sovereignty in the Constitution is all the more remarkable in light of the efforts of many of the Framers to dismantle state power. For example, the initial proposal for the Constitution, the Virginia Plan, sought to install a legislature based on the principle of proportional representation rather than one based on an equal vote for each state. Popularly elected representatives in the lower house would elect the members of the upper house, the Senate. Part of the plan provided the national government with the authority to veto any state legislation that "contravene the articles of union." The national veto over state legislation was the centerpiece of an effort to transform the states from their status as independent sovereigns under the Articles of Confederation to something more akin to the "lesser jurisdictions," of a "large Government," as James Wilson described it during the Convention.[50]

This was a sentiment shared by many of the Convention's leaders. In his famous speech before the Convention in June, Alexander Hamilton argued that the states should be "swallowed up" by the national government and called for the elimination of their independent sovereignty.[51] George Read of Delaware proposed "doing away [with] states altogether."[52] The only reason that the new plan of government ought to retain the states at all, Madison, Wilson, and Hamilton suggested, was because of the practical difficulties that a single government would encounter in administering so large a republic. "Were it practicable for the Genl. Govt. to extend its care to every requisite object without the cooperation of the State Govts.," Madison declared before the Convention, "the peo-

---

and partly national: in the operation of these powers, it is national, not federal: In the extent of them again, it is federal, not national: And finally, in the authoritative mode of introducing amendments, it is neither wholly federal, nor wholly national.") (cited in note 47).

[49]Id. at 256.

[50]1 Max Ferrand, The Records of the Federal Convention of 1787, at 323 (Yale University Press, 1966) ("Farrand").

[51]Id. at 287.

[52]Id. at 136.

ple would not be less free as members of one great Republic than as members of thirteen small ones."[53]

Despite these arguments, the delegates to the Philadelphia Convention created mechanisms for the states to protect themselves from the national government. As part of the Great Compromise that broke the deadlock between the large and small states, the Senate was to be composed of two senators chosen by each state legislature. The purpose was not just to protect the interests of small states such as Delaware and Rhode Island, but also to protect all of the states from the national government. As George Mason of Virginia, a delegate of one of the of the largest states, said, "the State Legislatures also ought to have some means of defending themselves agst. encroachments of the Natl. Govt."[54] Writing later as Publius, James Madison would echo Mason's theme: "[T]he equal vote allowed to each state, is at once a constitutional recognition of the portion of sovereignty remaining in the individual states, and an instrument for preserving that residuary sovereignty."[55]

Thus, Professor Wechsler was quite right to focus on the Senate as the representative of state interests in the national government, as the similarity of the Senate's structure to that of the Congress of the Confederation would have been clear to any member of the founding generation. By the end of the Convention, state sovereignty received such overwhelming support that the right of each state to equal representation in the Senate became the only clause forever protected from future amendment.[56] However, the Senate's role as protector of state sovereignty was not an unambiguous one.

As many others have remarked, ratification of the Seventeenth Amendment, which provided for the popular election of senators, diluted the ties between benators and their states *qua* states. Even if the people had not amended the Constitution, however, the Senate still would not be an institution wholly devoted to defending state sovereignty. In the minds of Madison and others, as Jack Rakove has written, "the Senate's representative character was incidental to its substantive functions and deliberative qualities."[57] The Framers intended the Senate to constitute, in point, a sort of privy council that would safeguard the interests of the nation as a whole. Thus, the Convention gave the Senate its special role in the treatymaking process and the power of advice and consent in the

---

[53]Id. at 357.

[54]Id. at 158–60.

[55]Federalist 62 (Madison), at 417 (cited in note 47).

[56]U.S. Const. Art. V ("no State, without its Consent, shall be deprived of it's equal Suffrage in the Senate."). For the debate on this provision and its unanimous adoption, see Farrand, at 629–31 (cited in note 50).

[57]Original Meanings, at 78 (cited in note 22); see also Vikram David Amar, Indirect Effects of Direct Election: A Structural Examination of the Seventeenth Amendment, 49 Vand. L. Rev. 1347, 1389–99 (1996).

appointment of federal judges and executive branch officials, both powers that had rested solely in the hands of the king under the British constitution.

These powers were given to the Senate, as Publius explained in *The Federalist Papers*, because the Senate would form a wiser and more stable body—due to the Senators' longer term of office—that could form and advance a more considered conception of the national interest. As Madison wrote in *The Federalist:* "The necessity of a senate is not less indicated by the propensity of all single and numerous assemblies, to yield to the impulse of sudden and violent passions, and to be seduced by factious leaders, into intemperate and pernicious resolutions."[58] In the realm of foreign affairs, Madison argued, "[w]ithout a select and stable [senate], the esteem of foreign powers will not only be forfeited by an unenlightened and variable policy . . . but the national councils will not possess that sensibility to the opinion of the world, which is perhaps not less necessary in order to merit, than it is to obtain, its respect and confidence."[59]

Two other elements of the Senate indicated that it would not perform a solely representative function on behalf of state sovereignty.[60] First, unlike the Continental Congress and the Philadelphia Convention, voting would not run along state-delegation lines, with each state delegation possessing an equal vote. Instead, each senator was to have an equal vote, hardly an ideal system if the Senate existed only to represent states as independent entities. Second, again unlike the Continental Congress, the Constitution provided for the payment of the salaries of the senators. When the Committee on Detail had proposed that states carry this financial burden, the Convention as a whole demanded that the national government pay the salaries of these officers of the national government. Oliver Ellsworth declared that he was "satisfied that otherwise too much dependence on the States would be produced." Another delegate argued that national salaries were necessary because, "[t]he Senate was to represent and manage the affairs of the whole, and not to be the advocates of State interests."[61] Although no ratifier of the Constitution could deny that the Senate was to play a significant role in representing state interests, the Senate's other qualities—made quite clear by the text of the Constitution—indicated that this would not be the Senate's only job.

The Senate's multiple functions—or the difference between its purpose of representation and its role in the operation of the national government—explain why the delegates to the Philadelphia Convention did not make the Senate the exclusive protector of state sovereignty. Instead, the members of the Philadel-

---

[58]Federalist 62 (Madison), at 418 (cited in note 47).

[59]Federalist 63 (Madison), at 422.

[60]See generally Original Meanings, at 170–71 (cited in note 22).

[61]2 Farrand, at 290 (cited in note 50). Cf. United States Term Limits v. Thornton, 514 U.S. 779 (1995).

phia Convention created another institution that could defend the states *qua* states: The federal judiciary.

It is beyond the scope of this essay to provide a complete discussion of whether the delegates to the Philadelphia Convention intended to give the Supreme Court the power of judicial review. Examining the question is not truly necessary for the purposes of this argument, because those who support the political safeguards of federalism thesis do not generally challenge the legitimacy of judicial review. Indeed, Professor Choper argues that nonjusticiability in federalism cases is necessary in order for the federal courts to exercise judicial review with greater authority in controversies involving individual rights.[62] To complete the approach of this essay, however, it is worthwhile to sketch out the historical evidence suggesting that the delegates to the Constitutional Convention believed that the federal courts would maintain the balance between federal and state power.

To be sure, as has been pointed out by others, the idea of judicial review itself was not discussed during the Philadelphia Convention with the same intensity as, for example, the question of state representation in the Senate.[63] Nonetheless, recent work suggests that several of the most influential delegates to the Constitutional Convention would have been intimately familiar with the concept of judicial review.[64] And it seems reasonably clear that the Framers believed that judicial review would play some role in preventing the national legislature from overstepping the constitutional limits on its powers. For example, the power of judicial review was one factor that led the Framers to reject a proposal for a council of revision, which would have exercised a veto on all legislation and would have included members of both the executive and the judiciary. Luther Martin argued that the council would give the judiciary "a double negative" over legislation, because "as to the Constitutionality of laws, that point will come before the Judges in their proper official character."[65] Judicial review, records

---

[62]2 Farrand, at 292 (cited in note 50).

[63]See Original Intent, at 89–123 (cited in note 22), for a summary and discussion of the critics and supporters of judicial review and their use of ratification era sources. The most significant works on the original intention behind judicial review include Raoul Berger, Congress v. the Supreme Court (Harvard University Press, 1969); 2 William W. Crosskey, Politics and the Constitution in the History of the United States (University of Chicago Press, 1953) ("Politics"); 1 Louis B. Boudin, Government by Judiciary (W. Goodwin, 1932); Charles G. Haines, The American Doctrine of Judicial Supremacy (University of California Press, 2d. ed. 1959); Charles Beard, The Supreme Court and the Constitution (Macmillan, 1912); Robert L. Clinton, Marbury v. Madison and Judicial Review (University Press of Kansas, 1989); Edward S. Corwin, The Doctrine of Judicial Review (P. Smith, 1914).

[64]William Michael Treanor, The Case of the Prisoners and the Origins of Judicial Review, 143 U. Pa. L. Rev. 491 (1994).

[65]2 Farrand, at 76 (cited in note 50).

from the Convention suggest, would extend to questions of federalism as well as the separation of powers. Judicial review, for example, provided the Framers with a reason not to provide the president with the power to remove federal judges. In opposing this proposal, John Rutledge argued, "[i]f the supreme Court is to judge between the U.S. and particular States, this alone is an insuperable objection."[66] If the Framers believed that the federal courts would exercise judicial review only over separation of powers or individual rights questions, there would have been no need for Rutledge's statement.

Of course much of the Framers' concern about the balance between the United States and "particular States" stemmed from their fear that the states would exercise too much power against the national government. The Framers addressed this problem, however, by using judicial review at the state as well as at the federal level. Once Madison's proposal for a national veto over state laws had failed, efforts turned toward the Supremacy Clause as the best check on encroaching state power. The Supremacy Clause, which declares that "[t]his Constitution . . . shall be the supreme Law of the Land; and the Judges in every State shall be bound thereby, any Thing in the Constitution or Laws of any State to the Contrary notwithstanding,"[67] imposes a requirement on state judges to invalidate unconstitutional state laws. In other words, Article VI appears to give state courts the power of judicial review over questions involving the powers of the federal and state government.[68] Since Article III gives the Supreme Court appellate jurisdiction over "arising under" cases, even if they originate in the state court system, it seems unlikely that the Framers would have believed that the federal courts could not exercise judicial review in federalism cases. And certainly this understanding was fulfilled by Article XXV of the Judiciary Act of 1789, in which Congress gave the Supreme Court appellate jurisdiction over state court decisions holding federal laws unconstitutional.[69]

There is no strong evidence that the Framers thought that judicial review ought to be exercised when the states were tipping the balance of power towards themselves, but not when the federal government tipped the scales in the other direction. Indeed, in either case, the judiciary would be performing the same

---

[66]Id. at 428. As Rakove correctly suggests, Madison's brief allusion in Federalist No. 39 also was a reference to judicial review over federalism questions. "In controversies relating to the boundary between the" national and state governments, Madison wrote, "the tribunal which is ultimately to decide, is to be established under the general government." Madison concluded that "The decision is to be impartially made, according to the rules of the Constitution; and all the usual and most effectual precautions are taken to secure the impartiality." Original Meanings, at 176 (cited in note 22).

[67]U.S. Const. Art. VI.

[68]See, for example, Herbert Wechsler, Toward Neutral Principles of Constitutional Law, 73 Harv. L. Rev. 1, 3–5 (1959); Judge Learned Hand, The Bill of Rights 28 (Harvard University Press, 1958).

[69]Charles Black, The People and the Court 23–25 (Macmillan, 1960).

function: drawing the proper line between federal and state power. To be sure, one could read Article VI as an authorization for state judges to exercise judicial review only over state laws. Any such reading, however, would also be a judgment on the power of the federal government. In order to determine whether a state law is in conflict with federal law, a court first must determine whether the federal law itself is a legitimate exercise of constitutional power.

Furthermore, the Constitutional Convention failed to draw any distinctions in the text of the Constitution between different types of constitutional cases. Article III simply provides that the "Judicial Power shall extend to *all* Cases, in Law and Equity, arising under this Constitution." The text of the Constitution does not distinguish between federalism cases and individual rights cases, or cases of state power versus cases of national power. The Constitution's text is surely the best piece of evidence concerning the intentions of the Philadelphia Convention, for it is this language that the delegates voted to send to the states for ratification. As we will see shortly, during the process of ratification the Federalists clearly articulated their belief that the federal judiciary would exercise judicial review over federalism questions. As I have argued, the understanding of the ratifiers should be of the highest relevance for our analysis, while that of the delegates to the Philadelphia Convention should be held in lower regard.

Notwithstanding the methodologies of original understanding analysis, the Philadelphia Convention's proceedings support the thesis that the Framers did not intend to place constitutional protections for state sovereignty on a lesser plane than other types of cases. The events of the summer of 1787 show that the delegates rejected strong efforts by Madison, Hamilton, and others to drastically reduce the structural independence of the states in the American political system. Instead, the drafters of the Constitution provided for the permanent presence and protection of the states, not just by guaranteeing equal state representation in the Senate, but also by creating written limitations on federal power, which were to be enforced by a new, independent federal judiciary. To any of the founding generation, these two innovations and their purposes would have been clear on their face.

## Judicial Review and Ratification

In determining whether the Constitution grants the federal courts the authority to invalidate legislation that encroaches on state sovereignty, we must place the highest value on the ratifiers' understanding of the Constitution. This conclusion derives from a normative judgment that it was the adoption of the Constitution by the representatives of the people, sitting in specially convened state ratifying conventions, that gives the Constitution its legal force. As previous writers have noted, this innovation of popular sovereignty made the American approach to government in the late eighteenth century unique in the Western world.[70] When the Federalists went to the states to defend their work, they argued that the actions of the Convention had no legal force at all, but that the act of ratification would give the Constitution its "value and authority," its "character of authenticity and power."[71] To the extent that history matters, it is the original understanding of the ratifiers that we should seek to enforce.

Ratification was by no means a smooth political process, even by today's standards. After the Philadelphia Convention, there was no physically unified forum in which debate could occur; events had moved to the 12 state ratifying conventions, which were separated by both geography and time. Lacking the almost instantaneous communications we enjoy today, the Framers relied on letters and newspapers carried by horse or sea for information. The ratification struggle did not occur solely in the conventions; a parallel debate also took place in the public square, where the printed pamphlet and newsletter was the preferred means of communication. Although ratification was an up-or-down question, the very complexity and breadth of the subjects treated by the Constitution meant that the debate would be broad, complex, and unmanaged. A glance through the many volumes of the definitive documentary record of the struggle, the *Documentary History of the Ratification of the Constitution,* shows that the debate had no mechanism for quality control: Pieces ranged from the sophistication of *The Federalist Papers* to bits of song and bad poetry.[72]

It would be understandable to look at this diverse mass of information and conclude that the ratifiers had no single understanding, that the ratification debates had no consistent or common themes. This might be the case with some clauses of the Constitution that were discussed only briefly or not at all. This was not so, however, with questions of federalism. As we shall see shortly, the question of state sovereignty was perhaps the leading intellectual issue that

---

[70]Gordon Wood, The Creation of the American Republic 306–89 (University of North Carolina Press, 1969).

[71]Merrill Jensen, et al., eds., 2 Documentary History of the Ratification of the Constitution 484 (State Historical Society of Wisconsin, 1976) ("Documentary History") (Speech of James Wilson before the Pennsylvania ratifying convention on Dec. 4, 1787) ("the late Convention have done nothing beyond their powers. The fact is, they have exercised no power at all. And in point of validity, this Constitution proposed by them . . . claims no more than a production of the same nature would claim, flowing from a private pen. It is laid before the citizens of the United States, unfettered by restraint; it is laid before them to be judged by the natural, civil, and political rights of men." Id. at 483). See also Federalist 40 (Madison), at 263–64 (cited in note 47) ("the powers [of the Convention] were merely advisory and recommendatory; that they were so meant by the States, and so understood by the Convention; and that the latter have accordingly planned and proposed a Constitution, which is to be of no more consequence than the paper on which it is written, unless it be stamped with the approbation of those to whom it is addressed.").

[72]Original Meanings, at 94–96 (cited in note 22).

dominated the ratification debates, with the question of the need for a Bill of Rights coming in a close second. In fact, these two issues—federalism and individual rights—were theoretically closely intertwined, as both raised the same fundamental questions concerning the limits of the federal government's enumerated powers and the institutional means necessary to enforce them.[73]

When we examine the debates concerning the question of federalism and judicial review, a pattern emerges: While the Framers believed that the political branches at times would guard state sovereignty, they did not believe that these protections should be exclusive. Instead, by the end of the ratification process, it seems evident that the founding generation understood that the federal courts—exercising the power of judicial review—also would check national legislation that trampled on the states.

This understanding became clear as the ratification debates evolved through the give-and-take between the Federalists and the Anti-Federalists. If the Anti-Federalists shared any common argument, it was that the Constitution created a "consolidated" government in which the national authority would absorb the states. When Federalists found that simply repeating the mantra that the national government was one of enumerated powers would not satisfy the Anti-Federalists, the debate shifted to the question of institutional enforcement of the Constitution's written limits on federal power. Anti-Federalists warned that written limits would be of little use if Congress possessed such unlimited institutional power that it could overcome any resistance to its unconstitutional actions. Federalists initially responded that Congress would not overstep the Constitution's written limitations because the states were well represented in the political process. When these arguments did not prove wholly convincing, the Federalists presented the judiciary as another means to enforce the limits on congressional power over the states.

When the proposed Constitution went to the states, opponents objected that the federal government would destroy the state governments. As the Federal Farmer, one of the more thoughtful and moderate Anti-Federalist authors, wrote:

> But as to powers, the general government will possess all essential ones, at least on paper, and those of the states a mere shadow of power. And therefore, unless the people shall make some great exertions to restore to the state governments their powers in matters of internal police; as the powers to lay and

---

[73]For example, as I have argued elsewhere, the question of whether the Constitution recognized unenumerated rights under the Ninth Amendment was closely related at the time to the question of what check existed on the national government and its powers. See Declaratory Ninth (cited in note 26); see also Thomas B. McAffee, The Original Meaning of the Ninth Amendment, 90 Colum. L. Rev. 1215 (1990) ("Original Ninth"); Suzanna Sherry, The Founders' Unwritten Constitution, 54 U. Chi. L. Rev. 1127 (1987).

collect, exclusively, internal taxes, to govern the militia, and to hold the decisions of their own judicial courts upon their own laws final, the balance cannot possibly continue long; but the state governments must be annihilated, or continue to exist for no purpose.[74]

This "annihilation" argument was repeated by Anti-Federalists in every state from which we have records and was one of the central issues debated in the first state in which ratification was contested, Pennsylvania. Soon after the Pennsylvania ratifying convention approved the Constitution on December 12, 1787, by 46–23, the losing Anti-Federalists published a "dissent," declaring: "We dissent . . . because the powers vested in Congress by this constitution, must necessarily annihilate and absorb the legislative, executive, and judicial powers of the several states, and produce from their ruins one consolidated government, which from the nature of things will be *an iron handed despotism.*"[75]

Anti-Federalists used the open-ended clauses of the Constitution as ammunition in this initial attack. They argued that the Necessary and Proper Clause, when combined with the Supremacy Clause and the General Welfare Clause, which they read to vest in Congress the power to pass all laws necessary for the "common Defence and general Welfare," would permit the federal government to legislate on all subjects. According to the minority who dissented from Pennsylvania's ratification, these three clauses gave Congress power that "is so unlimited in nature; may be so comprehensive and boundless in its exercise, that this alone would be amply sufficient to annihilate the state governments, and swallow them up in the grand vortex of general empire."[76] Wrote Brutus: "The inference is natural that the legislature will have an authority to make all laws which they shall judge necessary for the common safety, and to promote the general welfare. This amounts to a power to make laws at discretion."[77] The Constitution's own clear limits on federal power could not sufficiently mitigate the potential breadth of these clauses. Further, since Congress would have independent sources of revenue and could raise a dreaded standing army, Anti-Federalists believed that the national government would experience little difficulty in enforcing its illegal measures. According to the Federal Farmer, Congress would be unable to enforce its laws "without calling to its aid a military

---

[74]Letter II From the Federal Farmer, October 9, 1787, in Bernard Bailyn, ed., 1 The Debate on the Constitution: Federalist and Antifederalist Speeches, Articles and Letters During the Struggle over Ratification, at 258 (Library of America, 1993) ("Debate").

[75]Dissent of the Minority of the Pennsylvania Convention, Pennsylvania Packet, Dec. 18, 1787, in id. at 536.

[76]Id. at 540. Because they were one of the earliest groups of Anti-Federalists to put their objections to the Constitution in writing, the Pennsylvania minority's views were repeated by their allies throughout the nation.

[77]Brutus V, N.Y. Journal, Dec. 13, 1787, in id. at 500.

force, which must very soon destroy all elective governments in the country, produce anarchy, or establish despotism."[78]

Federalists responded to this argument by maintaining that the federal government, unlike those of the states, was one of only enumerated and defined powers. All other remaining powers and rights would remain with the states or with the people. As Publius wrote in *Federalist No. 14:*

> [T]he general government is not to be charged with the whole power of making and administering laws. Its jurisdiction is limited to certain enumerated objects, which concern all the members of the republic, but which are not to be attained by the separate provisions of any. The subordinate governments which can extend their care to all those other objects, which can be separately provided for, will retain their due authority and activity.[79]

In regard to state sovereignty, this principle of limited enumeration meant that any power not expressly granted to the federal government was retained. Wrote Publius in *Federalist No. 32:* "[A]s the plan of the Convention aims only at a partial Union or consolidation, the State Governments would clearly retain all the rights of sovereignty which they before had and which were not by that act *exclusively* delegated to the United States."[80] At this early stage in the argument, the defenders of the Constitution did not elaborate on *who* would enforce the boundaries of federal power, should Congress overstep them. For them, it was merely enough to argue that the Constitution's written limitations on federal power would be sufficient.

The Federalists' *expressio unius* argument proved singularly unsuccessful. In particular, the Federalists initially had difficulty responding to two related Anti-Federalist arguments that "parchment barriers" would not contain the national government. First, Anti-Federalists argued that the Constitution violated the ancient principle—*imperium in imperio*—that two governments could not exist within the same territory. Violation of this principle would force the national government to eliminate the states in order to vindicate its own authority, the Anti-Federalists argued. Second, Anti-Federalists turned to Montesquieu's famous argument that a republic could exist only within a small territory.[81] Ac-

---

[78]Letter from the "Federal Farmer" to "The Republican" II, Examine Coolly Every Article, Clause, and Word (Oct. 8, 1787), reprinted in 1 id., at 258. On Anti-Federalists fears of a standing army, the Federalist response, and their significance concerning the ongoing debate over war powers, see Continuation of Politics (cited in note 26).

[79]Federalist 14 (Madison), at 86 (cited in note 47).

[80]Federalist 32 (Hamilton), at 200.

[81]Original Meanings, at 182 (cited in note 22). See also David Wallace Carrithers, ed., Charles Louis de Secondat, Baron de la Brede et de Montesquieu, 8 The Spirit of the Laws, ch. 16, at 176 (University of California Press, 1977) ("It is natural to a republic to have only a small territory; otherwise it cannot long subsist.").

cording to the Anti-Federalists, the large size of the United States, which extended farther than any other republic in history, would force the central government to become despotic in order to be effective. Both principles, drawn from the examples of ancient history that had such great effect on the founding generation, had the virtue of being well known throughout the colonies and therefore required little explanation.

Throughout the states, the Federalists raised the political safeguards argument to fend off these powerful claims. In one of the first major public defenses of the Constitution, James Wilson in his Pennsylvania State House Yard speech asked rhetorically: "But upon what pretence can it be alleged that [the Constitution] was designed to annihilate the state governments?" In answer, Wilson showed that the presidency was selected by electors chosen by rules of the state legislature, that senators were elected directly by the state legislature, and that even representatives were chosen by an electorate defined by the state legislature. "If there is no [state] legislature," said Wilson, "there can be no senate," or president, or House.[82] Publius in *Federalist No. 45* agreed:

> Without the intervention of the State Legislatures, the President of the Without the intervention of the State Legislatures, the President of the United States cannot be elected at all. . . . The Senate will be elected absolutely and exclusively by the State Legislatures. Even the House of Representatives, though drawn immediately from the people, will be chosen very much under the influence of that class of men, whose influence over the people obtains for themselves an election into the State Legislatures.[83]

In fact, Publius predicted that the influence of the states perhaps might be too strong: "Thus each of the principal branches of the federal Government will owe its existence more or less to the favor of the State Governments, and must consequently feel a dependence, which is much more likely to beget a disposition too obsequious, than too overbearing towards them."[84]

In making this argument, the Federalists recognized that the states, as representatives of the people, also were parties to the great contract known as the Constitution. As Publius would comment a few months later in *Federalist No. 62:* "[T]he equal vote allowed to each state [in the Senate], is at once a constitutional recognition of the portion of sovereignty remaining in the individual states, and an instrument for preserving that residuary sovereignty."[85] So represented in the national government, both large and small states would "guard by every possible expedient against an improper consolidation of the states into one

---

[82]James Wilson, Speech in State House Yard, Oct. 6, 1787, in 1 Debate, at 67 (cited in note 74).

[83]Federalist 45 (Madison), at 311 (cited in note 47).

[84]Id.

[85]Federalist 62 (Madison), at 417.

simple republic."[86] As Oliver Ellsworth, under the pseudonym A Landholder, wrote in response to Anti-Federalist Elbridge Gerry: "State representation and government is the very basis of the congressional power proposed."[87] Federalists repeated these arguments not only in the press, but also in the state ratifying conventions.[88] Asked James Madison during the Virginia ratifying convention: "Are not the States integral parts of the General Government?"[89] Alexander Hamilton declared, "the senators will constantly be attended with a reflection, that their future existence is absolutely in the power of the states."[90]

Professors Wechsler and Choper are to be praised for restoring to us this understanding of the structure of the Constitution. It is undeniable that the Framers understood that each of the components of the political branches would be "dependent," in Madison's words, on the state governments. Senators did rely upon their appointment by the state legislatures, which could be assumed to be more solicitous of state sovereignty than any other actor in the national political system. The president is elected by a College of Electors who are chosen "in such Manner as the [state] Legislature may direct," and the members of the House are elected by voters according to qualifications set by the state legislature. One might even suggest that the original structure of the Constitution was designed to protect the rights of the states just as much as it was intended to protect the rights of individuals. For example, Article I, Section 9's limitations on Congress contain restrictions that favor both the states[91] and the individual.[92] And as noted earlier, the Federalists responded to arguments that states' rights were jeopardized by emphasizing the strict enumeration of the federal govern-

---

[86]Id.

[87]Oliver Ellsworth, A Landholder IV, Connecticut Courant, Nov. 26, 1787, in 1 Debate, at 237 (cited in note 74).

[88]See also Federalist 45 (Madison), at 311 (cited in note 47); Federalist 46 (Madison), at 317–19; James Madison to Thomas Jefferson, Oct. 24, 1787, in 1 Debate, at 197 (cited in note 74); The Republican, Connecticut Courant, Jan. 7, 1788, 1 id. at 715; James Wilson, Opening Address, Philadelphia Ratifying Convention, Nov. 24, 1787, 1 id. at 796; Charles Cotesworth Pinckney, South Carolina Ratifying Convention, May 14, 1788, 2 id. at 589; James Madison, Virginia Ratifying Convention, June 6, 1788, 2 id. at 619–21; Alexander Hamilton, New York Ratifying Convention, June 25, 1788, 2 id. at 811.

[89]James Madison, Virginia Ratifying Convention, June 11, 1788, in 2 Debate, at 658 (cited in note 74).

[90]Jonathan Elliot, The Debates in the Several State Conventions on the Adoption of the Federal Constitution 317–18 (J. Lippincott Company, 1876) (Alexander Hamilton in New York ratifying convention) ("Elliot").

[91]See, for example, Art. I, § 9, cl. 1 (restriction on congressional authority to regulate slave trade); Art. I, § 9, cl. 4 (tax in proportion to state population); Article I, Section 9, cl. 5 (no tax or duty on state exports); Art. I, § 9, cl. 6 (no port preference).

[92]Art. I, § 9, cl. 2 (suspension of writ of habeas corpus); Art., § 9, cl. 3 (prohibition on bills of attainder and *ex post facto* laws).

ment's limited powers. Thus, the statements of those who framed our Constitution support the Wechsler/Choper insight that the very structure of the federal government would protect the states.

But while the history of the Constitution's ratification highlights the preeminent role that the Senate was to play in maintaining federalism, there is no evidence that these political mechanisms were originally understood to be the *exclusive* means for curbing federal power. In fact, because the Anti-Federalists remained unpersuaded by the political safeguards theory, the Federalists emphasized other checks on congressional power, most notably the judiciary.

Anti-Federalist arguments remained unanswered because of yet a third, allegedly universal, principle of eighteenth-century political science: that any group of rulers would seek to expand their power at the expense of the people. "[T]he records of all ages and of all nations," one Anti-Federalist wrote, showed *"that the liberties and rights of the people have been always encroached on, and finally destroyed by those, whom they had entrusted with the power of government."*[93] Anti-Federalist Brutus agreed: "It is a truth confirmed by the unerring experience of ages that every man, and every body of men, invested with power, are ever disposed to increase it, and to acquire a superiority over every thing that stands in their way."[94] Such had been the lesson of the Roman Republic's transformation into the Roman Empire, and, Anti-Federalists feared, such would be the future of the United States.

To the critics of the Constitution, these lessons of history proved that, because of their political nature, the political safeguards of federalism would be no safeguard at all. According to Anti-Federalist writers, the senators and representatives, once elected as members of the national government, would pay little attention to the needs of their constituents or of their states. Due to the large distances of the country, the people would have little knowledge of their elected representatives, and, conversely, their elected officials would feel little need to represent their distant constituents.[95] In modern parlance, an "inside-the-beltway" mentality would seize the minds of congressmen, with the result that accountability and responsibility between the representative and the represented would dissipate. As the links of representation between constituent and official disappeared, the new government would find it easy to rule by corruption and force. As the minority of the Pennsylvania ratifying convention put it: "The permanency of the appointments of senators and representatives, and the controul the congress have over their election, will place them independent of the sentiments and resentment of the people, and the administration having a greater interest in the government than in the community, there will be no consideration

---

[93]"A True Friend," 14 Documentary History, at 373 (cited in note 71).

[94]Brutus I, New York Journal, (Oct. 18, 1787), 13 id. at 416.

[95]See, for example, Brutus IV, New York Journal, (Nov. 29, 1787), 14 id. at 300–01.

to restrain them from oppression and tyranny."[96] Anti-Federalists had turned Madison's famous argument in *Federalist No. 10* on its head: The great size of the republic would lead to less, not greater, democratic government.[97]

Parchment barriers, according to the Anti-Federalists, could not stand before the natural instinct of the rulers to expand their powers. Indeed, having raised the specter of an unaccountable and distant federal Congress, the Anti-Federalists then turned the political safeguards argument back upon the Federalists. State representation in Congress only made it possible for the states to attempt to ensure that the constitutional limitations on federal power would be observed; it could not guarantee that Congress would never pass unconstitutional legislation. Worst of all, thought the Anti-Federalists, if congressmen became corrupted by the false idol of federal power, they would be the only judges of their own authority, which would soon become limitless. Anti-Federalist writer Brutus, for one, asked who could define the limits of the general welfare and common defense clause in Article I, Section 8. "Are these terms definite, and will they be understood in the same manner, and to apply to the same cases by every one?" he asked rhetorically. "No one will pretend they will. It will then be matter of opinion, what tends to the general welfare; and the Congress will be the only judges in the matter."[98] In a different paper, Brutus noted that "[n]o terms can be found more indefinite than these, and it is obvious, that the legislature alone must judge what laws are proper and necessary for the purpose."[99]

If Congress were the only judge of its own powers, then the safeguards of a written Constitution would become meaningless. As Brutus concluded, every expansion of federal power would be constitutional, *ipse dixit,* because Congress had already given its approval by passing the legislation: "The government would always say, their measures were designed and calculated to promote the public good; and there being no judge between them and the people, the rulers themselves must, and would always, judge for themselves."[100] Anti-Federalists made similar arguments in other states. The Pennsylvania dissenters, for example, argued that Article VI's grant of supremacy to laws made in pursuance of the Constitution would be a blank check for national power. "In our opinion," they said, "'pursuant to the constitution' will be co-extensive with the *will* and

---

[96]Dissent of the Minority of the Pennsylvania Convention, 1 Debate, at 548 (cited in note 74); see also Brutus IV, New York Journal, Nov. 29, 1787, 1 id. at 426; Letter Federal Farmer II, 1 id. at 254–59.

[97]See Akhil Amar, The Bill of Rights as a Constitution, 100 Yale L. J. 1131, 1139–42 (1991) ("Bill of Rights").

[98]Brutus VI, New York Journal, Dec. 27, 1787, in 1 Debate, at 618 (cited in note 74).

[99]Brutus V, New York Journal, Dec. 13, 1787, in id. at 500; see also Thomas Wait to George Thatcher, Jan. 8, 1788, id. at 728.

[100]Id. at 619.

*pleasure* of Congress, which, indeed, will be the only limitation of their powers."[101] Anti-Federalists not only rejected the political safeguards of federalism theory in much the same way the dissenters in *Garcia* would two centuries later, they also appropriated the Federalists' institutional arguments to show that Congress in fact would expand, rather than restrain, the exercise of its powers over the states.

Once they were pressed to the wall by the force of these arguments, the Federalists first began to articulate publicly a theory of judicial review. Initially, Federalists had argued that if Congress exceeded its powers, the people themselves could rise up against Congress with the support of the state governments.[102] This argument, however, carried little weight, because such an extreme form of popular sovereignty undermined the need for a written Constitution. Instead of continuing to rely upon the political safeguards theory, the Federalists switched their response to the arguments that would justify judicial review and would appear two decades later in *Marbury v. Madison*. Supporters of the Constitution argued that the Constitution was the supreme law of the land, and because the judiciary was the expositor of the laws, it would have the authority to declare unconstitutional any unjustified exercise of congressional power.

James Wilson's speech before the Pennsylvania ratifying convention is most telling on this point. During the convention he conceded that the political safeguards could not guarantee that Congress would not pass unconstitutional acts. In response to Anti-Federalist William Findley's arguments that the Constitution was just a plan for the "national consolidation" of all government, Wilson chose to turn to the judiciary, rather than to the Senate, as the ultimate guardian of state sovereignty:

> [U]nder this constitition, the legislature may be restrained, and kept within its perscribed bounds, by the interposition of the judicial department. . . . I had occasion, on a former day, to state that the power of the constitution was paramount to the power of the legislature, acting under that constitution. For it is possible that the legislature, when acting in that capacity, may transgress the

---

[101]Dissent of the Minority of the Pennsylvania Convention, 1 id. at 538.

[102]As James Madison wrote:

But ambitious encroachments of the Federal Government, on the authority of the State governments, would not excite the opposition of a single State or of a few States only. They would be signals of general alarm. Every Government would espouse the common cause. A correspondence would be opened. Plans of resistance would be concerted. One spirit would animate and conduct the whole. The same combination in short would result from an apprehension of the federal, as was produced by the dread of a foreign yoke; and unless the projected innovations should be voluntarily renounced, the same appeal to a trial of force would be made in the one case, as was made in the other.
Federalist 46 (Madison), at 320 (cited in note 47).

bounds assigned to it, and an act may pass, in the usual *mode,* notwithstanding that transgression; but when it comes to be discussed before the judges—when they consider its principles, and find it to be incompatible with the superior power of the constitution, it is their duty to pronounce it void.[103]

Wilson, second perhaps only to Madison in his influence upon the Constitution, saw no inconsistency between the political safeguards and a potent judicial review of federalism questions. Nor did he believe that the political safeguards were the exclusive protection against overweening federal authority. In fact, in the very passage just quoted, Wilson goes on to note that the people can always vote either representatives or senators out of office if they do not respect the constitutional limitations on their power. "The congress may be restrained," Wilson asserted, "by the election of its constituent parts,"[104] and one of those parts, he reminded the Pennsylvania Convention, represented the states. Ultimately, the people always could pass a constitutional amendment to reverse illegal exercises of congressional power. Or, as Wilson put it rather pithily, "they may revoke the lease, when the conditions are broken by the tenant."[105] But, as the excerpted passage makes clear, these remedies for federal transgressions coexisted with the safeguards created by judicial review.

Wilson's statements were not chosen randomly. Instead, they were part of a sophisticated, long-running dialogue between Federalists and Anti-Federalists throughout the states. Admitting the force of Anti-Federalist arguments that Congress could not be trusted to keep its own power within constitutional limits, the Federalists pointed to the separation of powers as an additional bulwark for federalism. For example, Virginia Governor Edmund Randolph published a letter criticizing the Constitution because it provided Congress with general and ambiguous grants of power that could be used to swallow up the state governments. Writing under the pseudonym Americanus, John Stevens of New York answered by conceding that while the necessary and proper clause might be ambiguous, the judiciary would be present to prevent its abuse:

But it may be asked in what manner is this *discretionary* power to be kept within due bounds? I answer, that the Constitution itself is a *supreme law of the land,* unrepealable by any *subsequent law:* every law that is not made in conformity to *that,* is in itself nugatory and the Judges, who by their oath, are bound to support the Constitution as the *supreme law of the land* must determine accordingly.[106]

---

[103] James Wilson, Pennsylvania Ratifying Convention, Dec. 1, 1787, in 1 Debate, at 822–23 (cited in note 74).

[104] Id. at 823.

[105] Id.

[106] John Stevens, Americanus VII, Daily Advertiser, Jan. 21, 1788, in 2 id. at 60.

Publius, the author of the Federalist, similarly saw no conflict between the political safeguards and judicial review. In fact, Publius initially indicated that both the judicial and executive branches would have the obligation to refuse to enforce congressional enactments that overstepped constitutional bounds. In *Federalist No. 44,* for example, Publius responded to the Anti-Federalist concern about the open-ended Necessary and Proper Clause by invoking the separation of powers:

> If it be asked, what is to be the consequence, in case the Congress shall misconstrue this part of the Constitution, and exercise powers not warranted by its true meaning? I answer the same as if they should misconstrue or enlarge any other power vested in them, as if the general power had been reduced to particulars, and any one of these were to be violated; the same in short, as if the State Legislatures should violate their respective constitutional authorities. In the first instance, the success of the usurpation will depend on the executive and judiciary departments, which are to expound and give effect to the legislative acts.[107]

Thus, the Federalists suggested that the federal judiciary, under its authority to hear cases and controversies arising under the Constitution, and the president, under his power to execute the laws, would check congressional infringements on state sovereignty.

In *The Federalist No. 78,* Publius responded more directly, and most famously, to Brutus's charges that Congress could not be trusted to control the exercise of its own powers. All at this point agreed that "[n]o legislative act therefore contrary to the constitution can be valid," because this was inconsistent with the model of delegated and enumerated powers.[108] But because of the Anti-Federalist assault, the question had became one of institutional competence, of which branch had the authority to deem a law constitutional. According to Publius, the legislature had the first cut on the question, but not the last: "If it be said that the legislative body are themselves the constitutional judges of their own powers, and that the construction they put upon them is conclusive upon the other departments, it may be answered, that this cannot be the natural presumption, where it is not to be collected from any particular provisions in the constitution."[109] Publius's statement elaborated on his earlier argument that each branch had a duty to interpret the Constitution and restrain the other branches from unconstitutional actions. Although Congress had the power to decide on the constitutionality of its own enactments, its determinations on this score had no binding weight on the other branches. If the Constitution wanted Congress to

---

[107]Federalist 44 (Madison), at 305 (cited in note 47).

[108]Federalist 78 (Hamilton), at 524.

[109]Id. at 524–25.

have the last word, there would have been a clause in the Constitution expressly providing for it.

It is thus in the context of the ratification debate over the political safeguards theory that we must understand *Federalist No. 78*'s famous discussion of the purposes and operation of judicial review. That essay does not deny that Congress can protect the states by refusing to enact laws that extend beyond its delegated powers. Hamilton emphasizes, however, that Congress is not the ultimate judge of constitutionality. Because the Constitution is the supreme law, Congress cannot judge its own enactments to be superior to it. Instead, as the expositors and enforcers of the law, the courts are better suited to maintain the Constitution's checks on congressional power. As Publius wrote: "The interpretation of the laws is the proper and peculiar province of the courts. A constitution is in fact, and must be, regarded by the judges as a fundamental law. It therefore belongs to them to ascertain its meaning as well as the meaning of any particular act proceeding from the legislative body."[110] Further, to allow Congress to be the final judge of the constitutionality of its enactments would be to allow Congress to place its authority before that of the people: "[T]he constitution ought to be preferred to the statute, the intention of the people to the intention of their agents."[111] If Congress did pass a statute contrary to the Constitution, the legislature would be acting *ultra vires,* and its judgment as to its constitutionality could have no weight: "[W]here the will of the legislature declared in its statutes, stands in opposition to that of the people declared in the constitution, the judges ought to be governed by the latter, rather than the former."[112]

The Federalists repeated their reliance upon judicial review in other state conventions. For example, in the Connecticut ratifying convention, the argument was taken up by no less than Oliver Ellsworth, who wrote the widely published Landholder pamphlets during the debates in the press, who as a senator would draft the Judiciary Act of 1789, and who would become chief justice of the Supreme Court. In response to objections that two governments could not co-exist within the same territory, Ellsworth responded:

> This constitution defines the extent of the powers of the general government. If the general legislature should at any time overleap their limits, the judicial department is a constitutional check. If the United States go beyond their powers, if they make a law which the constitution does not authorize, it is void; and the

---

[110]Id.
[111]Id.
[112]Id.

judicial power, the national judges, who to secure their impartiality are to be made independent, will declare it to be void.[113]

In the Virginia ratifying convention, John Marshall, the future chief justice, listed many of the subjects, such as property or contract law, that he believed to be outside of Congress's delegated powers. Responding to George Mason's claims that Congress could enact general legislation throughout the country, Marshall declared: "Can [Congress] go beyond the delegated powers? If they were to make a law not warranted by any of the powers enumerated, it would be considered by the Judges as an infringement of the Constitution which they are to guard:—They would not consider such a law as coming under their jurisdiction.—They would declare it void."[114] Marshall, like Publius, Ellsworth, Wilson, and the other Federalists, saw the authority of judicial review as the federal institution of last resort, as the last bulwark against a Congress intent on grabbing power: "To what quarter will you look for protection from an infringement on the Constitution, if you will not give the power to the Judiciary? There is no other body that can afford such a protection."[115] Article III, Section 2's establishment of arising under jurisdiction, Marshall opined, guaranteed that the Court would have the authority to intervene in cases where the federal government surpassed the written limitations on its power.

Perhaps surprisingly, some Anti-Federalists agreed with the Federalists that the national courts would be the ultimate arbiters of questions about national versus state powers. Brutus, perhaps the most astute Anti-Federalist writer on legal issues, concurred in the Federalist reading of Article III, Section 2. The courts "are authorised to determine all questions that may arise upon the meaning of the constitution in law. This article vests the courts with authority to give the constitution a legal construction, or to explain it according to the rules laid down for construing a law."[116] If a law were inconsistent with the Constitution, the courts would have the authority under Article III and Article VI to declare it void regardless of Congress's judgment of its constitutionality. Wrote Brutus:

In determining these questions, the court must and will assume certain principles, from which they will reason, in forming their decisions. These principles, whatever they may be, when they become fixed, by a course of decisions, will be adopted by the legislature, and will be the rule by which they will explain their own powers. This appears evident from this consideration, that if the

---

[113]Oliver Ellsworth, Connecticut Ratifying Convention Jan. 7, 1788, in 1 Debate, at 883 (cited in note 74).

[114]John Marshall, Virginia Ratifying Convention, June 20, 1788, in 2 id. at 731–32.

[115]Id. at 732–33. Marshall asked later in his June 20 speech: "If a law be executed tyrannically in Virginia, to what can you trust? To your Judiciary. What security have you for justice? Their independence. Will it not be so in the Federal Court?" Id. at 738.

[116]Brutus XI, New York Journal, Jan. 31, 1788, in 2 id. at 131.

legislature pass laws, which, in the judgment of the court, they are not authorised to do by the constitution, the court will not take notice of them; for it will
not be denied, that the constitution is the highest or supreme law. And the
courts are vested with the supreme and uncontroulable power, to determine, in
all cases that come before them, what the constitution means; they cannot,
therefore, execute a law, which, in their judgment, opposes the constitution,
unless we can suppose they can make a superior law give way to an inferior.[117]

Because the Constitution was the supreme law and the courts were the in-
terpreters of that law, concluded Brutus, the legislature must be bound by the
judiciary's decision on the constitutionality of enactments. "And I conceive the
legislature themselves, cannot set aside a judgment of this court, because they
are authorised by the constitution to decide in the last resort. The legislature
must be controuled by the constitution, and not the constitution by them."[118]
Since the three branches were independent, one could not attempt to interfere
with the constitutional duties of the other, and the duty of the judiciary was to
interpret the Constitution. Other Anti-Federalists in New York and Virginia
made similar arguments that assumed that the federal courts would exercise judicial review over federalism questions.[119]

Of course, the Anti-Federalists were not experiencing a conversion on the
road to Damascus. Rather, they argued that the intervention of the federal courts
would work only to expand, rather than restrict, federal power. First, the Anti-
Federalists believed that the courts would not be bound by the normal rules of
interpretation when construing the breadth of the Constitution's grant of powers.
Of particular concern was Article III, Section 2's grant of jurisdiction over all
cases arising under the Constitution "in Law and Equity." Quoting Blackstone
and Grotius, Brutus argued: "By this [the courts] are empowered, to explain the
constitution according to the reasoning spirit of it, without being confined to the
words or letter."[120] "In their decisions," he explained, "they will not confine
themselves to any fixed or established rules, but will determine, according to
what appears to them, the reason and spirit of the constitution."[121] Because the
Constitution, in Brutus's opinion, used such "general and indefinite terms," the
courts would find it easy to expand the federal government's power beyond the
intent of the Framers.[122] As an example, Brutus cited the Constitution's pream-

---

[117]Brutus XII, New York Journal, Feb. 7 & 14, 1788, id. at 172.

[118]Brutus XI, id. at 132.

[119]Samuel Osgood to Samuel Adams, Jan. 5, 1788, in 1 id. at 705–06; George Mason, Virginia Ratification Convention, June 19, 1788, 2 id. at 720.

[120]Brutus XI, 2 id. at 131.

[121]Id. at 132.

[122]For an extended discussion of the meaning of Article III, Section 2 and the Framers' thoughts on equity, see John Choon Yoo, Who Measures the Chancellor's Foot?: The

ble and argued that the courts would give the Constitution an equitable interpretation in the spirit of its goal to "form a more perfect union." The judiciary would invalidate any state laws that interfered with this objective, with the likely result that in order to "form a more perfect Union" it would soon become "necessary to abolish all inferior governments, and to give the general one compleat legislative, executive, and judicial powers to every purpose."[123]

Second, the Anti-Federalists declared that federal judges would be no more immune from the corrupting effects of power than the other members of the federal government. In their minds, the federal judiciary would have a powerful self-interest in expanding federal authority so as to increase their own jurisdiction and power. "[T]he judicial power of the United States will lean strongly in favour of the general government, and will give such an explanation to the constitution, as will favour an extension of its jurisdiction," warned Brutus.[124] This was, in essence, merely an extension of the Anti-Federalists' fear that Congress would seek to expand its powers and importance by sweeping more within its jurisdiction. "Every extension of the power of the general legislature, as well as of the judicial powers, will increase the powers of the courts; and the dignity and importance of the judges, will be in proportion to the extent and magnitude of the powers they exercise."[125] As the promulgator, rather than the interpreter, of the laws, Congress would follow the courts in the expansion of federal jurisdiction. Brutus predicted that "the judgment of the judicial, on the constitution, will become the rule to guide the legislature in their construction of their powers."[126]

Third, Anti-Federalists feared that the combination of an expansionist judiciary and an unchecked Congress would produce a dynamic that ultimately would annihilate the states. Because the unelected Supreme Court, rather than the states, or even the Congress, was the final expositor of the laws, no entity could reverse the Court's decisions, which inexorably would sanction ever more aggressive uses of federal power. As Brutus described it: "[T]he general legislature, might pass one law after another, extending the general and abridging the state jurisdictions, and to sanction their proceedings would have a course of decisions of the judicial to whom the constitution has committed the power of explaining the constitution."[127] Should the states attempt to resist these encroachments, "the constitutional mode of deciding upon the validity of the law, is with the supreme court, and neither people, nor state legislatures, nor the general leg-

---

Inherent Remedial Authority of the Federal Courts, 84 Cal. L. Rev. 1121, 1151–61 (1996).

[123]Brutus XII, New York Journal, Feb. 7, 1788, in 2 Debate, at 173–74 (cited in note 74).

[124]Brutus XI, id. at 133.

[125]Id. at 134.

[126]Brutus XII, id. at 172.

[127]Brutus XV, New York Journal, March 20, 1788, id. at 377.

islature can remove them or reverse their decrees."[128] In the end, the separation of powers would pose no restraint on Congress's power, because in the eyes of the Anti-Federalists the different branches would have a joint institutional interest in expanding federal authority.

Federalists answered this vigorous attack by denying that the courts would be free to interpret the Constitution in any manner they chose. This explains why Publius devoted substantial portions of *Federalist No. 78, Federalist No. 81,* and *Federalist No. 83* to discussions of the canons of interpretation, perhaps not the most pressing issue to discuss during a debate on the nature of the nation's government. Publius sought to reassure his readers that the courts would not wield unchecked power: "To avoid an arbitrary discretion in the courts, it is indispensable that they should be bound down by strict rules and precedents, which serve to define and point out their duty in every particular case that comes before them."[129] But this was not an argument that the Federalists wished to push too hard, because it was not an argument they needed to continue. The Federalists and Anti-Federalists had by now reached some agreement about which institutions would address questions concerning the balance between federal and state authority. They differed only over how those questions would be resolved.

To summarize, the Framers—both Federalists and Anti-Federalists—understood the text and the structure of the Constitution to permit judicial review in cases questioning the scope of federal power. This conclusion does not deny that the Constitution, as originally understood, provided for state influence over federal decision making via the structures of the legislative and executive branches. In fact, both Federalists and Anti-Federalists anticipated that Congress would have the ability to curb its own actions when it threatened to overstep the boundaries set by the Constitution. The historical evidence, however, also shows the leading ratifiers had come to agree that while the national political process may have been a primary safeguard of federalism, it was not to be federalism's exclusive safeguard. If matters were otherwise, any act of Congress, no matter what its actual textual authorization, would be per se constitutional because of its enactment. After a lengthy, sophisticated, and detailed debate that spanned the distance and time of ratification, it had become clear that the Supreme Court's role was to be the ultimate protector of state sovereignty.

---

[128]Id.

[129]Federalist 78 (Hamilton), at 529 (cited in note 47). For discussion of the rules of statutory interpretation in the early American republic, see John Yoo, Note, Marshall's Plan: The Early Supreme Court and Statutory Interpretation, 101 Yale L. J. 1607 (1992).

# Sovereignty Then and Now

## States and Sovereignty

Judicial protection of the sates would be of little value if the states did not play an important role in the lives of the people. As the historical evidence from the Constitutional Convention and the ratification debates indicate, the Framers recognized that the states were to be a permanent feature of the national political landscape. As Chief Justice Chase would declare for the Court in *Texas v. White*,[130] a Reconstruction Era case that found that Texas had never ceased to be a state during the Civil War, the United States is "an indestructible Union, composed of indestructible States."[131] States existed, however, not just for the sake of existence, but for the purpose of effectuating the will of the people and for protecting their lives, liberty, and property. As James Madison wrote in *Federalist No. 46*, "[t]he Federal and State Governments are in fact but different agents and trustees of the people, instituted with different powers, and designated for different purposes."[132]

It remains for us to discuss, however, what the Framers believed those powers and purposes to be. Certainly, we could conclude that because the federal government is one of limited, enumerated power, all powers that are not encompassed in the Constitution's grants of power must be left to the states. Or, as Madison wrote in *Federalist No. 4:* "The powers delegated by the proposed Constitution to the Federal Government, are few and defined. Those which are to remain in the State Governments are numerous and indefinite."[133] This proposition would be enshrined in the Tenth Amendment, which declares that "the powers not delegated to the United States by the Constitution, nor prohibited by it to the States, are reserved to the States respectively, or to the people."[134] But in light of the broad sweep given to the Commerce Clause and other federal powers by the modern Court, it seems more worthwhile to identify those areas that the Framers believed would remain in the control of the states, despite the Constitution's grant of new powers to the national government.

Broadly stated, the Framers understood the Constitution to grant the national government primarily those powers involving foreign relations. The states would retain primary jurisdiction over almost all other domestic matters, such as taxation, judicial administration and law enforcement, and social and moral legislation. In defending the Constitution from Anti-Federalist claims that the Necessary and Proper Clause gave the national government unlimited powers,

---

[130]7 Wall. 700 (1868).

[131]Id. at 725.

[132]Federalist 46 (Madison), at 315 (cited in note 47).

[133]Federalist 45 (Madison), at 313.

[134]U.S. Const. Amend. X.

Madison declared that federal powers "will be exercised principally on external objects, as war, peace, negociation, and foreign commerce; with which last the power of taxation will for the most part be connected."[135] In contrast, state power would "extend to all the objects, which, in the ordinary course of affairs, concern the lives, liberties and properties of the people; and the internal order, improvement, and prosperity of the State."[136] Given that the Framers believed the nation's new national government and its isolation from Europe would render it relatively immune from the constant wars of the Continent, this meant that the national government would not often exercise its powers.

Article I, Section 8's grant of commerce clause authority constituted the only significant exception to this general division of authority between the national and state governments.[137] According to the Federalists, most of the other powers, such as "war and peace, armies and fleets, treaties and finance," had already been vested in the Congress of the Articles of Confederation.[138] The new Constitution merely made those powers more effective by eliminating the national government's reliance on the states and by giving the federal government the means to act directly upon its citizens. Some, most notably William W. Crosskey, have argued that the Framers enumerated Congress's powers in Article I, Section 8 not to give them to the federal government and take them from the states, but to vest them in Congress rather than the president.[139] Under this strained interpretation, the federal government becomes one of general police powers with the only exceptions to its authority declared in Article I, Section 9 and the Bill of Rights. Crosskey's work clearly misinterpreted the Constitution, the Articles of Confederation, and the British Constitution, for many of the powers in Article I, Section 8, had never belonged to the executive branch. Furthermore, providing Congress with a general legislative power would have undermined the purpose of a written Constitution.

A review of the case law, however, suggests that the Commerce Clause indeed has evolved into a virtual federal police power, *Lopez* and *Morrison* notwithstanding.[140] In *Jones v. United States,*[141] for example, just one week after

---

[135]Federalist 45 (Madison), at 313 (cited in note 47).

[136]Id.

[137]"If the new Constitution be examined with accuracy and candour, it will be found that the change which it proposes, consists much less in the addition of NEW POWERS to the Union, than in the invigoration of its ORIGINAL POWERS. The regulation of commerce, it is true, is a new power; but that seems to be an addition which few oppose, and from which no apprehensions are entertained." Id. at 314.

[138]Id.

[139]1 Politics, at 409–508 (cited in note 63). For a modern adherent, see Herbert Hovenkamp, Judicial Restraint and Constitutional Federalism: The Supreme Court's *Lopez* and *Seminole Tribe* Decisions, 96 Colum. L. Rev. 2213, 2233–36 (1996).

[140]Neither decision, for example, overruled cases such as Wickard v. Filburn, 317 U.S. 111 (1942) (Congress may regulate purely intrastate production of wheat), or Perez

deciding *Morrison,* a unanimous Court reversed a federal arson conviction for the burning of a private home, but not because the federal government should never prosecute "paradigmatic common-law state crime."[142] Rather, the Court found that "an owner-occupied dwelling" used for no other purpose simply did not fall within the statutory requirement that the property in question be "'used in interstate or foreign commerce or in any activity substantially affecting interstate or foreign commerce,'"[143] a holding that left both the logic and force of cases like *Wickard* intact.[144] Since the Court has experienced great difficulty in finding the outer limits of the Commerce Clause, a more useful inquiry would look to those areas that the Framers' understood to be wholly within state jurisdiction. This will also help us determine what the Framers believed they were protecting when they placed state sovereignty under the aegis of judicial review.

In defending the Constitution, the Federalists were often quite explicit about what areas would remain off limits to the federal government. In *Federalist No. 17* Alexander Hamilton included the "administration of private justice between the citizens of the same State, the supervision of agriculture, and of other concerns of a similar nature."[145] Other Framers declared in the state ratifying conventions that the federal government could not invade a state's authority to establish the common law rules governing property, contracts, trusts and estates, and other local matters.[146] The Framers never engaged in a thorough enumeration of all of the items under state control, because such a listing would have "involv[ed] a detail too tedious and uninteresting to compensate for the instruction it might afford."[147] No listing was necessary, because the principle of a na-

---

v. United States, 402 U.S. 146 (1971) (Congress may prohibit arson that occurs only in a single state), although the majority in *Morrison* did emphasize, in a footnote, that "the Constitution cannot realistically be interpreted as granting the Federal Government an unlimited license to regulate." *Morrison,* 120 S. Ct. at 1754 n.8.

[141]120 S. Ct. 1904 (2000).

[142]Id. at 1912.

[143]Id. at 1909 (quoting 18 U.S.C. § 844(i) (1994)).

[144]In a one paragraph concurring opinion, Justice Thomas, joined by Justice Scalia, demurred, stating that he "express[es] no view on whether the federal arson statute . . . is constitutional in its application to all buildings used for commercial activities." Id. at 1913 (Thomas concurring).

[145]Federalist 17 (Hamilton), at 106 (cited in note 47).

[146]See, for example, 3 Elliot, at 40 (Edmund Pendleton before the Virginia Convention) (cited in note 90); id. at 553 (John Marshall before the Virginia Convention); see also A Native of Virginia, Observations upon the Proposed Plan of Federal Government, Apr. 2, 1788, in 9 Documentary History at 692 (cited in note 71); Federalist 33 (Hamilton), at 206 (cited in note 47). I have relied upon Justice Thomas's opinion in United States v. Lopez, 514 U.S. 549, 590–93 (1995) (Thomas concurring), for sources on this point.

[147]Federalist 17 (Hamilton), at 107 (cited in note 47).

tional government of limited powers was clear to all. Hamilton even seems to have assumed that the distinction between federal and state power was so obvious that if the federal government, for example, sought to regulate the "law of descents," it would "be evident that in making such an attempt [the federal government] had exceeded its jurisdiction and infringed upon that of the State."[148]

The Framers did not want to preserve these areas of state autonomy solely for its own sake. As will be explored in more detail in the next section, the Framers deeply feared that the national government would seek to burst the written restrictions on its powers. Federal officials would do so not to help the rich and powerful, or the weak and needy, but to grab power for their institution. In the Framers' minds, the states were to serve as an important bulwark against this possibility. Allowing states to regulate much of the daily lives of their citizens would make those citizens more loyal to the state governments, and therefore more likely to support their states in opposing an overweening national government.

This relationship between state sovereignty, citizen loyalty, and maintaining checks on the federal government becomes clear when we examine *The Federalist*'s discussion of state law enforcement. Hamilton identified "the ordinary administration of criminal and civil justice" as one of the most important powers to be left in the hands of the states.[149] The justice system was so important, in Hamilton's mind, not because states would be more efficient than the national government at law enforcement, but because "[t]his of all others is the most powerful, most universal and most attractive source of popular obedience and attachment."[150] An effective protection of life, liberty, and property, Hamilton argued, "contributes more than any other circumstance to impressing upon the minds of the people affection, esteem and reverence towards the government."[151] By allowing the states to perform effectively and win the support of their citizens, *The Federalist* concluded, the Constitution sought to bolster state power so as to check the national government. Wrote Hamilton:

> The great cement of society which will diffuse itself almost wholly though the channels of the particular [state] governments, independent of all other causes of influence, would ensure them so decided an empire over their respective citizens, as to render them at all times a complete counterpoise and not infrequently dangerous rivals to the power of the Union.[152]

---

[148]Federalist 33 (Hamilton), at 206.
[149]Federalist 17 (Hamilton), at 107.
[150]Id.
[151]Id.
[152] Id. at 107–108.

In this conception, judicial review becomes necessary to protect the state's ability to check the federal government. If the federal government is permitted to invade more and more of the jurisdiction of the states, then the states will be unable to maintain the support of their citizens. So weakened, the Framers feared, the states would prove to be little obstacle to a national government intent on seizing absolute power. Sovereignty is not maintained for sovereignty's sake, but instead is necessary to check those driven by power for power's sake. As we will see shortly, maintaining state sovereignty and checking national power, the Framers believed, ultimately would lead to greater liberty for the people.

## State Sovereignty, Judicial Review, and Rights

The Framers' view of the role of judicial review and federalism was very much in keeping with their understanding of constitutional law, which, I would suggest was quite different from the way most constitutional scholars view the subject. Underlying the political safeguards of federalism approach to judicial review is a concern over individual rights. Only by abstaining from federalism or separation of powers controversies, this theory maintains, can the Court preserve the political capital that allows it to protect individuals from an oppressive majority. This approach is very much in keeping with the manner in which the Constitution is taught and studied, with a division between the structural elements of the Constitution and its rights-bearing provisions.

But as Akhil Amar has suggested, the Framers did not understand the Constitution to embody this neat separation between structural issues on the one hand, and individual rights on the other.[153] The Bill of Rights and the structural elements of the Constitution should be viewed as a whole, and just as the Constitution itself has certain protections for individuals, such as the Ex Post Facto Clause, the Bill of Rights has much to say about federalism. Indeed, when one examines together the debates about whether to have a Bill of Rights and whether the Court should review federalism questions, it becomes clear that the Federalists and Anti-Federalists were really arguing about the same conceptual issue. Rather than federalism and individual rights, both debates were about controlling the central government. Above all, the Framers were not concerned so much about whether individuals would have the unimpeded right of free expression, as they were concerned about restraining a federal government that someday might lose touch with the people and act in its own self-interest. As I have argued elsewhere in regard to the Ninth Amendment, the main purpose of the First Amendment and much of the Bill of Rights, which was added in response

---

[153]Bill of Rights (cited in note 97).

to Anti-Federalist demands, simply was to deny the federal government power, rather than to define the rights of the individual.[154]

The Framers' unified understanding of federalism and rights becomes clear when the Bill of Rights and its history are briefly examined. A reading of the Bill of Rights reveals that many of its guarantees are not written as individual rights as such, but as restrictions on what the federal government may do with its enumerated powers. Thus, the First Amendment does not speak of the individual's right to free speech or freedom of religion, as did several of the state declarations of rights at the time, but instead says that "Congress shall make no law respecting" those subjects. The Third Amendment forbids the federal government from quartering troops; the Fourth Amendment forbids the issuance of warrants without probable cause; the Eighth Amendment forbids excessive bails and fines, or cruel and unusual punishments. These amendments do not define, in positive law, the rights of the individual. Instead, they are simply a list of actions that the federal government may not take, much like those listed in Article I, Section 9.

Indeed, one need only read to the end of the bill, when one encounters the Ninth and Tenth Amendments, to fully understand the link between federalism and the Bill of Rights. It is in these two amendments that individual rights and federalism are expressly linked. The Ninth Amendment states that "[t]he enumeration in the Constitution of certain rights shall not be construed to deny or disparage others retained by the people." Thus, the Ninth Amendment is, at a minimum, a rule of construction forbidding the expansion of federal power by negative implication,[155] and, as I have argued, an explicit recognition of other popular rights, such as the right to alter and abolish government, that impose further restraints on the operation of federal power.[156] The Tenth Amendment states that "[t]he powers not delegated to the United States by the Constitution, nor prohibited by it to the States, are reserved to the States respectively, or to the people." The federalism aspects of this amendment, the last of the Bill of Rights, could not be clearer. It declares expressly what the Federalists had argued was already implicit in the structure of the Constitution: that the federal government would be one of delegated powers, and as such it could not act beyond those limitations.[157]

Furthermore, the Bill of Rights, to the extent that it protects rights rather than restricts powers, recognizes rights that belong to those in the majority, rather than the minority, to the states, rather than to individuals. Thus, the First Amendment does not give the individual a right to associate, but instead de-

---

[154]Declaratory Ninth (cited in note 26).

[155]Original Ninth (cited in note 73).

[156]Declaratory Ninth, at 972–86 (cited in note 26).

[157]United States Term Limits, Inc. v. Thornton, 514 U.S. 779, 846–50 (1995) (Thomas dissenting).

clares that Congress cannot abridge the right of "the people" to assemble or to petition the government. The Bill of Rights' use of "the people," rather than the individual, emphasizes that the rights protected are those of the majority—the people's right to keep and bear arms, for example—against an oppressive central government.[158] It will be recalled that this was precisely the same concern the Federalists sought to address with their arguments concerning the political safeguards of federalism and, ultimately, judicial review. Further, the Constitution recognizes intermediate institutions whose roles are to be preserved: established state churches, state militias, and the jury. All of these entities imposed successive checks on the powers and reach of the federal government, and both the church and the militia were critical to state authority.[159] In fact, in including these provisions in the Bill of Rights, the Framers quite consciously understood them to defend principles of federalism, as much as individual rights.

Although there are no records of the state ratifications of the Bill of Rights, the records we have of its drafting indicate that its purpose was to use judicial review to check Congress. In this sense, the Bill of Rights was significant because it gave individual rights the *same protections* that the Constitution already had given to the states. In initially debating the need for amendments, James Madison argued that "I do conceive that the constitution may be amended; that is to say, if all power is subject to abuse, that it is possible the abuse of the powers of the General Government may be guarded against in a more secure manner than is now done."[160] Further, in discussing the enforceability of the Bill of Rights, Madison explicitly declared that both the federal courts and the states would ensure that the federal government would not encroach on the rights of the people:

> If [these amendments] are incorporated into the constitution, independent tribunals of justice will consider themselves in a peculiar manner the guardians of those rights; they will be an impenetrable bulwark against every assumption of power in the legislative or executive; they will be naturally led to resist every encroachment upon rights expressly stipulated for in the constitution by the declaration of rights. Besides, this security, there is a great probability that such a declaration in the federal system would be enforced; because the State Legislatures will jealously and closely watch the operations of this Government, and be able to resist with more effect every assumption of power, than any other

---

[158]When state constitutions and declarations of rights used the terms the "rights" of "the people," they referred specifically to popular sovereignty rights needed to control and, if necessary, abolish the government. Declaratory Ninth, at 974 (cited in note 26).

[159]Bill of Rights, at 1157–74 (cited in note 97).

[160]James Madison, House of Representatives, June 8, 1789, in 2 Bernard Schwartz, The Bill of Rights: A Documentary History 1025 (Chelsea House Publishers, 1971).

power on earth can do; and the greatest opponents to a Federal Government admit the State Legislatures to be sure guardians of the people's liberty.[161]

If the Bill of Rights were solely about individual rights, there would be little need for the state legislatures to join the federal courts in enforcement. But reliance on the states makes perfect sense when it is "assumption[s] of power" that must be guarded against. When that is the task, the Framers saw no inconsistency, as we saw earlier, in having both the federal courts and the States—either independently or through the federal government itself—involved in opposing unconstitutional exercises of power.

Another way to examine this point is to ask whether the Framers believed that the federal courts would be the primary enforcers of individual rights. Certainly, as the dissenters in *Garcia* noted, the political safeguards theory can apply to individual rights as easily as it does to federalism. Because individuals are adequately represented in the federal government—they directly elect members of the House and Senate, and indirectly choose the president—does not the political safeguards theory demand that individuals rely upon the political process to safeguard their rights? As Justice Powell put it, "[o]ne can hardly imagine this Court saying that because Congress is composed of individuals, individual rights guaranteed by the Bill of Rights are amply protected by the political process."[162] During the ratification debates, the Framers rarely mentioned that the federal courts would become the guardians of individual liberties. In fact, they discussed judicial review of federalism more often than they did judicial review of individual rights. With passage of the Bill of Rights, the Framers raised individual rights to the same level as federalism in terms of their importance, and, ultimately, their protection by the courts.

One final way to examine the link between state sovereignty and individual rights is to recall the Framers' understanding of the role of the former in protecting the latter. As we saw earlier, the revolutionaries had come to view the state legislatures as the primary guardians of the people's rights and liberties against the Crown and Parliament. This understanding continued under the Articles of Confederation and the new Constitution. The Framers agreed that state legislatures would play two important roles in regard to rights. First, the states would continue to bear the primary responsibility for defining and enforcing individual rights. While the national government's powers "will be exercised principally on external objects, as war, peace, negotiation, and foreign commerce," Madison wrote in *Federalist No. 45,* "the powers reserved to the several States will extend to all the objects, which, in the ordinary course of affairs, concern the lives,

---

[161]Id. at 1031–32.

[162]Garcia v. San Antonio Metro. Transit Authority, 469 U.S. 528, 565 n.8 (1985) (Powell dissenting).

liberties and properties of the people."[163] This was the creative role that Justice Brennan believed states should adopt in defining individual rights more broadly than the federal government.[164]

In addition to creating individual rights, states also were to serve as the primary defenders of those rights against a national government that sought to exceed the boundaries of its powers. Even if parties within the national legislature failed to restrain Congress, Hamilton wrote in *Federalist No. 26*, "the state Legislature, who will always be not only vigilant but suspicious and jealous guardians of the rights of the citizens, against incroachments from the Federal government, will constantly have their attention awake to the conduct of the national rulers and will be ready enough, if any thing improper appears, to sound the alarm to the people and not only to be the VOICE but if necessary the ARM of their discontent."[165] In addition to blocking unwarranted federal action through their participation in the selection of the national government, state legislatures are to protect the people's rights by organizing outside opposition to the national government.[166] States performed this function not only by acting as something of a trip wire to detect illegal federal action, but also by acting as loci and organizers of resistance. As Hamilton put it, states "can at once adopt a regular plan of opposition, in which they can combine all the resources of the community. They can readily communicate with each other in the different States; and unite their common forces for the protection of their common liberty."[167] Ultimately, this resistance could take a military form, as Madison argued: "[T]he existence of subordinate governments to which the people are attached and by which the militia officers are appointed, forms a barrier against the enterprises of ambition, more insurmountable than any which a simple government of any form can admit of."[168]

In this dual way, the continued existence of states as quasi-independent sovereigns is crucial to the preservation of individual liberty. Removing one of the primary institutional checks on the power of Congress—judicial review—in order to better protect individual rights would have made little sense to the Framers. They would have seen the disintegration of state sovereignty as a potential threat to individual rights, first because it would prevent innovation in their creation, and second because it would eliminate a check on the national government's ability to invade those rights. Judicial review, therefore, had two

---

[163]Federalist 45 (Madison), at 313 (cited in note 47).

[164]William J. Brennan, State Constitutions and the Protection of Individual Rights, 90 Harv. L. Rev. 489 (1977).

[165]Federalist 26 (Hamilton), at 169 (cited in note 47).

[166]Larry Kramer, Understanding Federalism, 47 Vand. L. Rev. 1485 (1994) ("Understanding Federalism").

[167]Federalist 28 (Hamilton), at 180 (cited in note 47).

[168]Federalist 46 (Madison), at 321–22.

salutary effects in regard to individual rights: it not only protects those rights, it also protects other institutions that are charged with guarding rights.

This essay also shows that the Framers' understanding of state sovereignty and judicial review anticipated some of the concerns raised in recent scholarship concerning the legislative process. Public choice scholars argue that the legislative process should be considered to be a market, in which the product—legislation—is determined by the efforts of organized groups to achieve their special interests.[169] Under this theory, congressmen further their interests by seeking to maximize their chances for re-election. Congressmen will provide legislation to those groups that can provide the most campaign donations and political support—in other words, legislation goes to the highest bidder. Such legislation often will not further the public good, because private groups will be likely to seek laws that generate narrow benefits for their members, at the expense of costs that are imposed on the diffuse, unorganized general public. Reaction to this thesis has been two-fold. There are those who argue that this pluralism ought to be accepted, and that courts must enforce statutes in order to give effect to the legislative bargains between interest groups.[170] In other words, groups should get what they pay for. Others believe that interest group theory justifies more active judicial review that prevents private groups from using the legislative process in ways that do not further the public good.[171]

The Framers clearly anticipated the possibility that organized factions would seek to use the legislative process to the detriment of the public good. Abuse of the legislative process, after all, is not a phenomenon of the twentieth century. James Madison's solution, set out in *Federalist No. 10,* was to create a large republic, in which "clashing interests" would cancel each other out due to the large number of interests and the great expanses of distance and time. Because Madison believed that "the most common and durable source of factions, has been the various and unequal distribution of property,"[172] his answer to the

---

[169]Daniel A. Farber & Philip P. Frickey, Law and Public Choice: A Critical Introduction 12–17 (University of Chicago Press, 1991). The summary of the public choice approach here is necessarily brief; for a comprehensive description of interest group theory and its faults, see generally Einer R. Elhauge, Does Interest Group Theory Justify More Intrusive Judicial Review?, 101 Yale L. J. 31 (1991).

[170]See, for example, William Landes & Richard Posner, The Independent Judiciary in an Interest-Group Perspective, 18 J. L. & Econ. 875 (1975).

[171]William N. Eskridge, Politics Without Romance: Implications of Public Choice Theory for Statutory Interpretation, 74 Va. L. Rev. 275 (1988); Cass R. Sunstein, Interest Groups in American Public Law, 38 Stan. L. Rev. 29 (1985); Cass R. Sunstein, Naked Preferences and the Constitution, 84 Colum. L. Rev. 1689 (1984); Jerry L. Mashaw, Constitutional Deregulation: Notes Toward a Public, Public Law, 54 Tul. L. Rev. 849 (1980); Martin Shapiro, Freedom of Speech: The Supreme Court and Judicial Review 17–25, 31–40 (Prentice-Hall, 1966).

[172]Federalist 10 (Madison), at 59 (cited in note 47).

problem of interest group legislation seems limited to laws involving economic interests. In a sense, then, the Framers believed that the political safeguards would work, but only when it came to economic legislation.

But what the Framers emphasized during their debate over federalism appears to be unnoticed by public choice scholars. The Framers would have agreed with modern thinking concerning the potential for a gap between the duty of representation and the incentives created by personal interests; in other words, they realized that the interests of legislators would not necessarily match the interests of their constituents. Under the founding generation's conception, however, legislators' interests would not naturally fall into line with those of powerful factions either. Instead, the greater fear was that the people's representatives would pursue their own *institutional* interests, and that these interests would lead them to expand national power despite the Constitution's written enumerations. As we saw earlier, the statement of the minority at the Pennsylvania ratifying convention is illustrative: "The permanency of the appointments of senators and representatives, and the controul the congress have over their election, will place them independent of the sentiments and resentment of the people, and the administration having a greater interest in the government than in the community, there will be no consideration to restrain them from oppression and tyranny."[173] While an interest group might seek to capture rents by paying congressmen to infringe on federalism and state sovereignty, federal legislators also might seek to expand their power for power's sake, without benefiting an interest group.

As members of the federal government, legislators would possess the driving interest to expand the power of the federal government, even perhaps if it did not benefit them in terms of political support. The founding generation feared that Congress would seek to grab more power from the states in order to enhance their own institutional power, prestige, and glory. Some public choice theorists would express this as the idea that federal legislators always would seek to expand national powers, because a broader national jurisdiction would allow them to regulate more issues, which would then allow them to attract more political support from more coalitions interested in those issues.[174] Others might argue, however, that under certain conditions the self-interested federal legislator would defer to state regulations, specifically when a group has made an investment in certain state laws, or when customized state law has been tailored to the needs of local interest groups, or when the federal government seeks to avoid

---

[173]Dissent of the Minority of the Pennsylvania Convention, 1 Debate, at 548 (cited in note 74); see also Brutus IV, New York Journal, Nov. 29, 1787, id. at 426; Letter Federal Farmer II, id. at 254–59.

[174]Jonathan R. Macey, Federal Deference to Local Regulators and the Economic Theory of Regulation: Toward a Public-Choice Explanation of Federalism, 76 Va. L. Rev. 265, 269–74 (1990) ("Federal Deference").

politically risky issues.[175] In the Framers' eyes, however, the problem extended beyond preventing the legislature from providing special benefits to organized groups. The Framers chose to extend judicial review to federalism questions precisely because they did not trust legislators to pursue the interests of their constituents above their own institutional interests. The Framers feared that congressmen would seek power solely for their love of power.

Legislators were not the only threat to a limited Constitution; some Framers even feared that the states and their people could not be trusted to protect federalism. Congressmen might represent popular interests back home, but those popular interests might not always represent the states *qua* states. Alexander Hamilton made this point during the ratification debates in New York. During the ratifying convention, Anti-Federalist Melancton Smith proposed an amendment that in part would have allowed the state legislatures to recall their senators. In defending the amendment, Smith argued "that as the senators are the representatives of the state legislatures, it is reasonable and proper that they should be under their controul."[176] Hamilton successfully defeated the amendment by arguing that, while senators did represent the states in the federal government, senators were there to defend the *rights* of the state first, and its *interests* second. Said Hamilton:

> The [constitutional convention] certainly perceive[d] the distinction between the rights of a state and its interests. The rights of a state are defined by the constitution, and cannot be invaded without a violation of it; but the interests of a state have no connection with the constitution, and may be in a thousand instances constitutionally sacrificed.[177]

As Hamilton explained, it was precisely because the short-term interests of a state and its people might seek to overcome the longer-term good of maintaining the boundaries on federal power that, in part, the Constitution gave senators six-year terms: "To prevent this, it is necessary that the senate should be so formed, as in some measure to check the state government, and preclude the communication of the false impressions which they receive from the people."[178] Continuing Hamilton's point, we cannot be sure that the Senate or the Congress are going to be full-time guardians of federalism either, hence the need for a judicial role in policing the balance between federal and state powers.

---

[175]Id. at 274–290.

[176]Melancton Smith, New York Ratifying Convention, June 25, 1788, in 2 Debate, at 805 (cited in note 74).

[177]Alexander Hamilton, New York Ratifying Convention, June 25, 1788, in id. at 813.

[178]Id. at 811.

A state's popular interests and a state's institutional rights became more detached at the time of the ratification of the Seventeenth Amendment, which removed state legislatures from the process of selecting senators. State legislatures, as opposed to the people of a state, were perhaps the only institutions that had a consistent, long-term interest in protecting state sovereignty. It seems telling that since the passage of the Seventeenth Amendment, state governmental entities, such as legislators, attorney generals, and governors, have had to organize into national interest groups to make their interests known in the political process. Other institutions, such as political parties, that allow states to influence the political process have also grown in strength.[179] The very presence of these groups and outside mechanisms indicate that the political safeguards have failed. States should not have to organize into *national* lobbying groups if, as the political safeguards theory holds, they could pursue their interests directly through their elected representatives in Congress. One could catalogue other developments, such as the nationalizing effect of changes in technology, economics, and culture, that also have diminished the respect for local concerns in the halls of Washington.[180]

The disparity between a state's popular interests and its institutional rights may explain why the federal government has been able to expand its powers so dramatically in the last 60 years. To be sure, the Supreme Court opened the door by granting Congress substantial deference in the exercise of its Commerce Clause powers, but the Court did not force Congress to run through with the speed it has. The political safeguards theory predicts that Congress will restrain itself, because the states will prevent their senators and representatives from invading the sovereignty of the states. Today's great mass of federal regulation, however, makes more sense when we consider the Framers' insight that the momentary interests of a state and the institutional or constitutional interests of a state at times may conflict.

Another way to view this point is to view the relationship among the states as a competitive one, in which each state seeks to maximize the welfare of its inhabitants. A significant determinant of state welfare today is the great pool of federal funds available through a variety of national programs. Sometimes federal funds will not be available without a corresponding loss of state sovereignty. For example, in order to receive funds a state often must accept federal conditions on how the money is spent, such as with highway construction or welfare programs, or a state must transfer partial decision-making authority to federal regulators.[181] If the 50 states are in competition for these funds, then the states that are most willing to surrender some of their autonomy will be the ones that acquire the most federal money. Therefore, those states that are most willing

---

[179]See generally Understanding Federalism (cited in note 166).

[180]Id. at 1503–14.

[181]See, for example, South Dakota v. Dole, 483 U.S. 203 (1987).

to surrender some aspects of their sovereignty will be the states that maximize the welfare of their inhabitants. To borrow from a concept in corporate law, there will be a "race to the bottom" in order to attract federal funds.[182] But unlike the race to the bottom theory, this destructive competition arises not from state efforts to attract private commercial activity, whether it be business incorporations or industrial plants, but from state efforts to attract federal largess and support.

Judicial review provides an important check on the temptation to surrender state sovereignty voluntarily. To some extent, judicial review may guard against the threat of legislative instability predicted by Arrow's Theorem or the possibility of unconstitutional actions taken in the states in the heat of emotion.[183] Just as importantly, however, judicial review prevents states that are fully informed from sacrificing their sovereignty for some greater financial gain. Put in public choice terms, federalism and the maintenance of a federal government of limited, enumerated powers may be a positive externality that no individual state acting individually or collectively fully internalizes. In this sense, the Framers viewed federalism as a normative good that ought to be promoted despite any state's momentary interest in reducing its rights.

In this regard, the Framers' decision to use judicial review to enforce federalism provides new insights for the ongoing discussion concerning the value of federalism. In recent years, there has been renewed interest in legal scholarship concerning the costs and benefits of federalism. Supporters of a rejuvenated respect for state sovereignty argue that states can bring important advantages to the execution of good public policy. First, federalism is a decentralized decision-making system that is more responsive to local interests and preferences. States can tailor programs to local conditions and needs and can act as innovators in creating new programs.[184] Economists have found that under certain conditions, smaller governments can provide a more efficient allocation of resources that

---

[182]Whether such a race to bottom exists in corporate law, or other areas of law, due to the competition among states, is open to debate. See, for example, Judge Ralph Winter, State Law, Shareholder Protection and the Theory of the Corporation, 6 J. Legal Stud. 251 (1977); Richard L. Revesz, Rehabilitating Interstate Competition: Rethinking the "Race to the Bottom" Rationale for Federal Environmental Regulation, 67 N.Y.U. L. Rev. 1210 (1992).

[183]James Madison wrote in Federalist 62 concerning the "propensity of all single and numerous assemblies to yield to the impulse of sudden and violent passions" and the problem of "mutability in the public councils." Federalist 62 (Madison), at 418–19 (cited in note 47).

[184]Michael W. McConnell, Federalism: Evaluating the Founders' Design, 54 U. Chi. L. Rev. 1484, 1493–1500 (1987); Deborah Jones Merritt, The Guarantee Clause and State Autonomy: Federalism for a Third Century, 88 Colum. L. Rev. 1, 8–10 (1988). For a useful exposition of the profederalism arguments, see David L Shapiro, Federalism: A Dialogue 58–106 (Northwestern University Press, 1995).

maximizes the well-being of their citizens.[185] State governments compete for households and businesses by enacting efficient policies; in the long-run this competition produces overall efficiency.[186] Indeed, for much of our nation's history, the states did play the primary role in developing economic programs designed to enhance their citizens' welfare.[187] Recent writing has also stressed that a decentralized state system enhances democracy, either by increasing political participation at the state and local level or by reducing the opportunities of powerful interest groups to receive rent-seeking legislation at the national level, thereby increasing the costs of passing such legislation.[188]

As noted earlier, however, the Framers believed that the chief role states would play in their relationship with the federal government would be the protection of the people's liberty. Although limiting the power of the federal government might produce inefficiencies, the Framers believed that this cost was necessary in order to guard against potential tyranny by a federal government filled with self-interested, ambitious politicians. In this sense, the Framers' discussions indicated their belief that federalism brought advantages by diffusing power. To be sure, creating different power centers and decentralizing decision-making authority can be different things. Indeed, Malcolm Feeley and Ed Rubin have argued that many of the benefits observers commonly associate with federalism are those that arise from the decentralization of power, and that states are only convenient administrative divisions.[189] No doubt they are correct on this point, but they overlook the crucial benefit that states bring because of their independent sovereignty. As separate political units, states can oppose the exercise of power by the national government, even if the national government and the

---

[185]Charles Tiebout, A Pure Theory of Local Expenditures, 64 J. Pol. Econ. 416 (1956). I have relied upon the works of my colleague, Daniel Rubinfeld, to guide the way through the economics literature on federalism. See Robert P. Inman & Daniel L. Rubinfeld, Making Sense of the Antitrust State Action Doctrine: Balancing Political Participation and Economic Efficiency in Regulatory Federalism, 75 Tex. L. Rev. 1203 (1997) ("Making Sense"); Daniel L. Rubinfeld, The Economics of the Local Public Sector, in 2 Alan Auerbach and Martin Feldstein, Handbook of Public Economics (North-Holland, 1987).

[186]Of course, for this to be true, a number of conditions must exist: (i) publicly provided goods and services are provided at minimum average cost; (ii) a perfectly elastic supply of jurisdictions exists; (iii) households and business have full information about each jurisdiction's policies; (iv) mobility is costless; (v) no interjurisdictional externalities or spillovers exist. Making Sense, at 17 (cited in note 185).

[187]See, for example, Harry N. Scheiber, Federalism and the American Economic Order, 1789–1910, 10 L. & Soc'y Rev. 57 (Fall 1975); Harry N. Scheiber, Property Law, Expropriation, and Resource Allocation by Government, 1789–1910, in Constitutional Order, at 132 (cited in note 40).

[188]Federal Deference (cited in note 174).

[189]Federalism Notes (cited in note 12).

people believe that centralization of power at that moment is good public policy. By allowing, or even encouraging, the federal and the state governments to check each other, the Framers' Constitution seeks to create an area of liberty that cannot be regulated by either government. Dividing political power between the two levels of government appears even more effective in light of the presence of a separation of powers in both governments. As James Madison wrote in *Federalist No. 51:* "In the compound republic of America, the power surrendered by the people, is first divided between two distinct governments," federal and state, "and then the portion allotted to each, subdivided among distinct and separate departments," in other words, the legislative, executive, and judicial branches.[190] "Hence a double security arises to the rights of the people. The different governments will controul each other; at the same time that each will be controuled by itself."[191]

As I argued earlier, the Framers did envision that individual liberties would receive protection through the competition between federal and state governments to provide rights to their citizens. But this was not the only way, in the Framers' minds, that federalism would become the shield of liberty. Freedom also would arise from the inefficiencies that the Framers built into the federal system itself. The nation's governments simply would not be able to regulate all the issues of life because, even if they could overcome the internal checks created by their separation of powers, their external powers would come into conflict and cancel each other out. In a sense, this conclusion is somewhat at odds with the public choice approach to federalism sketched above, because in this conception federalism does not exist purely to advance efficiency. Instead, in some cases federalism can prevent the national government from enacting policies that produce national benefits that outweigh the costs.

The Framers believed this deliberate inefficiency to be necessary in order to protect liberty. However, an absence of judicial review over federalism questions would abort the Framers' design. The Framers created judicial review in order to prevent any of the branches or levels of government from exceeding the written limitations on their powers. The federal courts would prevent the states from frustrating the legitimate exercise of national power, and, on the flip side of the coin, they would block the national government from infringing the independent sovereignty of the states. From this clashing of institutional interests, the Framers hoped that liberty would result. Ironically, by creating a theory designed to protect individual rights at the expense of federalism, the advocates of the political safeguards of federalism may have undermined the Framers' most effective mechanism for guarding individual freedom.

---

[190]Federalist 51 (Madison), at 351 (cited in note 47).
[191]Id.

CHAPTER FIVE

# Revolution or Retreat?

## Mark R. Killenbeck

One of the most interesting aspects of the current federalism debate is that we know so much and yet so little about the current Court's views in these matters. Arguably, most of the meaningful judicial handwriting is on the wall for both the friends and foes of the current take on federal-state relations and the Tenth Amendment. "Federalism," Chief Judge J. Harvey Wilkinson recently observed, is "the promise of the future."[1] By this he meant that it now seems both necessary and appropriate to seek solutions to pressing problems at the local level, and to adjudicate disputes about the proper locus of authority in a manner that accords appropriate primacy to the states. The Supreme Court has, quite simply, become an ally of the states rather than their adversary. A controlling balance in favor of the states has been struck, with the current majority unlikely to retreat from the various lines it has drawn and the dissenting justices similarly unwilling to reexamine their own take on these matters.

There is then every reason to believe that, taken together, the Court's recent federalism opinions comprise perhaps the single most important body of decisions since the aptly described Constitutional Revolution of 1937. The simple fact that the Court has for the first time in almost 70 years found acts of Con-

---

[1] J. Harvey Wilkinson III, Federalism for the Future, 74 S. Cal. L. Rev. 523, 524 (2001) ("Future").

gress beyond its Commerce Clause authority is proof positive that something profound is happening. And, especially for the authors who have contributed to this collection, there are ample grounds—as in the cases of Professors Leuchtenburg and Rakove—to harbor profound reservations about the directions in which the majority is taking us and—as does Professor Yoo—to express satisfaction that these are matters for the Court itself, rather than simply for the political process.

But these realities, important as they may be, do not necessarily mean that the doctrines the Court is articulating will ultimately produce fundamental or lasting transformations in the woof and warp of federal-state relations. As important as they are, it is entirely possible that many of the decisions issued to date simply articulate a series of adjustments that, when all is said and done, leave largely intact prior assumptions about the proper scope of federal power and the residual sovereignty of the states. And while the developments to date are worthy of our attention, it also eminently appropriate to ask what the future might hold.

Can we, for example, equate the demise of the Gun Free Schools Zone Act in *United States v. Lopez* with the invalidation of the Child Labor Act in *Hammer v. Dagenhart? Hammer* was, after all, part and parcel of a series of opinions in which the Court left most such matters beyond the ambit of both federal and state regulation. The same, however, cannot be said of *Lopez,* which proceeds on the assumption that the reality of state authority to deal with such matters is the very reason the Court should be unwilling to recognize parallel or competing authority at the federal level. Indeed, it is worth recalling that Alfonso Lopez was originally arrested and charged by state authorities for violations of state law,[2] and that it was only after the Bureau of Alcohol, Tobacco and Firearms and a federal grand jury intervened that state charges were dropped and the case became a federal matter.[3] I have been unable to find anything in the record that indicates how the incident came to federal attention or why the federal government elected to prosecute a matter already properly before state authorities. The fact that the state had both detected the conduct and initiated legal action does, however, raise questions about whether the federal measure, which may well have been proper under previous Commerce Clause doctrines, was in fact necessary.

---

[2]See United States v. Lopez, 514 U.S. 550, 551 (1995) (Lopez "was arrested and charged under Texas law with firearm possession on school premises"). What the Court does not note is that Texas apparently took these matters quite seriously, as the state offense charged was a third-degree felony. See Respondent's Brief at 2, United States v. Lopez, No. 63–1260.

[3]See *Lopez,* 514 U.S. at 551 ("[t]he next day, the state charges were dismissed after federal agents charged [Lopez] with violating the Gun Free School Zones Act of 1990.").

In a similar vein, does the loss of the civil remedies provision of the Violence Against Women Act in *United States v. Morrison* stand in *pare materia* with the denial of a private cause of action for redemption of state bonds in *Hans v. Lousiiana?* The two cases are hardly comparable, in that one involves a simple economic matter and the other a brutal assault. But an argument can be made that *Hans* effectively extinguished all rights and remedies for the aggrieved debtor. The same cannot, however, be said of *Morrison* or, for that matter, *Alden v. Maine* or *Board of Trustees of the University of Alabama v. Garrett,* which left intact the important elements of the underlying statutory scheme,[4] recognized the power of the federal government to enforce those statutory proscriptions,[5] and reaffirmed the right of the individual to pursue injunctive relief against recalcitrant states.[6]

This does not mean that *Lopez, Morrison, Alden,* and *Garrett* are not significant in and of themselves, or that individuals alarmed by the restrictions on federal power articulated in these decisions have no cause for alarm. The record of the states in many of these matters is uneven, and if history demonstrates anything it is that recourse to the states often leaves certain disfavored groups at the mercy of a political process that is at best inhospitable to their claims.[7] Indeed, it was precisely this reality that led to the passage of the Violence Against

---

[4]See United States v. Morrison, 120 S. Ct. 1740, 1752 n. 5 (2000) (noting that Violence Against Women Act includes "a federal remedy for [interstate] gender motivated crime" that has been "uniformly upheld . . . as an appropriate exercise of Congress's Commerce Clause authority"); Alden v. Maine, 527 U.S. 706, 759 (1999) ("The State of Maine has not questioned Congress's power to prescribe substantive rules of federal law to which it must comply.").

[5]See *Alden,* 527 U.S. at 759–60 (noting that "history, precedent, and the structure of the Constitution make clear that, under the plan of the Convention, the States have consented to suits" by the United States to enforce the Fair Labor Standards Act).

[6]See Board of Trustees of the University of Alabama v. Garrett, 121 S. Ct. 955, 968 n. 9 (2001) ("Title I of the ADA still prescribes standards applicable to the States. These standards can be enforced by the United States in actions for money damages, as well as by private individuals in actions for injunctive relief under Ex parte Young, 209 U.S. 123 (1908).").

[7]Interestingly, Judge Wilkinson maintains that important aspects of this heritage have changed and that "for the first time there is reason to believe that ceding authority to state and local governments may actually advance race relations" given that "America will have not racial or ethnic majority by the year 2050." Future, at 526–27 (cited in note 1).

Women Act,[8] and it is noteworthy that, for whatever reasons, 36 states filed *amicus* briefs in support of the private civil remedy and only one opposed it.[9]

It is then simply much too early to in the game to maintain that we can offer definitive answers to many of the questions that these decisions raise. Professors Leuchtenburg and Rakove are, given their particular views on these matters, justifiably apprehensive about what the future holds, as am I. There is, however, a world of difference between the record fashioned by the pre-1937 Court and that of the Rehnquist Court to date, which has sustained at least as many measures as it has overturned. Indeed, the fact that the Court has hardly hewn a consistent line in these matters is especially noteworthy. In this regard, those enraged by the result in *Morrison* might find at least some comfort in *Jones v. United States,* decided just one week later, in which reaffirmed the "Congress' [ability] to invoke its full authority under the Commerce Clause" to regulate matters "affecting commerce."[10] And one arguably need look no farther than *Bush v. Gore* to find evidence that the very same five justices that have insisted on state primacy in certain matters are quite willing, for arguably legitimate reasons, to accord the states secondary status in appropriate instances.[11] The *per curiam* opinion, for example, while describing "the State legislature's power to select the manner for appointing electors" as "plenary,"[12] makes it clear that this authority must yield to that of the Supreme Court and the federal Constitution. And Chief Justice Rehnquist, in his concurring opinion, maintained that while "[i]n most cases, comity and respect for federalism compel us to defer to the decisions of state courts on issues of state law," there are "exceptional cases" in which such cannot be the case.[13]

A similar solicitude for matters federal was apparent in the Court's current Term in *Cook v. Gralike,*[14] in which the Court invalidated a voter-initiated amendment to the Missouri Constitution that, among other things, imposed certain sanctions on candidates for Congress unwilling to support a particular approach designed to impose term limits on United States senators and representatives. Writing for the Court, Justice Stevens emphasized that the Missouri measure was not a mechanism designed in the light of what the Court has de-

---

[8]See *Morrison,* 120 S. Ct. at 1773 (Souter dissenting) ("It was against this record of failure at the state level that the Act was passed to provide the choice of a federal forum in place of state-court systems found inadequate to stop gender-based violence.").

[9]Id.

[10]120 S. Ct. 1904, 1909 (2000).

[11]I use the qualifier "arguably" here deliberately, recognizing (but expressing no opinion regarding) the argument that the majority decision was an exercise in naked partisan politics.

[12]Bush v. Gore, 121 S. Ct. 525, 529 (2000).

[13]Id. at 534 (Rehnquist concurring).

[14]121 S. Ct. 1029 (2001).

scribed as a state's "'broad power' to prescribe the procedural mechanisms for holding congressional elections."[15]  Rather, "Article VII is plainly designed to favor candidates who are willing to support the particular form of a term limits amendment set forth in its text and to disfavor those who either oppose term limits entirely or would prefer a different proposal."[16]  That, the Court held, exceeded the powers delegated for, as Justice Kennedy emphasized in his concurring opinion, "[a] State is not permitted to interpose itself between the people and their National Government as it seeks to do here."[17]

The unevenness of the Court's work product should not, however, be allowed to obscure the fact that taken on their own terms the decisions issued to date are extremely important, with those who ignore the warning signs they have placed in the path of federal power doing so at their peril.  This seems especially clear given that a continuing and potentially far more expansive skepticism about the nature and scope of the commerce power is evident in the Court's most recent pronouncement on these matters, *Solid Waste Agency of Northern Cook County v. United States Corps of Engineers.*[18]  In that decision, the Court held that a Corps definition of the term "navigable waters" that would have extended Corps supervision to certain wetlands frequented by migratory birds exceeded the authority delegated by Congress.  The opinion, written by the chief justice and joined by his usual federalism allies, arguably did little more than parse the terms of the statute and give effect to congressional intent.[19]  A close reading of the majority opinion, however, reveals substantial reservations about the authority of Congress to "impinge" the "States' traditional and primary

---

[15]Id. at 1038 (quoting Tashjian v. Republican Party of Connecticut, 479 U.S. 208, 217 (1986)).

[16]Id.

[17]Id. at 1040 (Kennedy concurring).  The chief justice, in an opinion joined by Justice O'Connor, agreed that the measure was invalid, but disagreed on the grounds, arguing that the provision violated the First Amendment.  Only Justice Thomas indicated anything that approached a willingness to sustain state authority in this instance, repeating his argument from his dissent in the *Term Limits* decision that "because they possess 'reserved' powers, 'the people of the States need not point to any affirmative grant of power in the Constitution in order to prescribe qualifications for their representatives in Congress, or to authorize their elected representatives to do so.'" Id. at 1041–42 (quoting United States Term Limits, Inc. v. Thornton, 514 U.S. 779, 846 (1995) (Thomas dissenting)) (Thomas concurring).  Since "the parties conceded the validity of th[e] premise" with which he disagreed, however, Justice Thomas concurred in the holding of the Court. Id. at 1042.

[18]121 S. Ct. 675 (2001).

[19]See id. at 682–83 (maintaining that the majority has simply parsed the statute in the light of a congressional refusal "to [clearly] readjust the federal-state balance").

power over land and water use."[20]  And one need only look at the series of lower court opinions embracing the logic of *Lopez* and *Morrison,*[21] and the roster of federal measures challenged but not yet placed in peril, to understand the potential significance of both the Court's recent decisions and the willingness of litigants to now challenge measures that might once have been deemed sacrosanct.[22]

Assuming, however, that the die is cast—and this seems an especially appropriate assumption given the ascendency of George W. Bush to the presidency—there are additional questions as yet unanswered and decisions not yet issued that are prefigured in and will likely expand upon those the Court has given us to date.  In *Alexander v. Sandoval,*[23] for example, one important source of current federal authority over the states, the Spending Clause, initially seemed to be at issue in a decision that refused to recognize an implied cause of action for injunctive relief against a recipient of federal financial assistance. The core issue, whether the state of Alabama may, pursuant to an amendment to its constitution that makes English the official state language, require that its driver's license examination process be administered in English only, was itself timely and interesting.  The more intriguing question is, however, what if anything the current Court will eventually make of the spending power, a means of securing state compliance with federal directives that, ironically, finds its current expansive scope in yet another Rehnquist opinion, *South Dakota v. Dole.*[24] The Court did not reach that question in *Alexander,* but future challenges to that power will most certainly soon be at its door.

Other cases have been or will be accepted for review, and will come before the Court in its October 2001 term.[25]  The truly interesting question is then how

---

[20]Id. at 684.  Justice Stevens dissented, in an opinion joined by his usual allies in these matters, Justices Souter, Ginsburg, and Breyer.

[21]For two representative examples, see United States v. Faasse, 227 F.3d 660, vacated and en banc review granted, 234 F.3d 312 (6th Cir. 2000) (holding that Congress may not criminalize, via the Child Support Recovery Act of 1992, the failure to pay child support when the state itself has refused to do so); United States v. King, 2001 WL 111278 (S.D.N.Y., Feb. 13, 2001) (same).

[22]See, for example, Gerling Global Reinsurance Corp. v. Low, 240 F.3d 739 (9th Cir. 2001) (reversing a district court decision that the California Holocaust Victim Insurance Relief Act violated the Commerce Clause).

[23]121 S. Ct. 1511 (2001).  The lower court opinion is Sandoval v. Hagan, 197 F.3d 484 (11th Cir. 1999).

[24]483 U.S. 203 (1987).

[25]The Court has, for example, signaled its intention to pursue further its reshaping of the sovereign immunity doctrines by granting review in a case that may signal troubles ahead for one of the significant remnants of the prior regime, *Ex parte Young.* See *Mathias v. WorldCom Technologies, Inc.,* cert. granted, 121 S. Ct. 1224 (2001) (directing the parties to brief and argue whether an action seeking prospective relief under the Tele-

far the current majority is willing to go, and what lies ahead in the light of potential Bush appointments to the Court.[26] For example, as much as one might applaud or disagree with the results reached in *Lopez* and *Morrison,* it is difficult to disagree with the majority's assumption that carrying a gun in a school zone or raping a woman is not in and of itself commercial activity. The real question is the extent to which one believes that discrete local activities, regardless of their nature, in certain ways affect commerce, and as such fall within the ambit of the aggregation doctrine embraced by the Court in *Wickard v. Fillburn* and its successors. To date, only Justice Thomas has made continuously and unmistakably clear his desire to discard a doctrine he has characterized as "rootless and malleable."[27] But, as I have indicated, there is language in the majority opinion in *Solid Waste Agency* that, if not itself signaling agreement with the full scope of the Thomas position, most certainly provides reason to believe that further restrictions on the commerce power are in the offing.

The Court has also so far refused to question perhaps the most important aspect of current doctrines, the authority of Congress to regulate the states themselves under the assumption that state activities either constitute or substantially affect commerce. As I noted in my introduction to this volume,[28] the current doctrines governing the exercise of that power developed in a line of cases that culminated in the Court's acceptance of a political process approach to such matters in *Garcia v. San Antonio Metropolitan Transit Authority.*[29] That authority was secured, however, by a tenuous five-to-four majority that overruled a

---

communications Act of 1996 may be maintained pursuant to the *Ex parte Young* doctrine). The lower court opinion is Illinois Bell Telephone Co. v. WorldCom Technologies, 179 F.3d 566 (7th Cir. 2000). The grant of review is interesting if for no other reason than Justice O'Connor has recused herself, raising the specter of a potentially evenly divided Court if prior voting alignments persist.

[26]While it may or may not be true that Bush appointees to the Court will fulfill his campaign pledge to seek individuals in the mold of Justices Scalia and Thomas, it is worth noting that he has made clear his affinity with the directions in which the Court has been moving. See Terry Eastland, Un-impinging the States, Wash. Times, Mar. 11, 2001, at B1; Robert Pear, Shifting of Power from Washington Is Seen Under Bush, N.Y. Times, Jan. 7, 2001, at § 1, 1.

[27]United States v. Morrison, 120 S. Ct. 1740, 1759 (2000) (Thomas concurring). Justice Thomas argues that "the very notion of a 'substantial effects' test under the Commerce Clause is inconsistent with the original understanding of Congress' powers and with this Court's early Commerce Clause cases." Id. For competing assessments of this claim, compare Randy E. Barnett, The Original Meaning of the Commerce Clause, 68 U. Chi. L. Rev. 101 (2001), with Grant S. Nelson and Robert J. Pushaw, Jr., Rethinking the Commerce Clause: Applying First Principles to Uphold Federal Commercial Regulations but Preserve State Control over Social Issues, 85 Iowa L. Rev. 1 (1999).

[28]See No Harm in Such a Declaration?, at 13–14.

[29]469 U.S. 528 (1985).

prior Rehnquist opinion, *National League of Cities v. Usery.*[30] The lynchpin in the Court's analysis in *Garcia* was, as Professor Yoo notes, and disputes, the assumption that these matters are best left to the political process, with Congress providing both the appropriate interpretation of its own authority and the proper avenue for redress in those instances when the states disagreed with a given congressional decision. The central tenet in recent decisions does not, however, appear to be a rule that "the principal and basic limit on [federal power] is that inherent to all congressional action—the built-in restraints that our federal system provides through state participation in federal government action."[31] It is, rather, that the relationship between states and nation are elements of a "federal balance the Framers designed . . . that this Court is obliged to enforce."[32]

That being the case, it seems logical, if not inevitable, that the *Garcia* principle will soon be questioned and, if the predictions of the current chief justice are fulfilled, discarded.[33] For one of the salient aspects of the recent federalism opinions is the fact that the Court has reserved for itself the role as ultimate arbiter of both the meaning of the Constitution and the extent to which individual federal statutes pose the danger of "obliterating the Framer's carefully crafted balance of power between the States and the National Government."[34] It is then not a terribly great leap from *Lopez* and *Morrison,* in which the Court reserved to itself the right to determine if the underlying private conduct was in fact a commercial activity, to a future decision in which, in a properly presented case, the Court decides that many if not most state government activities are in fact attributes of state sovereignty, rather than mere commercial transactions.

Is it then appropriate to now equate the changes in federal-state relations that the Court has fashioned with those it undertook in the 1930s in response to and defense of the New Deal? Is this, to purloin the phrase popularized by Professor Ackerman, a constitutional moment, within which the Court is "placing a new problematic at the center of American political life"?[35] Or are these decisions in certain important respects "much ado about very little," reflections of an adjustment in approach that is controversial not for what it portends, but rather because the cases involve issues that are in many respects visceral? The collec-

---

[30]426 U.S. 833 (1976).

[31]Id. at 556.

[32]United States v. Lopez, 514 U.S. 549, 583 (1995) (Kennedy concurring).

[33]See *Garcia,* 469 U.S. at 580 (Rehnquist dissenting) ("I am confident" that the principle exempting states from such regulations will "in time command the support of a majority of this Court").

[34]*Morrison,* 120 S. Ct. at 1755.

[35]Bruce Ackerman, A Generation of Betrayal?, 55 Fordham L. Rev. 1519 (1997). Professor Ackerman characterizes the New Deal as one such moment, and would presumably view the Court's current quest as potentially yet another. See generally Bruce Ackerman, 2 We the People: Transformations (Belknap Press, 1998).

tive judgment of the individuals who have contributed to this collection is that this is indeed an extraordinarily important point in the development of the nation. And while the legacy of the Rehnquist Court cannot yet be written, it is very likely that most individuals describing William Rehnquist's tenure as chief justice will place the reshaping of federal-state relations at the top of their list of defining characteristics. There is a certain degree of irony in this for, as Jeffrey Rosen has aptly observed, "[t]he word 'federalism' tends to make most people's eyes glaze over."[36] There is little doubt, however, that whatever its decisional incarnation, federalism has become for all intents and purposes the hallmark of the Rehnquist Court,[37] and it is telling how many of the recent opinions have issued from his chambers.

The various essays in this volume provide the readers with the information and perspectives required to assess for themselves the legitimacy of the current decisions, their importance for the nation, and a sense of where matters might next progress. They describe a situation within which a majority of the current members of the Supreme Court seem likely to remain skeptical about federal statutes that lie at the margins of congressional power and especially inhospitable toward measures that authorize or expand private causes of action against the states. These are matters of considerable importance for us all, both as citizens of the nation and, presumably, individuals interested in the Constitution and how it structures our government and our lives.

It is then well worth recalling the words with which this volume began, those of the Tenth Amendment, which speaks of a reservation of power not simply to the states, but also to the people. Each individual must decide whether they believe that the Tenth Amendment imposes substantive limitations on federal authority or, as was the understanding prior to the recent spate of federalism decisions, simply describes an allocation of power specified in the text itself. That inquiry is, however, an appropriate one, for the Tenth Amendment itself makes abundantly clear what the Preamble promises, that the ultimate authority in these matters is in fact reserved to "We the People."

---

[36]Jeffrey Rosen, The Next Court, N.Y. Times, Oct. 22, 2000, § 6 (Magazine), at 74.

[37]See, e.g., Erwin Chemerinsky, The Hypocrisy of Alden v. Maine: Judicial Review, Sovereign Immunity and the Rehnquist Court, 33 Loy. L.A. L. Rev. 1283, 1283 (2000) ("When constitutional historians look back at the Rehnquist Court, they undoubtedly will say that its most significant changes in constitutional law were in the area of federalism."); Larry D. Kramer, Putting the Politics Back Into the Political Safeguards of Federalism, 100 Colum. L. Rev. 215,. 218 (2000) (describing a "current Supreme Court [that] is plainly willing, perhaps eager to rethink its position").

# Case Index

# Subject Index

# About the Contributors

**Mark R. Killenbeck** is the Wylie H. Davis Professor of Law at the University of Arkansas, Fayetteville. He is the author of a number of studies on American Constitutional history and law, among which is "Pursuing the Great Experiment: Reserved Powers in a Post-Ratification, Compound Republic" (1999 *The Supreme Court Review* 81), within which he develops more fully many of the perspectives expressed in his introduction to this collection.

**William E. Leuchtenburg** is the William Rand Kenan Professor of History at the University of North Carolina at Chapel Hill and a visiting professor of legal history at Duke Law School. He is the author of several of the most important studies of the Roosevelt presidency and the New Deal, and his work has garnered substantial critical praise, including the Bancroft and Parkman Prizes. He is past president of both the American Historical Association and the Organization of American Historians. His contribution to this volume is based on his Jefferson Memorial Lecture, delivered at the University of California, Berkeley, in December 1995.

**Jack N. Rakove** is the Coe Professor of History and American Studies at Stanford University. He is a prolific author whose work probes deeply into the intersection between politics and political thought during the era from the American Revolution through the 1790s. He also has a special interest in the role of historical thinking in contemporary constitutional disputes and in the life and thought of James Madison. His book, *Original Meanings: Politics and Ideas in the Making of the Constitution* (Knopf, 1996), won the Pulitzer Prize for history.

**John Choon Yoo** is professor of law at Boalt Hall, the University of California, Berkeley. He is a former clerk to Justice Clarence Thomas of the United States Supreme Court and served as general counsel to the United States Senate Committee on the Judiciary. His work routinely appears in the nation's preeminent law journals, and emphasizes the use of historical materials as a means of gaining important perspectives on current constitutional issues.